Introducing Cultural and Media Studies

Introducing Cultural and Media Studies

A Semiotic Approach

Tony Thwaites

Lloyd Davis

Warwick Mules

First edition published as *Tools for Cultural Studies* 1994
This edition published as *Introducing Cultural and Media Studies: A Semiotic Approach* 2002 by
PALGRAVE
Houndmills, Basingstoke, Hampshire RG21 6XS and
175 Fifth Avenue, New York, N. Y. 10010
Companies and representatives throughout the world

PALGRAVE is the new global academic imprint of
St. Martin's Press LLC Scholarly and Reference Division and
Palgrave Publishers Ltd (formerly Macmillan Press Ltd).

ISBN 0–333–97248–1 hardcover
ISBN 0–333–97247–3 paperback

This book is printed on paper suitable for recycling and made from fully managed and sustained forest sources.

A catalogue record for this book is available from the British Library.

Library of Congress Cataloging-in-Publication Data

Thwaites, Tony.
  Introducing cultural and media studies : a semiotic approach /Tony Thwaites, Lloyd Davis, and Warwick Mules.
    p. cm
  Rev. ed. of: Tools for cultural studies, published in 1994 by Macmillan Education Australia.
  Includes bibliographical references and index.
  ISBN 0–333–97248–1
1. Culture—Study and teaching. 2. Semiotics. 3. Mass media—Social aspects. I. Davis, Lloyd, 1959– II. Mules, Warwick. III. Thwaites, Tony. Tools for cultural studies. IV. Title.

HM623.T59 2002
306'.071——dc21   2001059838

10   9   8   7   6   5   4   3   2   1
11   10   09   08   07   06   05   04   03   02

Printed in Great Britain by Creative Print and Design (Wales), Ebbw Vale

Contents

Preface to the revised edition

This book is a revised edition of *Tools for Cultural Studies: An Introduction*. This was originally published in 1994 by Macmillan Education Australia, and aimed specifically at the Australian market. We were delighted to find that the book soon gained a wider circulation so, while we have kept the original arrangement and progression of the argument, we have deliberately also addressed that wider audience in this edition.

This new edition contains several quite new sections, and also provides further development of a number of topics familiar from the first edition. There is a new and fuller discussion of myth in Chapter 3, which finds echoes throughout the later chapters; similarly, Chapter 7 elaborates further on the concept of discourse. The examination of ideology in Chapter 8 is enriched by important discussions of interpellation and hegemony. Throughout, there are new examples, new connections among sections, new exercises and suggestions for classroom work. In particular, the growth of the Internet since our last edition has given us much new material for discussion in the text, as well as a wealth of online resources for the student. All the guides to resources have been thoroughly updated, both in the annotated 'Sources and further reading' sections at the end of each chapter and in the bibliography.

Acknowledgements

There are always many people to thank. In particular, we would like to express our gratitude to Kim Wilkins and Anna Bemrose, who provided the research assistance on this edition; to Catherine Gray at Palgrave, for her unfailing encouragement and enthusiasm for the project; to Peter Debus, who did the same for us in the first edition; and, of course, to our families.

The authors and publishers also wish to thank the following for permission to reproduce copyright material: Figure 1.3: Yves Saint Laurent; Figure 1.6: Kelloggs Australia; Figure 2.4: Uncle Ben's of Australia; Figure 3.1: *BBC Good Food*, Redwood Publishing; Figures 3.3, 3.5: Printed with permission, the *Toowoomba Chronicle* and the *Courier-Mail*; Figure 3.6: from Stephen Jay Gould, *The Mismeasure of Man* (Harmondsworth: Penguin, 1981) and John S. Haller, Jr, *Outcasts from Evolution: Scientific Attitudes of Racial Inferiority, 1859–1900* (Urbana, Illinois: University of Illinois Press, 1971); Figure 3.7: *Time*; Figure 3.8: Andrew Chapman; Figure 4.1: Printed with permission of Rothmans of Pall Mall (Australia) Limited; Figure 4.2: Campbell's Soups, Australia; Figure 4.3: Revlon Manufacturing Ltd.; Figure 4.4: Sony; Figures 5.3, 5.4: Mirror Australian Telegraph Publications; Figure 5.5: 1990 American Express International Inc. All rights reserved. Reprinted with permission; Figure 6.1: Potter Warburg Asset Management; Figure 6.2: Simona Pty Ltd; Figure 6.3: Unilever Foods; Figure 7.1: ad for United States Rubber, the *Saturday Evening Post*, 23 April 1960; Figure 7.3: *Morning Bulletin*, Rockhampton Australia; Figure 8.3: Reprinted with permission, the *Sunday Mail*, Brisbane Australia; Figure 8.4: News Ltd; Figure 8.5: Craig Golding, *The Sydney Morning Herald*; Figure 9.2: Sheridan Cotton Man, 1985, Sheridan, 34 Wilson St, South Yarra, Victoria Australia 3141; Figure 9.3: Austral International/Rex Features; Figures 9.6, 9.8: Poem and commentaries cited in I. A. Richards, *Practical Criticism* (London: Routledge & Kegan Paul, 1964), pp 162–64, 174–76.

Reading this book

This book can be read in several ways, depending on the detail you are after.

One way, of course, is to read it all the way through, beginning to end. If you do this, you will be following a developing argument in which each stage builds on and reworks earlier concepts. The book is designed so that it can be used as the main or even the sole set textbook for an introductory module. Each chapter is followed by exercises which can be used for further investigation in the classroom, and an annotated selection of further reading and resources. In the course of a semester, it will give you a familiarity with some of the more pervasive ways in which cultural studies has developed and is practised, and will give you a firm grounding for further work in the area.

But this book is also designed to be used in other, more flexible ways. It can be used in conjunction with other textbooks (many of which it suggests in the 'Sources and further reading' sections at the end of each chapter), to develop a particular emphasis. Major sections or single chapters can be read individually: they aim to be enriched by earlier sections and chapters rather than unintelligible without them. Each chapter is broken up into fairly short subsections by descriptive headings, to make directed browsing as easy as possible.

Through its indexing and contextual definitions, the book can also be used as a reference to the main semiotic concepts in use in cultural and media studies. Rather than provide a glossary of decontextualised terms, it aims to give you definitions which are surrounded by demonstration and discussion of just how a particular term works.

Definitions of key terms are placed in boxes, like this. Taken together, the boxes provide a glossary of basic terms, and direct you to fuller discussion in the main text.

The main text is unboxed, and in the same font you are reading now. Major occurrences of **key concepts** are indicated by **bold** type. Important subsidiary concepts are often in *italics*. Breakout boxes are often used for relatively autonomous examples; these can be read on their own as well as for the light they shed on the issues discussed in the main text surrounding them.

There are three main sections to the book. The first, 'Cultural signs', introduces some of the basic concepts of semiotics. The second, 'Cultural texts', looks at some of the ways in which texts work socially and culturally. The third, 'Cultural practices', turns to the large-scale questions of how these processes produce us as cultural beings. A final chapter opens the book out to other sorts of research, debate and investigation in cultural studies.

Approaching cultural and media studies

CONTENTS

Culture

If it is obvious that cultural studies involves studying culture, what may not be nearly so obvious is just what culture is. We are going to approach it in a way common to much (though not all) of cultural studies: as a matter of meanings.

> **Culture** is the ensemble of social practices by which meanings are produced, circulated and exchanged.

Let's take the implications of this a bit at a time. Culture is that aspect of the social which is concerned with **meanings**. There are, of course, many other aspects of the social, with many other concerns (economic, legal, governmental, educational, etc.), but in some senses culture would seem to be a very basic one. One can at least imagine what societies might be like without money, exploitation, government or the like – there's an entire branch of fiction, the utopian romance, which does as much. A society which does not produce and circulate meanings, however, is strictly inconceivable.

In its concerns with the practices of meaning, culture overlaps into economic, legal and governmental areas. It is not at all clear where one might end and the other begin. Perhaps, then, rather than take meaning and its practices as a strictly defined area within the social world, we should see it more as an emphasis, a point from which to see things. Constructed in this way, cultural studies is a series of questions about what we can say about a variety of areas (governmental, legal, economic, etc.) if we approach them as practices of meaning. If, for example, economics is concerned with the

1

production, circulation and consumption of wealth, some of the things cultural studies will be interested in might include how wealth acts as a meaningful sign, the various meanings it produces, and the ways in which those meanings are circulated and exchanged.

Culture is the site of the **production of meanings**, not the expression of meanings which exist elsewhere. Meanings come about in and through social relations, those among people, groups, classes, institutions, structures and things. And because they are produced, circulate and are exchanged within the social world, these meanings are *never entirely fixed*. Some meanings may be quite stable, of course, but others may be highly and rapidly variable. This variability means that although meanings always come about in a social context, we must also say that they are *never wholly determined by that context*. Meanings migrate from one context to another, sometimes ending up very far from where they started – they are always getting displaced, diverted, reworked and exchanged. This is not something which goes wrong in the transmission of meanings. Rather, it is itself the very process of meaning. A document is intelligible, after all, even if we don't know its author or the circumstances under which it was written. A photograph makes sense even if we've never met the people posing for it. This is not to say that meaning is ever *free from context*: all it means is that a knowledge of the author or the sitters provides a *different sort of context*.

Lastly, we should simply add that culture is not a single unified process, but an **ensemble** of practices. These may work together very tightly, but in other cases they may be in considerable conflict with one another. We shall have to keep the disparate natures of cultural practices clearly in mind as we proceed.

Framing the question

Here we will examine some of the ways in which meanings operate in their social usages. From that, we will ask how these processes can best be described in general terms, in a **model**.

Often, especially in older textbooks, you will find meaning described in terms of the **communication** of a message between two points, something like this:

sender ⟶ ⟶ receiver
message

There are quite a few variations on this, and quite a few reasons why we find them all unsatisfactory here. The most obvious one is that this model simply doesn't answer the question we're interested in, of how meanings come to be produced in the social world. It says nothing about the social, simply assuming meaning's already there, rolled up in the message. What's more, it assumes this meaning simply travels intact from one point to another, like a solid projectile.

Neither does it help to modify this model to take into account possible interferences with the projectile:

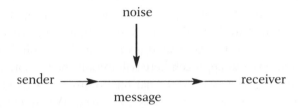

This still doesn't help us understand how meanings come about, and though it nods in the direction of the ways in which meanings alter in circulation and use, it writes all this off as just a matter of purely external, accidental interference, which it calls by the catch-all term 'noise'. Even modified, this model is not going to be much use to us in trying to figure out how it is that meanings can be so enormously flexible and varied, or how it is that those variations may nevertheless have considerable, if complex, regularity.

In short, what we will be interested in here is all the ways in which meaning is a more complex matter than the accurate and efficient transmission of a message.

To investigate this, we will have to look more carefully at some features of cultural sign-activity. From these, we will try to put together some different models of what is happening, in an attempt to account for some of that variety. We will treat these models critically. At each stage, we will want to know not only where they can usefully be called into play, and where they seem to provide some genuine understanding of the processes they model, but also where their *limits* are. What questions do each of the models allow us to ask? Just as important, what questions do they *not* provide for? And how, as we try to ask at the end of each chapter, can we get to ask new questions?

We want to encourage a critical attitude not only to all the disparate phenomena of culture, but also to the models which provide ways of thinking about them. It's necessary to know some of the main conceptual schemas which inform the enormous volume of literature on cultural studies, and also something about how they work, and why. The critical approach we'd like to foster here would be one which is also capable of opening up other approaches, raising other questions: approaching things differently.

Approaches

We don't for a moment claim that this is the only way of approaching cultural studies. The field is too diverse for that, too full of the hubbub of its multiple, disparate, diverging voices. The way we take here is largely that of an influential **semiotic** stream which developed historically out of linguistics.

Though semiotics is far from uncontested, it is still the basis for much introductory pedagogical material. We see several possible advantages in this, which we hope to take up here. Semiotics opens up a vast amount of critical material; it works well in the classroom, leading quickly to hands-on investigations; and it has generated a varied and valuable body of critique. For these reasons, our approach here will initially be semiotic, though as the book progresses we seek to open that out to others, many of which extend well beyond the semiotic as originally conceived. We are not trying to advocate a particular theoretical model, which it will be the reader's job to apply dutifully and accurately to a number of actual situations. We use some classical semiotics to raise questions about what signs do within the social world, and, just as importantly, about how these might be thought through. Other questions include the conceptual tools that might need to be developed to do that, and the limits of their use. What kinds of concepts do we need and what do we want them to do? How do we go about developing them?

SOURCES AND FURTHER READING

Raymond Williams's *Keywords: A Vocabulary of Culture and Society* (London: Fontana, 1988) has a valuable short essay on the many and varied meanings of culture, which Williams suggests (p. 87) is 'one of the two or three most complicated words in the English language'. Williams is generally regarded as one of the founders of cultural studies in its British version. For a brief history of how cultural studies developed in the UK, see Graeme Turner's *British Cultural Studies: An Introduction*, 2nd edn (New York: Routledge, 1996).

The sender-message-receiver model is generally known as Shannon and Weaver's model. Claude Shannon was an American engineer who in 1948 published an influential technical paper on the mathematics of telecommunications. This was a highly technical piece, which addressed a very practical problem in the construction of telephone systems: how much information can be sent without distortion down a line of given characteristics? In the following year, Shannon and Weaver published their book, *The Mathematical Theory of Communication*, from which this model comes. Most use of the Shannon and Weaver model in the human sciences is content to take the diagram and ignore the mathematics. You will find the technicalities of Shannon's theories explained in John R. Pierce, *An Introduction to Information Theory: Symbols, Signals and White Noise*, 2nd edn (New York: Dover, 1980).

A measure of the sheer diversity of cultural studies is the huge volume edited by Lawrence Grossberg, Cary Nelson and Paula Treichler, and simply named *Cultural Studies* (New York: Routledge, 1992), which came out of the 1990 conference on 'Cultural Studies Now and in the Future' at the University of Illinois at Urbana-Champaign. The conference drew papers from some of the best-known names in cultural studies in the English-speaking world, some 42 of which (plus transcripts of discussions) are gathered into this large-format volume of almost 800 pages. Similarly wide-ranging collections of material are *The Cultural Studies Reader* (London: Routledge, 1993), edited by Simon During, and *Contemporary Literary Criticism and Cultural Studies* (New York: Longman, 1998), edited by Robert Con Davis and Ronald Schleifer. These volumes bring together many important essays and issues in the field.

There is a wealth of cultural studies material available online, and it is growing all the time. This book will generally refer only to stable sites whose URL is unlikely to change, and in particular those with their own collections of up-to-date links to further resources.

Daniel Chandler's Media and Cultural Studies site at the University of Wales, Aberystwyth (www.aber.ac.uk/media) is one of the best and most comprehensive websites of its kind. It has sections on semiotics and textual analysis, TV, radio, film, music, advertising, gender, ethnicity, written and spoken language, visual images, and a lot more. The site is geared to student needs, and in particular assessment. There are links and suggestions for further reading, in print and online, and the whole site is searchable and thoroughly indexed. Similarly rich and wide-ranging sites are PopCultures, Sarah Zupko's Cultural Studies Centre (www.popcultures.com), Robin Markowitz's Cultural Studies Central (www.culturalstudies.net), Rob van Kranenburg's Scholê (simsim.rug.ac.be/schole), and Mick Underwood's Cultural, Communication and Media Studies Infobase (www.cultsock.ndirect.co.uk/MUHome/cshtml). The Voice of the Shuttle is a huge collection of links in almost every field of the humanities, put together by Alan Liu at the University of California at Santa Barbara; its cultural studies listings are at vos.ucsb.edu/shuttle/cultural.html.

A note on World Wide Web resources

When you use Web resources, it is vital to keep in mind that the Web is like an enormous vanity press. Anyone with an Internet account can publish almost anything they like, as long as it's not defamatory and observes copyright. There are no general editorial standards or requirements of accuracy. You will find all sorts of material on the Web. Some of it is very valuable; a lot of it isn't; and some of it can be downright misleading.

As a result, it is absolutely important that you know just what weight you should give – if any – to material you find online. In general, you have to exercise more scepticism and discernment than you do with print. The New Mexico State University Libraries have a fine page on Web evaluation, along with a series of examples to try yourself on: 'The Good, the Bad, and the Ugly: or Why It's a Good Idea to Evaluate Web Sources' (lib.nmsu.edu/instruction/eval.htm). While we have been very selective in our choice of Web resources for this book, the Web's capacity for rapid change means that nothing absolves you from the need to evaluate for yourself any of the sites we mention, or to which they link in their turn. All of the Web resources listed in this book were current at the time of preparation of this book.

PART I

Cultural signs

CHAPTER 1

Some aspects of signs

CONTENTS

An opening move: the sign

In the Introduction, we set a very broad agenda for cultural studies: its object of study will be the social production of meanings. Here we had better start with the actual location of meaning:

> A **sign** is anything which produces meanings.

This is a very broad description, but it does allow us to keep in mind the three points emerging from the Introduction's brief discussion. They might act as guiding principles in our investigation:

1 Signs are not just comments on the world, but are themselves things *in* the world – and specifically, in the social world.
2 Signs do not just convey meanings, but *produce* them.
3 Signs produce *many meanings*, not just one meaning per sign.

This chapter will attempt to outline in a very broad way some of the aspects of the sign which we will investigate. We will use two examples (Figures 1.1 and 1.2) to ask general questions about the ways signs function. These examples are complex, compound signs – **texts** of signs, in fact – but they are also commonplace. It's that banality of meaning we want to examine here.

Content

One of the more obvious things a sign can do is *refer* to something. In different ways and to varying extents, each of the letters in Figures 1.1 and 1.2 is concerned with conveying certain information about certain topics, such as the facts and events of Sam's life, from his address to his educational qualifications and professional experience. They refer to things in the world and the relations among these things: they represent, depict, propose as real, make statements, stand for. Whether these are true or false is not the point here: what we will call the sign's **referential function** is simply the way in which it proposes something to be the case.

A sign's **referential** function is its ability to invoke a *content*.

It may be tempting to see the referential function as the principal feature of a sign. It is certainly a very important factor, and one which may be highly valued. Nevertheless, as we shall shortly see, it is hardly the only function. These texts do various things that cannot be reduced to conveying information: they attempt to persuade, for example, or seek to establish or maintain relationships.

Codes

As you read the two texts, you no doubt very quickly become aware of what *sort* of text they are. They are both letters (one printed, one electronic), rather than, say, film reviews, advertisements, transcripts of interviews, limericks or mathematical arguments. In fact, you almost certainly realised that *before* you started reading them, from cues in the very layout and typeface. You doubtless also realised that they were different kinds of letter: one of them is a job application, and the other is a personal communication.

Signs suggest ways in which they may be read: they cue in certain **codes** for interpreting them. The *type* of text it is (its **genre**, as we'll later call it) is a very powerful example of this process. Knowing what sort of a text it is sets up a complex set of expectations about what it will say, and how. These need not be adhered to, nor do they have to be consistent: a text may thwart as much as satisfy the expectations it sets up, and this allows for quite complex plays of meanings.

Figure 1.2 is a case in point. Emails are often far more casual than letters on paper: they're often done on the fly, with little or no concern for spelling or misprints, and a freely conversational grammar and syntax. The codes

Figure 1.1

23 Avenue Road
Springfield 14037
25 October, 2001

Ms Lauren Hazard
Personnel Manager
UnityBank
3142A Mawson Street
Chisholm 10066

Dear Ms Hazard

**Application for position of Technology Policy and
Development Officer, ref UB/BMT/102001**

I would like to apply for this position. I have enclosed my
CV, academic record, and the requested list of three referees.

This year I shall be completing my studies at Chisholm
University of Technology, where I've been majoring in
Business Studies and Technologies, and English
(Communications and Cultural studies). As the enclosed copy
of my academic record shows, my results have been consis-
tently good. I have a particular interest in online commerce,
and Web database and security design.

Because I've been interested in a career in banking, last year
I decided to investigate, as a semester-long self-directed
research project for credit within my BST major, the impact
of e-commerce on the relationships of bank branches and
local community in my home town of Springfield. I wanted
to know what services were most used by the customers of
these banks, and in particular how banks were working with
small businesses to help them expand or improve their online
financial management and facilities. In this, I worked closely
with the manager of the Shelbyville Central branch of
UnityBank, Mr David Field. I presented Mr Field with a copy

of the final document, and over the next six months was employed as a part-time consultant under the UnityBank Branch Initiative Scheme, implementing as a trial several of the measures I had investigated in the project. This has been written up favourably in UnityBank's *UnityNews*, and I understand several other branches are now undertaking similar trials. I have included details of the project, and of the later consultancy work.

As well as this, over the last two years I have working part-time as a freelance consultant in Web design for a number of local businesses. The details are listed in my CV, along with the URLs of sites I have designed. As you will see, some of these are complex sites, involving online access to databases and secure credit-card facilities. I have had experience in using world processors, Web editors, desk-top publishing, and most of the major accounting software packages.

I'd particularly enjoy working for UnityBank because its forward-looking approach to the new technologies in an environment in which the customer is always the focus of attention. I am familiar with and am excited by the recommendations outlined in the UnityBank report on Initiatives in Technology, and feel I have a lot to offer in achieving those goals. I would be more than happy to discuss this with you further at an interview.

Yours faithfully

Samuel G West

Samuel G. West

Enclosures:

- Curriculum vitae
- List of referees
- Academic record
- Dossier of research project

Figure 1.2

Samuel West, 10:17AM 10/25/01 + 9000, oh, nothing much

X-Sender: st33487@studentmail.cu.edu
X-Mailer: Windows Eudora Version 5.0 (32)
Date: Thurs 25 Oct 2001 10:17:53 + 1000
To: Vivian Carter <vivid99@hotmail.com>
From: Samuel West <st33487@studentmail.cu.edu>
Subject: oh, nothing much

great to arrive home after a hard day in the
library and find a breath of canada waiting for
me. :) hey, a real live letter, on *paper* and
all!

you might be getting out warm clothes and seeing
the trees starting to get that threadbare look,
but it goes the other way round here. summer's
started early here, and with a vengeance: it even
hit 33 a couple of days ago. and in october! the
air conditioning in the library broke down the
other day, leaving me sweltering over a stack of
company reports. i would have taken them out and
sat down under a tree with them all if they'd
have let me get them out the door, but no such
luck: I sometimes i think the thing i envy you
most at the moment is the cool weather. (*and*
that you might even get some skiing in before
you come back!)

so how does it feel now that you've not only
finished and submitted all the work, but have
also had a couple of weeks totally free? enjoy
it--you've certainty deserved it! and *don't*,
whatever you do, worry about whether it'll get
through or not. the bit of the thesis you sent
back to me looked traffic to me. i don't know
what canadian examiners are looking for, but i'm
sure they recognise quality when they see it.
relax, enjoy all the things you've been too busy
to enjoy until now. well, not *too* much;) spare
the occasional thought for me slogging on here at
home. i'm almost finished here, too: two more

Printed for Vivian Carter <vivid99@hotmail.com>   1

intensive days in the library should do it, and
then there are only the exams to worry about,
but they'll be fine.

just wanted to get a quick message off to you to
say i'd got yours, and how great it was—as
always—to hear from you. once i've got this
library work out of the way in a couple of days,
i'll sit down and write you a proper letter
back, a long one, get you up to date ('up to
date', it's only a week since the last one, do
you think i must be in love?), a *real* letter
rather than all these emails. (i've just been
doing a job application at one of the terminals
in the student union, and thought i might as
well keep going with a quick note to you. more
about that later.) watch the mails.

anyway, take care of yourself, and roll on december! can't wait.

as always, all my love

sam

~~~~~~

```
+--------------+
| ~~      @    |        Write me:
| =====        |
| =====        |        Samuel West
+--------------+        st33487@studentmail.cu.ed
```
~~~~~~

which dominate them are those of spoken rather than written language. But because they nevertheless *are* written, they lack all of the cues which normally go with speech: tone of voice, gestures, facial expressions. To get round this, they often use a range of smileys and other graphic signs intended to stand in for these.

This email, though, seems to be suggesting that email's even a little *too* casual, and that a handwritten letter might provide that extra sense of genuine feeling just because of the little bit of extra work involved in it, or its slightly old-fashioned feel as a medium:

> once i've got this library work out of the way in a couple of days, i'll sit down and write you a proper letter back, a long one, get you up to date ('up to date', it's only a week since the last one, do you think i must be in love?), a *real* letter rather than all these emails. (i've just been doing a job application at one of the terminals in the student union, and thought i might as well keep going with a quick note to you. more about that later.) watch the mails.

This is an overt example of cueing, where the passage is actually suggesting how the text could, or should, be read.

That signs in general include some sort of **metalingual function** like this indicates that a sign's meaning is far from a given fact. Instead, it is something to be actively worked out or negotiated, and always subject to renegotiation.

A sign's **metalingual** function suggests the *codes* by which the sign might be understood.

The idea of code is quite a crucial one in any study of signs, and we will be elaborating on it throughout the book, particularly in Chapters 2 and 3. In Chapter 5, we will turn to a more detailed examination of genre and the roles it plays.

Format

Before you even started reading Figure 1.1, various aspects of its formal layout probably suggested to you that here was a letter of some sort – features such as the indented address and date, and the opening and closing salutations. Other features – the font, the blocked paragraphs, even the use of the space of the sheet of paper – suggest a business letter in particular. But these are purely *formal* aspects of the document. They depend not on what is said, but on how it's said: how the sign deploys its formal features, including the space and medium in which it exists.

> A sign's **formal functions** involve its formal structure and the format which it takes.

The formal function is tied closely to the material **support** of the sign: what it is made of. Different supports are capable of producing different sorts of formal function. Print is generally on paper, and is restricted to written language and static images; the television screen gives a relatively small image, but with motion and sound; the film screen gives a larger image, with different proportions; and so on.

The two examples shows how various functions may be linked. The formal function (the layout) also works metalingually, suggesting the type of document: we recognise a letter by the addresses which head it, and the salutation, 'Dear ____'; we recognise the printout of an email by the header and footer, the signature block, the lack of punctuation, the smileys and ASCII art. In both cases, one sort of meaning first gets cued in by the formal function, and then this immediately gets taken up by the metalingual function.

Address

Another very important set of functions involved in all sign activity is that of their **address**. Signs address.

Consider some of the problems involved in address. Signs may go astray, and be received by other than those for whom they were intended. The letters in our examples are *addressed to* 'Ms Lauren Hazard' and 'Vivian'; but their *actual receivers* include you reading this book, whom they do not address. Nor do signs necessarily come from where they say they do. Letters may lie, or can be forged. In cases like this, the perhaps quite imaginary place they are *addressed from* may differ considerably from their *actual sender*. (These letters are addressed from 'Sam West', but it's quite possible they were written by the authors of this book.)

For these reasons, we should start off by making an important distinction: between the actual sender and receiver of a communication, on the one hand, and the ways these are represented in it, on the other.

> The **addresser** of a text is the position it constructs as its source: where it *says* it is from.
> The **sender** is its *actual* source.

> The **addressee** of a text is the position it constructs as its destination:
> where it *says* it is going.
> The **receiver** is its *actual* destination.

Sender and receiver are actual people. Addresser and addressee, on the other hand, are purely constructions of signs. They are like fictional characters in that they have no existence other than in signs, and they may bear very little resemblance to the actual sender and receiver. Nothing either of the letters can do can guarantee that they are telling the truth: that Sam really does have some experience in banking, or that he is fondly counting the days until Vivian arrives home. Each of them *constructs* a Sam, and a different Sam in each case: a diligent student and prospective employee on the one hand, a fond lover on the other. It is these constructed figures of addresser and addressee we react to, and which make the text intelligible even if we do not have any access to the real sender and receiver. (Indeed, in this case how could we? For all we know, Sam, Lauren Hazard and Vivian may be entirely fictitious characters.)

The relationships between these two sets of terms, sender and receiver on the one hand, and addresser and addressee on the other, may be quite complex. Different senders may share the same addresser. For instance, the agony column of a magazine may always appear under the same proper name, but the actual writers may vary from week to week. Likewise, different receivers may share the same addressee: think of the thousands of actual readers addressed by a newspaper headline, or the thousands of viewers who hear a television newsreader's 'Good evening'.

On the other hand, the one sender may produce a number of different addressers: we construct ourselves differently in our words, depending on whether we are applying for a job or writing to an absent loved one. And correspondingly, one receiver may be addressed as a number of different addressees: any one person plays a number of different roles (friend, colleague, parent, spouse, daughter or son), each of which brings a different mode of address.

To speak of sender and receiver in all of these cases, then, we would have to know (or guess at) what is happening in the minds of actual people, and this knowledge may not be available to us. When we speak of addresser and addressee, though, we are speaking of something that happens in texts, made up of signs, which we have right in front of us. We are speaking of how those texts set up and construct certain roles or positions within the text, available for both sender and receiver to occupy. Sender and receiver are actual people; addresser and addressee are not people at all, but ways texts have of addressing us. The two sets of terms are logically quite distinct from each other, and belong to two different orders of being.

Though these may seem fine distinctions, they are crucial. They suggest that we may be able to talk about what happens in texts in specifically *textual* ways, without having recourse to hypotheses about what their sender may have intended them to mean, or without having to guess about what their effects on a single given receiver might be. In short, the separation of addresser from sender and addressee from receiver is what lets us do semiotics rather than psychology.

A sign's **expressive** function is its construction of an *addresser*.
A sign's **conative** function is its construction of an *addressee*.

There is another very important factor to consider here. As well as constructing the positions of addresser and addressee, any sign must also establish a **relationship** between the two.

The classic case of a sign which functions mainly like this is the word 'hello'. It serves to establish the possibility of communication. Depending on the tone of voice with which it's said, it may work to open up or close off an interchange. There are more complex examples in the two letters we've been using. Their salutations each set up a certain relationship: 'Dearest Vivian' is much more affectionate than 'Dear Ms Hazard' (the metalingual functions indicate that that 'Dear' is not the expression of affection it might be elsewhere, but a purely ritual greeting). Throughout the job application, the syntax and diction maintain this respectful, distanced but businesslike and eager relationship between addresser (this perhaps fictitious 'Sam', the enthusiastic possible employee) and addressee (the unknown 'Ms Hazard').

A sign's **phatic** functions are the ways in which it constructs a *relationship* between addresser and addressee.

In its expressive and conative functions, the sign delineates a group including both addresser and addressee. The phatic effect of this is to mark out something like a *community* within which the exchange is taking place, even if this community should be a temporary one with only two people in it. The phatic is what binds addresser and addressee together in the act of the exchange of signs. Conversely, though, in marking out a group like this, the phatic also excludes those who are not part of it. The phatic function links addressers and addressees in all sorts of degrees of social inclusion and exclusion.

Some sort of phatic functioning is unavoidable in any sign activity. If an exchange of signs implies a common code within which the exchange can take place, then that exchange will on the broadest scale phatically include those with access to the code and exclude those without it: whatever other phatic functions it might have, a letter in English will exclude non-English users. A particular way of speaking may bind a group together and give it an immediately recognizable identity, to itself and others. Phatic functions can be enormously complex and subtle ways of discerning insiders, and the degree of their belonging.

One of the important phatic effects of the job application letter is to place Sam *already* within that group of 'business-minded people'. It suggests that he is already in spirit, if not yet in fact, part of the business community, aware of and working according to its values. The phatic community the letter to Vivian sets up is much narrower: its references to the particular relationship between them, and the experiences they share, tend to narrow that community down to two.

> The conative, expressive and phatic functions are the sign's **functions of address**.

As Figure 1.3 shows, signs which are visual and representational may often display considerable complexity in their functions of address, particularly through the *gaze*. We shall be dealing with further aspects of the functions of address in Chapters 8 and 9 in particular.

Context

It only remains to say that all of these functions depend on the social context of the sign. The social situations in which a sign is used may determine the appropriate content, type of sign and coding, who is being addressed, by whom and how, and the phatic community it constructs.

> A sign's **contextual** functions indicate the *context* in which it operates.

One of the key questions to be asked of all the various conceptual models we develop in this book will be the extent to which they are capable of taking into account the complexities of contextuality.

Figure 1.3 The gaze, the gift

To say that this advertisement is sent by a perfume company to women who are potential customers of its product would be to say little of the actual complexities of its address

The bodies of the man and the woman form a plane which contains most of the focal points of the photograph. It is marked out in particular by the man's face (exactly side-on, he is looking along this very plane), the woman's shoulders (emphasised by the pads of her suit) and her left arm, with its hand or her hip). The woman's body thus meets your gaze as viewer: she addresses you in her *bodily stance.*

Of the two characters, the man's attention is given wholly to the woman, but as her eyes, smile and pose show, the woman's attention is directed away from him, at a right angle, towards the camera and thus seemingly directly out of the plane of the picture, towards the position of the viewer. The effect is that her eyes appear to meet your own; the picture looks back at you looking at it. He addresses her, but *her gaze* addresses you, and your act of looking at her. Her smile shows that in the phatic bond set up by the returned gaze, where each of you is simultaneously in the position of addresser and addressee, you are in complicity, sharing knowledge.

Somewhat in front of this plane the two bodies mark out, the woman's right hand is holding a bottle of perfume, whose Yves Saint Laurent label is clearly displayed facing the viewer. The *bottle* addresses you; the woman holding the bottle addresses you with her *gesture*. Her hand holds the perfume out from the plane of the two lovers, between them and you. It is a gift, for you. Her gaze emphasises the motion: while her eyes are looking directly at you, if she were looking in the direction her head is tilted, she would be looking directly at the bottle of perfume. Her eyes, making the offer, have gone from perfume to you. What she is giving you is what the perfume has given her: the affections and undivided attention of the man next to her, who is unaware of this complicity between the two of you, but whom you cannot help but see in the background plane every time your eye moves to the perfume.

(And who is this woman who addresses you, offering you not only a perfume but a grand passion? Her *scarf* says it all with its YSL logo: she is the manufacturer, the product itself, offering itself to you in a conspiracy of pleasure.)

The seven functions

Figure 1.4 shows how we can now summarise and diagram these various functions. There are several points we should note about them.

First, all these functions are necessary for any sign activity to take place. That is, a sign must:

- work within a system of references and codings;
- be describable in terms of formal attributes which allow us to distinguish it from other signs;
- set up relationships of address; and
- operate within, and vary according to, specific concrete situations.

Figure 1.4 The functions of the sign

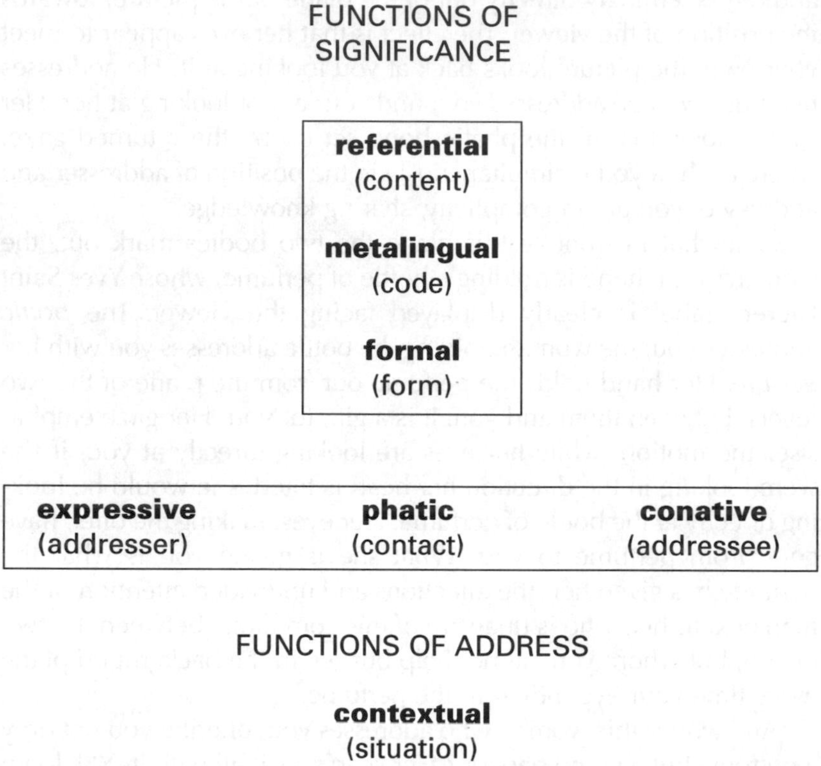

FUNCTIONS OF
SIGNIFICANCE

referential
(content)

metalingual
(code)

formal
(form)

| **expressive** | **phatic** | **conative** |
| (addresser) | (contact) | (addressee) |

FUNCTIONS OF ADDRESS

contextual
(situation)

This is an adaptation of a well-known model by the linguist Roman Jakobson. His original model, which is frequently cited in other textbooks, has six functions rather than our seven. Following Hymes's revision, we have separated out content and context. Our *formal function* is a reworking of Jakobson's *poetic function*: we have generalised its meaning somewhat, and renamed it to mark the difference (and also to avoid the implication that this function is synonymous with ideas such as a conative aesthetic pleasure, or the metalingual coding of a text as poetry). For similar reasons, our *expressive* function reworks what Jakobson calls the *emotive* function, which may misleadingly imply it is concerned with emotionality. (Think of a scientific paper: for it to be properly scientific, the addresser constructed by its expressive or emotive function must be dispassionate and *un*emotional.)

Second, though all of them are necessary for there to be a sign, in any given sign certain of these functions may be predominant. The language of a scientific paper demands a high emphasis on the referential, but day-to-day work with colleagues in a laboratory will certainly require an emphasis on the phatic.

Third, these functions are never independent of each other, but are constantly interrelating. Some of the possibilities are:

- *Certain functions may work together very closely.*
  Expressively, the addresser of the second letter is constructed as fond, thoughtful, solicitous, reassuring, and looking forward to the addressee's return. Conatively, the addressee is constructed as an object of affection, hardworking, intelligent, deserving. Phatically, the letter constructs the relationship between addresser and addressee as one of close affection, even love. In this case, those three functions work together in a strongly cohesive way.
- *Certain functions may overlap to a degree.*
  In the job application, the referential and the expressive functions largely coincide: an application has to convey a certain amount of information, and that information has to be about the addresser. They do not entirely coincide, however. As well as conveying information about the addresser, the expressive function is also concerned with constructing the addresser as having certain qualities – eagerness, earnestness, intelligence, politeness, etc.
- *Some functions may even work against others.*
  The email message uses the same typeface and a similar structure to the letter, even though it is a personal text rather than a business letter. Its formal aspects thus tend to cue in metalingual codes that are comparable to the job application, but codes which in this case are not particularly appropriate. The email recognises this, though, and in its referential and metalingual functions even tries to defuse the possibility of an aberrant coding by drawing attention to and openly contradicting the effects of the formal function. ('. . . a *real* letter rather than all these emails', etc.)
- *One function may trigger off another.*
  The font and layout of the application letter are part of its formal function. This, however, immediately triggers off certain metalingual functions, which suggest what sort of letter this is and thus what sorts of codes might be appropriate to bring to bear on it.

EXERCISES

Examine the ways in which the following examples work, in terms of the seven functions we have developed in this chapter. How do the metalingual and formal functions work in with the referential function? What sorts of address are these examples making? What contextual determinants and effects are there?

Figure 1.5

> **Desk, teak laminate** 1350 × 600,
> 4-drawer, steel frame plus chair adj
> height, swivel on castors, GC, $90
> Macarthur 5409 7658
>
> **Desk with 1 drawer**, cupboard
> on side with shelves, has a few
> scratches on outside of hutch,
> VGC, $130 Lancaster 7397 4014

Figure 1.6

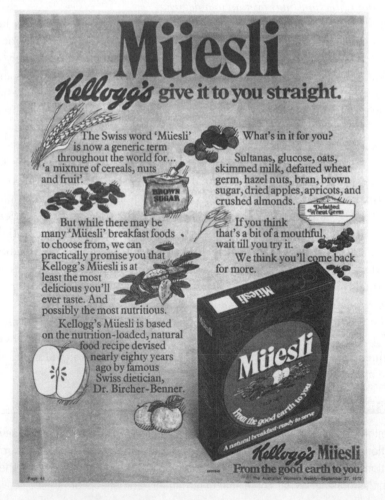

Figure 1.7

Figure 1.8

7.30 Just Shoot Me!
(PG)(R)(S). The staff prepare for
the annual softball game.
896436
8.00 World's Funniest
Animal Bloopers (G)(S). Dana
Meecham. 893349
8.30 Movie: Die Hard with a
Vengeance. (MIv)(R)(S).
(1995). A police officer and a
store owner must play a
bomber's deadly game. Bruce
Willis, Samuel L Jackson.
74991981
11.10 News. 6936165
6930681
11.15 Movie: A Life Less
Ordinary. (MIv)(S). (1997).
Two emissaries from heaven
are given the task of making
two people fall in love. Ewan
McGregor, Cameron Diaz.
4474404

Figure 1.9

Figure 1.10

Procedure:

1 Normal playback

Press the PLAY button (1).

- The PLAY indicator ▶ should appear in the display.
- Eliminate noise bars by using the TRACKING control (2).
- Adjust the picture with the SHARPNESS control (3), if needed

2 Still playback

To view a still picture, press the PAUSE button (4) when the VCR is in the normal playback mode.

- The PAUSE indicator | | and ▶ should appear in the display.
- If the VCR is left in Pause mode for more than 5 minutes, the unit automatically resumes playback to protect the tape and video heads.

Figure 1.11

SOURCES AND FURTHER READING

The classic statement of Jakobson's model is the first few pages of his paper 'Linguistics and Poetics'. Here Jakobson's main purpose – which is not ours – is to account for what he argues are the properties peculiar to poetic language. Our model is a free modification of this, which draws also on Dell Hymes's use of it in *Foundations in Sociolinguistics* (Philadelphia: University of Pennsylvania Press, 1974). More information on Jakobson can also be found at the Semiotics site of the University of Colorado at Denver (carbon.cudenver.edu/~mryder/itc_data/semiotics.html#jakobson) which is administered by Martin Ryder. For links to numerous relevant Internet sites, see the Semiotics page of Daniel Chandler's Media and Communications Studies site at www.aber.ac.uk/media/Functions/mcs.html.

Signs and systems

CONTENTS

Building a model

In the last chapter, we suggested that signs do many more things than merely refer. We briefly examined a few common situations in which signs are used, and saw that in some of these the referential function is not even necessarily an important part of what the sign does.

In this chapter, we will try to systematise some of these ideas about language processes. We will develop a detailed **model** of sign processes. As with all model-making, this will inevitably involve simplifying things somewhat, so there are bound to be aspects left out. We will try to pay attention to where these simplifications occur, but for the moment it should be stressed that this simplification may actually be one of the strengths of model-making. If for the moment we concentrate on only two or three carefully chosen aspects of signs, we may be able to provide a framework in which we can raise interesting questions about how signs work in general.

The particular model we're going to construct is **semiotics**, as it was developed in the work of the Swiss linguist Ferdinand de Saussure, in his posthumous *Course in General Linguistics* of 1916. Saussure's ideas have been taken up in many fields of the human sciences under the general term of **structuralism**. Though we are going to end up a considerable distance

from structuralism and semiotics, they will nevertheless be a very convenient point of departure for us. While there is a tendency for Saussurean
semiotics to be formal and abstract in its approach, throughout this book
we will be progressively more concerned with the *social* contexts in which
signs are used.

It is important to emphasise that semiotics is, precisely, a model. As we
will use it here, it lays no claim at all to be able to explain every aspect of
sign practices. We simply claim it as a useful way of picturing some of the
things which happen in them. It is a starting point, not the final truth
about signs: a set of tools which are very useful for some jobs but not
necessarily for others. Part of the skill, of course, always lies in picking the
right tools for the job. Semiotics provides an excellent framework for
asking some questions about signs, but is less useful for asking others. We
will consider these limits later on.

For our purposes, there are a couple of advantages in looking at semiotics in some detail here. First of all, it is a framework which is very
frequently invoked in cultural studies, even when it is debated. You'll find
the concepts we'll be developing mentioned almost everywhere in the literature. Second, semiotics is a very good example of just how much can be
got out of a relatively simple model. It starts off from two or three assumptions about signs, but builds this into a model which has very wide descriptive power.

Sign and referent

Our discussion in Chapter 1 has suggested that, even if it does seem the
most intuitively obvious aspect of language, referentiality may not be a
good place to start. Even the most common uses of language are just altogether too complex to be summed up in terms of the simple relationship
between a word and the thing it names.

As a first step towards constructing a theory of signs, then, we will take
the apparently drastic step of leaving the function of naming to one side.
That is, we are not initially going to assume we know anything at all about
how the sound 'cat' comes to refer to a particular sort of animal.

This may seem odd, but remember that it is purely a *tactical* manoeu-
vre, giving us a place to start from. It is not intended to deny the obvious
fact that the word 'cat' *is* in some way attached to a particular sort of
animal, or that we mostly don't have any difficulty in using it that way. For
most practical purposes, there is generally a reasonably clear link between
word and thing (though perhaps not always as clear as we'd like). For the
moment, though, we are not simply going to assume we know anything

about just what this link might be. While referentiality is certainly one of the *functions* a sign may have, one of its effects, it may not provide any explanation of how signs work. On the contrary, reference is one of the things we must explain about signs. If we start somewhere else, we may in the end be able to come back to the whole question of how words are connected to the world, but this time with some fresh ideas to work with. That is, instead of concentrating on the relationship:

$$\text{sign} \longleftrightarrow \text{referent}$$

we are going to concentrate on the *structure of the sign* itself.

Signifier and signified

What happens when something is perceived as a sign?
Take the sequence of sounds we write as 'cat'. Think about what happens when you recognise this sequence as a sign, not just a meaningless noise. Two things happen simultaneously in your mind:

1 You have a **mental impression** of the sound 'cat'.
2 This sequence of sounds also invokes in you a certain general and abstract **concept** – in this case, the concept of 'catness'.

This may seem a simple, even obvious point to make, but because it will be the basis of the entire system of semiotics we are going to build, we will take some time to discuss it before going on.

These two aspects of the sign have standard names. The mental impression of the sound is called the **signifier**; and the general concept invoked is the **signified**. In other words, one aspect of the sign does the signifying, the other aspect is what is signified. The relationship between the two is called **signification**.

We can generalise this distinction out to other types of sign, such as the written or graphic signs in Figures 2.1 to 2.4.

The **signifier** is the *sensory impression* of the sign: the mental image of marks on a page, or of sounds in the air, for example.
The **signified** is the *concept* the sign invokes.
The *relationship* between signifier and signified, the way in which a sensory impression 'points to' or invokes a concept, is called **signification**.

Figure 2.1 The spoken word 'cat'

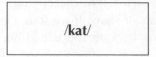

Figure 2.2 A sentence written in chalk on a blackboard

The two facets of the sign are often pictured like this:

$$\text{sign} = \frac{\text{signified}}{\text{signifier}} \updownarrow \text{signification}$$

There are several points to note here.

Signifier and signified are inseparable and simultaneous

The diagram tends to suggest that signifier and signified are separable parts of the sign, as though you could somehow make a cut between them and peel one away from the other. In reality, they are simply terms which are useful for emphasising the two different ways in which a sign must operate in order to be a sign. Signifier and signified always go together. Compare them to the two sides of an infinitely thin sheet of paper. You can cut through the paper any way you like, but in doing that you will not in any way separate front from back.

Signifier and signified are abstract mental entities

The sign itself is a mental construct, something which happens in our heads. What distinguishes a mere combination of sounds or graphic marks from a sign is a mental, cognitive activity. As a result, the two components of the sign, the signifier and the signified, must also be mental entities. This abstraction will allow us to formulate a very powerful and general concept of the sign.

First consider the signifier. Every time I hear the combination of sounds we write as 'cat', I am actually hearing a quite unique combination. The word

Figure 2.3 An amateur photo of a family pet

'cat' spoken by a man sounds different from the word spoken by a woman. Children sound different from adults. Geographical and class groups often tend to have their own distinctive accents. The same person will pronounce words differently according to where they come in a sentence, or the different functions they serve, or the comparative emphasis each is given. Say 'Cat? *What* cat?' and listen to the subtle differences between the two. Strictly speaking, each utterance is quite unique and unrepeatable. Even if

Figure 2.4 A magazine advertisement for cat food

READ *this* and you'll clearly see why
Whiskas® is good for your cat's eyes.

UNLIKE YOU, your cat can't eat carrots to help keep his eyes healthy. The fact is cats are carnivores (meat eaters) by nature. So they can't absorb nutrients like Vitamin A found in foods like carrots.

To keep his vision clear, your cat needs Whiskas every day. Being a complete and balanced meal, Whiskas has all the nutrients your cat needs daily like Taurine and Vitamin A (the nutrients for good vision). So every time he has his Whiskas, he's keeping his eyes healthy. And because Whiskas has the taste your cat loves, you can be sure he'll enjoy his meal every day. *Whiskas knows cats best.*

● WHISKAS is a registered trade mark © Uncle Ben's of Australia 1992   PATTS – W1631

you could make exactly the same sounds twice, the situation you'd be making them in would have changed.

Nevertheless, assuming a certain familiarity with accents and individual speech patterns, we tend to recognise the word 'cat' regardless of whether it's spoken by a Scots vet in a lecture, an angry Tasmanian breeder of rare mice, or a New York newsreader with a bad head cold. In order to do this, we make an abstraction from what we actually hear. In effect, we decide that certain features of the sounds we're hearing (pitch, individual variations, etc.) are really incidental and can be ignored. *What we are left with* after all these apparent incidentals have been stripped away is the signifier: the pure, abstract mental sound-impression 'cat'.

Something similar is true of the signified, too. The sign 'cat' doesn't signify because it invokes the image of this or that particular cat or type of cat: that would be the *referent*, which we've agreed to put out of play for the moment. The sign 'cat' *signifies* because it invokes a general and quite abstract concept of 'catness'.

In summary, the signifier is not the actual sounds heard, or the actual graphic marks seen, but the *mental impression* of them. Neither is the signified the actual thing referred to, but the *abstract concept* of the thing. The sign is not the actual mark or the sound, but a *conceptual entity*, the union of two conceptual others.

The signified is not the referent

It's important not to confuse these two: they're quite different things, so different that they belong to two quite different orders of being.

- The **referent** is something *other than* the sign, which the sign points to or stands for: an object in the world.
- The **signified**, on the other hand, is an *aspect of* the sign, a pure abstraction, a concept.

It's precisely because there is a difference between the two that I can understand perfectly well what you are *signifying* by the word 'cat', even though I have never met the particular cat to which you might be *referring*.

The link between signifier and signified is arbitrary

The signifier has no natural link with the signified. That is, there is no inherent and necessary reason that the sound-image or graphic-image 'cat' should automatically invoke the general concept of 'catness', or vice versa. The signified 'catness' can have other signifiers: the Latin word *felis*, for example, or a pictorial representation. The signifier 'cat', too, may in its turn have other signifieds than 'domestic feline'. It is also the name of a type of whip, a coal scow, and a bit of nautical tackle. One signified may have many signifiers; one signifier may have many signifieds. Even though there can be no signifier without a signified (and vice versa), the two nevertheless slide around over each other with a fair bit of freedom. In other words, by their very nature, signs do not have a *single* meaning but many.

This is not an absolute freedom: we could hardly argue that a sign can mean anything a user might want it to. Certain signifiers obviously do tend to get used in connection with certain sets of signifieds and not others (and vice versa), and this is not a matter for the individual user's choice. It is a decision that, as it were, has already been made for us by the language we speak and by the conventions of representation we use. (The next chapters will return to this point, to examine ways in which meanings get stabilised or contested.) That the connection between signifier and signified is arbitrary means that it is purely a matter of historical accident: there is nothing in the language system itself which would prohibit the possibility that, if history had been a little bit different, we would now associate different signifiers with the concept of 'catness', or different signifieds with the sound-image 'cat'.

Difference and value

We began by suggesting that a particular sign doesn't take on its meaning through the apparently direct link of reference, the relation between sign and object. Then we went on to suggest that even the more abstract link of signification (the relation between signifier and signified within the sign) is arbitrary. Because of this, the meaning of a sign cannot be due to some sort of essence of what the sign is in itself. There is no longer any such essence, as the sign is a sort of historical accident. How then *does* any sign take on meaning?

We already have the answer: from outside itself. We suggested in the first chapter that the meaning of a sign may depend on a variety of factors, including the situations and conventions in which it is used. The sign's meaning, that is, depends on what surrounds it: it is not a content hidden away somewhere 'inside' the sign.

Saussurean semiotics develops this idea in a narrower sense. Out of all the things outside the sign which may contribute to its meaning (everything we've called 'context', which potentially includes the entire situation and social world in which the sign is being used), Saussure considers only other signs within the system. That is, in the Saussurean system, a sign gets its meaning from *other signs*. The meaning it may get from things that aren't signs is not something Saussurean semiotics concerns itself with. Keep in mind that this is quite a restricted sense of meaning. We shall follow it for the moment, because even though it is restricted, the model we can build with it is still immensely suggestive.

If a sign gets its meaning from other signs, it works through a system of **differences** (from what it isn't), rather than of identity (with itself). It means something not because it has some fixed identity, but because it is different from other signs. We could put that in a succinct but paradoxical form by saying that what a sign *is* is due to what it isn't.

Let's make this more specific, by considering the case of our sign 'cat'. Again, we will consider both the signifier and the signified in turn.

We determined above that the actual sound-sequence 'cat' can vary considerably and yet still be recognised as a variation on the abstract, general sound-image which is the signifier. For this to occur, we need a system of sounds which can be distinguished from each other. If 'cat' and 'pat' are going to be different signifiers, we need to be able to distinguish between the sounds of 'c' and 'p'. What makes the sound-image 'cat' a possible signifier is not the qualities of the actual sounds themselves, but simply that we can distinguish them from other sounds. We can tell the difference between 'cat' and 'pat', 'mat', 'bat', and so on, or 'cat' and 'can', 'cap', 'cad', or 'cat' and 'cot', 'coat' or 'cut'.

Similarly, our general concept of 'catness' is defined in a network of differences. We can have a concept of 'catness' because we can distinguish this from other related concepts, like 'dogness', 'rabbitness', 'canaryness', 'fishness'. The sign 'big' only takes on meaning when it is part of a system which lets it be juxtaposed with 'little'. A big flea is of a different order of magnitude altogether from a big elephant, or a big (or even a very small) supernova.

You will recall that our earlier diagram depicted signification as a *vertical* relationship between signifier and signified. What we are suggesting now, as the source of the sign's meaning, is a set of *horizontal* relationships between signifier and signifier, and between signified and signified. These horizontal relationships determine a sign's **value**. A sign's signification is a function of its value. The relationship between signifier and signified for any particular sign depends ultimately on the relationships all the signs in the system have with one another:

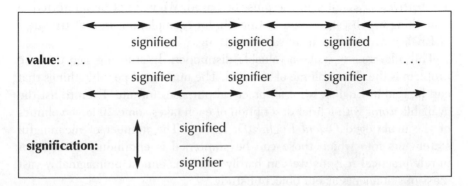

It may be useful to make a loose analogy with money here. A $10 note, say, buys a certain amount of one commodity, and a different amount of another. This is not because there is a direct and necessary relationship between an amount of money and an amount of a commodity: no law or principle says that $10 is inherently worth about 3.5 litres of milk. The relationship between the two is due to all sorts of other costs: those of buying, keeping and feeding cattle, of hiring labour, maintaining machinery, and processing and distributing the product. These in their turn depend other costs: the cost of hiring labour, for instance, is determined by factors such as the cost of living – to which of course, the cost of milk makes its own contribution. The cost of milk is rather like the vertical relationship of signification. The link between the signified commodity and the money which signifies it actually comes from the horizontal relationship it has with all the other costs in the economy.

Indeed, the very term 'value' which we have been using to describe signs comes, of course, from economics. Semiotics is basically an economic model of sign processes: it sees exchange as their essential feature.

System and acts

In discussing the signifier and signified, we have emphasised that neither of these corresponds simply to the actual sound or mark, or to the thing itself: both are abstractions. We are now going to make another, potentially very useful abstraction.

We have just decided that the sign's meaning doesn't arise within it, but from the entire system of relationships within which it exists, giving it value. The object we study in the semiotics we are building up here will have to be not the individual sign, but the entire system which gives any individual sign its meaning. Semiotics will not be concerned with individual or specific acts of sign use, but with the systems within which they operate and on which any particular case of sign use must be based. We will not be interested in everything which can be said in English, for example, but in the structures of English which allow us to say these things.

This allows us to make a valuable distinction. In studying sign use, the problem is the sheer volume of material. The number of possible things that can be said in English is for all practical purposes infinite. Even to list the available *words* with a brief description of each takes some 20 large volumes of the unabridged *Oxford English Dictionary*. The number of meaningful statements into those can be combined is enormous. Clearly, for purely practical reasons we can hardly take this almost unimaginably vast mass of statements as our object of study.

But this mass is not entirely chaotic. It has regularities. What if these statements are all produced according to a relatively small number of effective *rules*? If statements follow rules, then a knowledge of how the rules work should actually let us produce any possible statement: in effect, it will tell us everything we need to know about statements, and do it a lot more economically. While listing all possible English statements might be an infinite task, a list of the rules of English grammar fits pretty comfortably into a modestly sized book. Let us assume, then, for the sake of the model we are constructing, that *all actual sign usages follow conventional rules.*

This may be something of a simplification of the situation. Although it has certain advantages for our model, it may often be more useful to think of these regularities in other terms than rules that must be followed. Real sign practices may be more complicated matters. We shall take this up again in Chapter 9, but for the moment the hypothesis that signs follow rules will take us a valuable step forward.

If sign usages are rule-bound, we can separate the domain of signs into two conceptually distinct areas. We will give Saussure's original French terms for them, since there isn't a single pair of English words which makes quite the same distinction, and you'll find that most English texts on semiotics just adopt the French. They are:

---

parole (or **utterance**, or **speech**):
a given act or artifact of language, such as a spoken utterance, a conversation, a postcard, a novel, or a course handout; and

langue (or **code**, or **system**, or **the language**):
the system which enables such acts of *parole* to be produced.

Saussure also uses the term *langage* to refer indiscriminately to either of these, so in effect:

$$langage = langue + parole$$

Parole is made up of actual, concrete sign uses in the real world, and is potentially infinite. *Langue* is finite, but it is also abstract, something we infer behind the examples of *parole* we can observe. *Parole* has meaning only to the extent that it manifests, or is constructed according to, the system of *langue*. Semiotics is concerned with reconstructing the *langue* which underlies certain types of *parole*. We shall also have to ask about the relationship between them: how is the system *used* to produce utterances?

According to the semiotic model a sentence, for example, makes sense to the extent that it is constructed according to a system (which in this case is grammar). It is important to note that this system doesn't have to be what's often called 'good English usage' (which is really just the way in which certain dominant groups construct *their* English usage). It may be local, dialect, patois, jargon, slang, or whatever. The important point is that each of these does have its own system of regular and conventional uses, to which users' utterances broadly conform. To understand the utterance, you have to know something of the system.

Codes

We can sum this up quite simply. In practice, a single sign is capable of taking on many different meanings. This depends on the **code** or sub-system within which it is used and interpreted.

Take an example. I shake my head from side to side when asked a question. In most cases in Western usage, this is a quite obvious act of *parole* which signifies 'no'. In the system of bodily gestures of which it is a part, it is contrasted with a nod which means 'yes'. But this meaning depends on the system of gestures. In some other cultures, a shake of the head stands for 'yes', and is contrasted with other gestures meaning 'no'. The important thing is not whether the gesture for 'yes' is a shake or a nod, but simply that it has a consistent meaning within the system.

Another example: in western cultures, white stands for purity, and is traditionally worn at weddings, but in Chinese culture, white is a colour of mourning, and is worn at funerals. Meaning, then, is not the product of the sign itself, but of the code within which it is used.

Even within any given code, any number of **subsidiary codes** may also be operating. These may overlap, or they may be relatively separate from each other, even conflicting. Any example of *parole* may invoke and work from several different sub-codes at the same time. It will be useful to return to this later, when we come to consider genre.

Though this may seem altogether different from the model introduced in Chapter 1, what we have developed so far allows us to talk about some of the features of that model in much more detail. We have suggested, for example, that the meaning of a given sign comes from the code within which it operates. Another way of putting this is to say that *codes provide positions from which it is possible to speak or to mean*. To use terms we developed in Chapter 1, we could say that *codes construct possible positions for addresser and addressee*. What's more, as codes are social constructions, shared by a group, the positions they provide for addresser and addressee are necessarily social positions. Even though it tends to provide a rather formal analysis of signs (that is, according solely to their properties within a system), Saussurean semiotics nevertheless seems to open up possibilities for thinking of language in more fully social terms. We will discuss this shortly.

Synchrony and diachrony

A code is in effect a description of the state of the sign system at any given instant. It is something like a cross-section of the sign system at one point on the time axis. As a result, we can characterise it as a **synchronic** structure, and a semiotics like the one we have been developing here, which studies sign-systems by taking such a cross-section of them, we could accordingly call a **synchronic semiotics**.

Such a study necessarily leaves out much of the ways in which signs work. In considering them only as a system frozen in cross-section, it may have little to say about their historical aspects, or the ways in which such systems inevitably change with time. On its own, synchronic semiotics can have little to say about why the English spoken in London today is different from that spoken there 500 years ago, or how fashions, car designs and films have changed over the last fifty years. The aspects of signs which are time-bound rather than the product of a synchronic system are, by contrast, called **diachronic**.

The organisation of the system

It is all very well to say that sign acts are the result of a structured system, but what could that structure be? To complicate things, we are after a general theory which will work for all systems of meaning. Take our previous examples, Figures 2.1 to 2.4: is it possible to find principles of construction common to all of them?

The sentence (Figure 2.2) perhaps has the most obvious structure. It is made up of a number of clearly demarcated *elements* (words), which are *arranged* in a certain way, according to the rules of English grammar. Both of these contribute to the overall meaning. Alter either the choice of elements or the way in which they are arranged, and the meaning changes or even vanishes. 'On the mat sat the cat' means something very similar (but not exactly the same: Jakobson's model might suggest ways of pinpointing these differences). 'The dog sat on the mat' or 'The cat slept on the mat' are also meaningful, but in different ways. 'The mat sat on the cat' sounds rather improbable, but we can dismiss it only because it has a basic minimal intelligibility. Precisely because we know quite clearly what it means, we can dismiss it as different from the usual behaviour of cats and mats. The arrangement 'the The on sat mat cat', on the other hand, doesn't have even that intelligibility.

Is this true of the other examples? Take the advertisement of Figure 2.4. Is its overall meaning the result of both a set of elements and the ways in which these are combined? There may not seem to be anything as strict as a grammar at work here, but it is not too hard to isolate a basic set of elements whose arrangement is also crucial to the meaning. A convenient way of dividing up this advertisement would be to say that there are three basic elements: the photograph of the cat in extreme close-up, and taking up the top two-thirds of the page; the written text, taking up most of the bottom third; and the photograph of the can of cat food at bottom right. There would be other ways of doing it, and quite a few further subdivisions we could make, but for now let's take those three as a minimal set of elements. Does the way in which they are arranged affect the meaning?

Imagine how different the advertisement would be if the photos of the cat and the can of food swapped size and position. In its original full-page, full-colour magazine form, with the cat's eyes an electric yellowy-green and the whole face almost the same size as your own, the ad itself gives the arresting effect of staring back at you. Swap the order and size of the elements and that effect is altogether lost.

How about Figure 2.3, an amateur photograph of a family pet? Even here, we could argue that the meaning of the photograph comes from a certain set of elements (at very least, these would be the cat itself and the surroundings in which it is shown), and the way in which these are arranged (the cat is roughly central in the photo; it is also in front of the setting, not obscured behind it: those two aspects are, after all, precisely what leads us to call this a photo of a cat, rather than a photo of a garden path). And in Figure 2.1, the spoken word has clearly been broken down into three elements, the sounds, /k/, /a/ and /t/, which are combined according to the possibilities of English-language phonetics. Recombining them as /akt/ would have produced a different meaning altogether, whereas the arrangements /tka/ or /kta/ would have been nonsensical.

A commutation test

The concept of value lets us formulate a useful **commutation test** for determining, in a rather *ad hoc* way, three important aspects of the way a group of signs is working:

- what the significant elements of a given array of signs might be;
- what contribution they make to the overall significance; and
- what effect their particular arrangement may have.

Simply imagine what happens when one of the elements is changed, or the relationship between any two. The extent to which this imaginary change alters the overall meaning suggests the extent to which the original element is contributing to the array's meaning. It makes a big difference to the cat food advertisement if you swap the cat and the can, so we could expect the layout to be a big contributor to what the signs can mean.

Note that this commutation test is purely a preliminary step. It helps identify elements and relationships, but as yet it tells us nothing more about them, other than that they are significant to various degrees. It doesn't say anything at all about how they come to be significant, or what the implications of that might be. It is not yet a proper semiotic analysis, but it does provide a very useful basis for one, by giving a rough-and-ready idea of where to look.

Paradigm and syntagm

We can formalise these considerations by saying that *langue*, the code or system of signs, is organised along two axes: *selection* and *combination*. On the first axis, elements are selected. On the second, the elements which have been selected are now combined according to certain rules. Another set of names for these is the *paradigmatic* and *syntagmatic axes*.

> A **paradigm** is a set of signs, any of which are conceivably *interchangeable* within a given context.
> A **syntagm** is an ordered array of signs *combined* according to certain rules.

Paradigms are not fixed; they are determined by the criteria of the context and topic. Elements of the same paradigm can be broadly substituted for one another in a given syntagmatic context. In the two statements, 'The cat sat on the mat' and 'The dog sat on the mat', 'cat' and 'dog' both belong to the paradigm of *domestic mammal*. If the cat is mine and the dog belongs to the people next door, I may decide that they don't belong to the same paradigm at all (which would be *my pet*), and wonder what next door's dog is doing on my cat's mat.

In general, the less easy it is to substitute a given element for the original term, the more distant it is from the original paradigm set. If we broaden the paradigm set from *domestic mammals* to *mammals*, we start to get the possibility of less and less likely syntagms ('The dugong sat on the mat'). The further away we move, the less likely the syntagms we get. If the paradigm set is simply *nouns*, we have possibilities like 'The generalisation sat on the mat'. If we broaden it out even further, to anything at all, we might just end up with nonsense ('The of sat on the mat').

A syntagm, then, is the result of using a conventional rule to combine a series of elements from various paradigms:

---

elements of paradigms + rule = syntagm

Here we find the beginnings of a solution to a possible problem which arose earlier on. We said then that the link of signification between signifier and signified is arbitrary, and that therefore by their nature signs do not have a single fixed meaning; instead, they have potentially multiple and shifting meanings. How is it then that in our everyday lives we use signs as if their meanings were stable – as if we know what they mean? Why doesn't every attempted communication break down into a morass of ambiguities?

The answer is simple enough here. If any individual sign may have several *possible* meanings, the actual utterances in which a sign is used tend to narrow somewhat the field of *probable* meanings. In isolation, the word 'cat' may equally as well mean a domestic mammal, a whip, a coal scow, a bit of nautical tackle, a two-hulled boat . . . In fact, however, words never occur in isolation. They always occur in some context, and generally within some sort of syntagmatic statement, and this tends to narrow greatly the probable range of meanings. If the word 'cat' occurs in a syntagm such as 'The cat is on the mat', it is now much more probable that the cat in question is the domestic mammal rather than, say, the boat. The context and situation may make one particular meaning or set of meanings more probable again: it may not be the domestic mammal I mean if I say this sentence while wondering just where in the dungeon I left the thumbscrews, or while staring at the coal barge which has just crashed in through the wall. Paradigms provide a plurality of possible meanings; syntagms tend to narrow these down according to context. Paradigms expand; syntagms contract.

Semiotic systems in general

It is surprising how many activities can be described in this way. A recipe, for example, is a set of instructions (rules) showing you how to combine syntagmatically certain elements from a paradigm set of ingredients so as to produce the desired dish. Ordering food in a restaurant, you select elements from a number of paradigms ('appetiser', 'main course', 'dessert', etc.) and combine them according to certain customary rules (generally only one dish from each category, and following a given order). An outfit of clothing worn on a particular day syntagmatically combines elements from various paradigm sets ('shoes', 'hats', etc.) according to a code of dress which may vary according to time of day, occasion, economics, and – of course – gender.

'Errors of syntax' are of course always possible. I can utter a nonsensical 'sentence' like 'The the sat mat cat on', or combine the three letters into an illegitimate 'word' like 'tca'. To ice a fruit cake before cooking it and then add the fruit later is also, in the semiotic terms of this analogy, equivalent to producing a badly constructed statement: it goes against all the conventions (or 'grammar') of cookery.

Does this mean that all of these activities – preparing a meal, wearing clothes – are in some sense activities of signification: that is, that they are not just matters of satisfying a biological need or shielding oneself from sun or cold, but activities which produce meanings? Try the commutation test suggested earlier: does a bottle of cheap red wine carry the same meanings as a French vintage? What would it mean to eat your dessert first? Does an evening gown mean the same thing regardless of whether it's worn by a man or a woman?

It is perhaps not yet clear from our model just where these meanings might come from, or how they might function, but the model certainly seems to indicate the possibility of explaining such variations. Although it comes initially from the specific case of language, semiotics does seem to be broad enough to be able to describe non-linguistic or non-verbal social phenomena in terms of signification. Now we must try to describe just how such complex social meanings are produced. To do that, we shall first have to look at various ways in which signs within systems can interact with each other.

EXERCISES

1 Saussurean semiotics is based on a linguistic model. When Saussure defines signifier and signified, for example, he has spoken language in mind. Does this model work as well with graphic signs? (You may wish to refer back to the various graphic signs reproduced in this and the previous chapter.)

   Can we, for example, argue in the case of a photograph that the signifier and signified have only an arbitrary link? What precisely would 'arbitrary' mean in such a case? (Recall here that there is a careful distinction to be made between signified and referent.) How can we isolate individual signs from the continuum of a photograph? Does the commutation test help here?

2 Figure 2.5 suggests some activities and processes which can be understood in terms of semiotic system: that is, in each case there would seem to be a basic set of elements which develop meanings when they are combined according to the rules of a system. What other examples could be added to this list?

Does the idea of a system of rules work in quite the same way in each of these cases? Do the rules always have the same importance? What are the different effects, for example, of an irregular syntagm in a game of cards (an illegal play) and an irregular syntagm of clothing (odd socks, a colour mismatch, runners worn with a suit)? Can the application of the rules always be described as correct or incorrect? If not, what other factors should be taken into account, and how do you think the Saussurean model might accommodate them?

Figure 2.5 Paradigm and syntagm

elements of paradigm	+	rule	=	syntagm
words		grammar		sentence
ingredients		recipe		finished dish
clothes		codes of dress		complete outfit
items on menu		sequence of courses		order to waiter
playing cards		rules of game		sequence of play
letters, numbers, operators		algebra		equation
folds on paper		origami		paper animal
genes		genetic code		you

SOURCES AND FURTHER READING

Daniel Chandler's *Semiotics for Beginners* is an excellent online guide to elementary semiotics, with sections on all of the material covered in Chapters 2 and 3 of this book, a glossary of terms, advice on doing your own semiotic analyses in assignments, and suggestions for further reading. It is part of the Media and Communication Studies site at the University of Wales, Aberyswyth (www.aber.ac.uk/media). Follow the link from the Index. Chandler's *Semiotics: The Basics* (New York and London: Routledge, 2001) draws and expands on this site.

Mick Underwood's Cultsock site has a useful discussion of the material dealt with in this chapter and the next, though there are some differences in the concepts of connotation and connotation as we examine them in the next chapter (www.cultsock.ndirect.co.uk/MUHome/cshtml/semiomean/semio1.html). You can also check the entry on Saussure at the University of Colorado at Denver site on Semiotics (carbon.cudenver.edu/~mryder/itc_data/semiotics.html).

The principal source for much of the material dealt with in this chapter is of course Ferdinand de Saussure's *Course in General Linguistics* (London: Duckworth, 1983). Though the *Course* is one of the most influential texts text in linguistics, it has a complex and somewhat uncertain status: published in 1916, three years after Saussure's death, it was compiled from various sets of lecture notes by two of his former students. It's an approachable and interesting work, necessary reading if you're going to do advanced work in semiotics, structuralism or post-structural theories, and well worth looking at anyway. There are two translations available: the more recent, by Roy Harris, has the advantage of being able to draw on the 1972 critical French edition, which thoroughly revised the text from the original notes. It does, however, provide some opportunities for confusion. Rather than translate *signifié* and *signifiant* as the familiar *signified* and *signifier* (the terms we've used here), it chooses to translate them as *signification* and *signal*.

Jonathan Culler's *Saussure* (Ithaca, N.Y.: Cornell University Press, 1986) is a brief and very approachable introduction to the *Course*. For a more advanced discussion, see Roy Harris's *Reading Saussure* (London: Duckworth, 1987).

Saussure's *Course* is primarily linguistic, though he does suggest the future possibility of a general theory of signs to which he gives the name *semiology*. In his *Elements of Semiology* (London: Cape, 1967), Roland Barthes provides a sketch of what such a generalised science might be, supplementing Saussure with the work of later linguists such as Benveniste, Hjelmslev and Jakobson. Despite its title, this is not an introductory text: it's brief but demanding, though a book the advanced student will want to investigate.

Terence Hawkes' *Structuralism and Semiotics* (London: Methuen, 1977) is primarily addressed to students of literature, but it provides a clear and useful introduction to Saussure. The various essays in David Robey (ed.), *Structuralism: An Introduction* (Oxford: Clarendon Press, 1973) are also helpful. A couple of reference-type books on semiotics also offer useful definitions in the field: *Encyclopedia of Semiotics* (New York: Oxford University Press, 1998), which is edited by Paul Bouissac, and Winfried Noth's *Handbook of Semiotics* (Bloomington: Indiana University Press, 1995). Nick Lacey's *Image and Representation: Key Concepts in Media Studies* (New York: St Martin's, 1997) has some helpful discussions of semiotic concepts, as does Marcel Danesi's *Of Cigarettes, High Heels and Other Interesting Things: An Introduction to Semiotics* (Basingstoke: Macmillan – now Palgrave, 1999). Paul Cobley and Litza Jantz's *Introducing Semiotics* (Cambridge: Icon, 1999) is another accessible introduction.

Two more advanced studies of semiotic issues are Alec McHoul's *Semiotic Investigations: Towards an Effective Semiotics* (Lincoln: University of Nebraska Press, 1996) and David Holdcroft's *Saussure: Signs, Systems, and Arbitrariness* (Cambridge: Cambridge University Press, 1991).

Interactions of signs

An individual sign gains its meaning from its value in a system of signs. Signs invariably invoke other signs. Within paradigmatic sets and syntagmatic sequences, signs may associate with or substitute for each other in potentially very complex ways. In this chapter and the next, we will start to examine some of the basic mechanisms by which this can happen. We will then be in a position to start examining something of the social nature of signification.

Metaphor

Perhaps the most obvious way in which one sign can substitute for another is by *comparison*, or **metaphor**.

A **metaphor** is an implicit or explicit **comparison**.

'To make a pig of yourself' is a metaphor. It doesn't imply that you actually turn into a farmyard animal, but that your behaviour is in some way *like* that of a pig – perhaps that you're eating a lot, very fast and somewhat noisily. What is *described* is you; the paradigm into which you have been placed is that of 'things with disgusting eating habits'; what you are described *as* is another member of that paradigm, the pig.

Everyday speech is full of metaphor, ranging from the inventive ('As much use as pockets in socks') to the banal and familiar ('to make a pig of oneself', 'to follow like sheep', 'sour grapes', 'lion-hearted', 'to go flat out', 'to have egg on one's face', 'to be caught with one's pants down', 'a dog-in-the-manger attitude'). Nicknames may often be metaphorical. What aspects of former British Prime Minister Margaret Thatcher were metaphorised in the name 'The Iron Lady'? A former Australian Prime Minister, Paul Keating, was often called 'The Undertaker'. You don't have to be familiar with Australian politics of that era to suspect the nickname came either from his appearance or from his political behaviour. (In fact, it was both: tall, thin and always dressed in dark well-tailored Italian suits, Keating was renowned for his cuttingly sardonic demolitions of parliamentary opponents, and in turn attacked for presiding over an economy in recession.)

Metaphors may be visual as well as verbal. Figure 3.1, for example, compares the process of making a meal to that of making a movie. What is described is the familiar and perhaps mundane process of cooking, but it's described in terms of the somewhat less familiar and possibly more exciting process of shooting a film. The effect the metaphor has is to inject one sign with some of the meanings of another: the everyday process of preparing a meal is invested with some of the glamour and excitement of Hollywood.

Figure 3.2 is somewhat more oblique in its comparison. Here, some aspects of the large picture on the left are being compared – and transferred

Figure 3.1

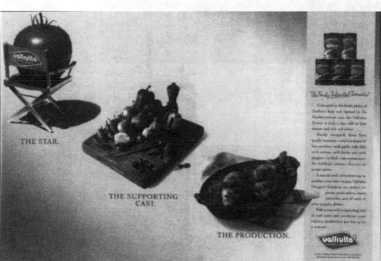

Figure 3.2

STILTON

— to the small one on the right. It may not be obvious just what Stilton cheese has to do with arriving by boat at a deserted shore somewhere on a vast lake or fjord at sunset, but the title running across the large picture makes the link: 'Stilton makes any meal a special occasion.' What they have in common is that they're both 'special occasions.' (Note here how the caption has almost acted as an equals sign, in that it's suggested just what the similarity is. Without it, the similarity might well remain a mystery.) By means of metaphor, a lump of animal fat has been invested with qualities of adventure, romance, escape – and whatever other qualities we might argue the large picture as signifying.

From the examples we've examined, it would seem that metaphor can have an interesting function of **transference**. That is, metaphor can in effect transfer certain qualities from one sign to another, which is thus invested with properties it might not originally have had. Tomatoes are not inherently glamorous, nor is cheese in itself adventurous.

Metaphors have both paradigmatic and syntagmatic effects.

Paradigmatically, they substitute one element of a paradigm set for another. To take a previous example, if you refer to a greedy person as a pig, you effectively place them in a paradigm set of voracious or disgusting eaters, and substitute for their name that of another member of that set. The paradigm sets may be obvious and familiar, or unfamiliar and more demanding of thought. Depending on how the paradigm set is chosen, metaphor can be used to describe the unfamiliar in familiar terms, or – going the other way – to describe the familiar in less familiar terms. The first can work to explain or illustrate. A child's science book, for example, might describe the human body as 'burning' food. This explains a complex and unfamiliar process (the breakdown and absorption of biochemicals) by placing it within a broader paradigm (chemical reactions in general) and from that substituting a simpler and more familiar example (burning). The latter case is more a strategy of defamiliarisation. In Raymond Chandler's *Farewell, My Lovely*, for example, the detective-narrator Philip Marlowe describes a big man as 'standing out like a tarantula on an angel cake'. The effect here is one of humour (and at the risk of explaining a joke, the paradigm set is 'things that are out of place'). Indeed, entire genres of jokes may rely on metaphoric transpositions of paradigms ('What do X and Y have in common?').

Syntagmatically, metaphor sets up a proposition. In effect, it says 'Since X and Y are both members of the same paradigm set, they are equivalent.' X and Y act as the subject and complement of a statement of identity: X is Y. Because you and a pig are sloppy eaters, you are effectively a pig.

Metonymy

Metonymy covers a much more diverse series of processes than metaphor.

To refer to a car as 'a motor' or as 'wheels' is a metonym which substitutes a part of the car for the whole thing. 'Britain has won its first gold medal for

> A **metonym** is an *association* of terms. One sign is associated with another of which it signifies a part, the whole, one of its functions or attributes, or a related concept.
> The general process of association is called **metonymy**.

this Olympics' goes the other way round, substituting the whole nation for the particular people in it who actually did the winning. A television news shot of troops and tanks on the move may metonymically invoke war. Many more things may be happening in that war, of course, from diplomatic negotiations to humanitarian aide to economic repercussions, but the troops and tanks stand for the entire conflict, including those aspects of it which don't easily lend themselves to visual representation: part for whole. To call a tall person 'Lofty' is to refer to them metonymically by an attribute. Movie stars easily come to stand for (and be typecast by) metonymic attributes (Meg Ryan is girl-next-door wholesomeness, Arnold Schwarzenegger is knowinglyexaggerated machismo, Harrison Ford is stalwart decency, Robin Williams is either fast-talking frenzy or sensitivity and self-discovery). Your signature is an attribute which metonymically stands for you: a metonym with legal status. To refer to a leader as 'Mr President' is to refer to him metonymically by his function.

Examples work metonymically, taking a specific example to illustrate a general case or an entire group: if asked to say what *beauty* is, it's tempting just to point to something beautiful rather than try to define it in the abstract. *Stereotypes* are metonymic too (we shall deal with them in more detail later on). They are like examples in that they take certain attributes and turn them into *characteristics of a group*; but what the stereotype then does is turn back onto the members of the group and ignore differences, treating members simply as examples of the general case, whether or not they actually possess that stereotypical attribute. The attributes on which the stereotyping is based may be anything from prevalent (such as a national or regional accent) to imaginary (insurance companies' figures, of course, show that on the whole women tend to be *better* drivers than men). It's hardly surprising that metonymy is often powerfully invoked in political discourse. When a politician refers to 'ordinary people' – as in 'Ordinary people have had enough,' or 'The average person wants [or doesn't want] *X*' – perhaps we should hear metonymy at work: what that politician is using to stand for everyone in the nation is that particular group defined as 'agreeing with me'.

Metonyms may be quite complex chains of association. Take, for example, 'The Crown', as in *The Crown* vs *Jane Smith*. Ms Smith is clearly not being sued by millinery. Instead, 'crown' is an *attribute* of its traditional wearer, the monarch; the monarch's *function* is nominal head of the British legal system; and lastly, 'The Crown' comes to stand for that legal system itself (*part for whole*). Metonymic links may be very powerful and subtle, and we shall have cause to return to them again when we consider myth later in this chapter.

As with metaphor, *visual* metonymy is also common. Again, advertising is a good source of examples. In many western nations, tobacco advertising is no longer permitted. In others, it is controlled in various ways: advertisements may not show the actual products themselves, or they may not show people using them. In some cases, they may not even show the packaging of the product. As a result, cigarette advertisements have often made particularly ingenious uses of metonymy to overcome some of these constraints while still remaining within the letter of the law. In each case, the impermissible sign (the cigarette itself, the packet, even the brand name) is invoked by a metonymic sign associated with it.

The well-known series of advertisements for Benson & Hedges cigarettes shows quite clearly one solution to the initial problem that one cigarette looks pretty much like another, no matter what the quality of the tobacco: they concentrate instead on the embossed gold foil packet that is the company's trademark. In fact, it is such a well-known trademark that it is no longer necessary even to show the cigarettes themselves. The packet becomes a metonym of the contents; indeed, it even becomes a 'truer' sign of the company than the product itself. Once goldness and the distinctive script of the brand name have been established as its signs, they can become more and more removed not only from the actual activity of smoking (which has never figured in these ads anyway), but even from any representation of the packet. In other ads in this series, the packet starts becoming a sort of visual pun on other objects: a mantelpiece, an easel, a float in a swimming pool. In still others, the key elements of goldness and script have been cut adrift from the packet altogether, and have become elements in an elaborate and seductive visual puzzle. The cunning campaign has resulted in an ad which is instantly recognisable, but for a product it nowhere mentions by name, depicts, or even shows the packaging – all by a progressive process of metonymy.

The most minimal and effective examples of this process are the famous Silk Cut ads, which rely on sumptuous photography and (again) a visual pun: the elements are a sheet of silk, of the same colour as the Silk Cut packet, and a cut. Where the Benson & Hedges ads truncated and dislocated the elements of the name of the product, here even the name is absent. The only thing which identifies the photograph as an advertisement – let alone as an ad for cigarettes – is the compulsory health warning. This reveals it as a cigarette ad precisely because it cites that one metonymic feature characteristic of all cigarette ads.

Metonyms too work both syntagmatically and paradigmatically. They suggest, but do not state, the completion of the whole whose attributes or parts have been signified. The metonym provides the paradigmatic example, the one which sums up the entire paradigm from which it is selected.

Metaphor and metonymy: a detailed example

Metaphor and metonymy are each quite simple concepts in themselves, though, as previous examples have shown, they are each capable of considerable elaboration and subtlety. Between them, these two mechanisms alone account for a surprising complexity of meaning.

Figure 3.3 shows a news photograph with its caption. It is not a particularly unusual example of local news photography, either in its subject matter

Figure 3.3

Taylor family all groomed for victory

After a landslide change of voting favouring the Liberals in the Groom by-election on Saturday, the new member, Mr Bill Taylor, his wife Jan and son Nick, 17, were all smiles yesterday.

or its execution. This is precisely why we have chosen it here: its very ordinariness will provide a useful demonstration of the sheer complexity of ways in which everyday meanings are constructed. That is, we are *not* interested here in finding some deeper and hidden meaning to this photo. What we want to do with the concepts we've developed so far – and particularly metaphor and metonymy – is to look at the obvious and widely accessible meanings, and ask how they come to be obvious. As we go through the discussion, ask yourself if this is in fact what we're doing. The semiotic concepts we're using may be still relatively new to you, but is the meaning they describe familiar to you already from the photo?

One of the first things to note is that the photograph doesn't simply function referentially. That is, it does a lot more than show us what the new member for Groom and his family might look like: it doesn't simply *identify* them for us, like a passport photo. It seems also to make various statements, about family life and public life, about being a politician: to suggest that being a politician, or a member of a family, *means* something in particular. In fact, the photograph even seems to equate the two. This is a picture which is ostensibly about the winner of a by-election, but it shows a family.

We can see how this works by starting off with the simple breakdown suggested in the last chapter. Can we simplify the picture somewhat, into a more manageable array of a small number of significant elements?

One fairly obvious way to do this is shown in Figure 3.4. What we've kept is four basic elements: the family group, the election poster, the setting, and the words which frame the picture. In a moment, we will break each of these down further, but they are a quite adequate starting point. (We are, after all, trying to describe and analyse this picture as extensively as we can with a minimal number of terms. The simplest models are often conceptually the most powerful.) When we diagram it in this way, it is easy to see the way in which the photograph is setting up a *metaphor*. The family group is on the left, the election poster is on the right: imagine a large equals sign suspended between them.

Let's look at each of the three groups of pictorial elements in turn, bringing to bear on them the suggestions made by the fourth group's verbal anchorage.

Family

Take the largest and most prominent single group of elements first: the group of three people, which takes up almost two-thirds of the width of the picture. Why, without any independent knowledge of the member for Groom, and even without reading the accompanying captions, do we see this

Figure 3.4 Signifying elements

as a family group? (Try a commutation test to see which aspects of the photo give this as a meaning. Would you read a single-sex group as family, for instance?) We make the *inference* of 'familyness' from features such as the particular combination of ages and sexes represented, the intimacy implied by the proximity of the various figures to each other, their stances, facial expressions, and the positions of their hands. All of these are *signs* of 'familyness' available in the photo for us to read. Even if the three figures were in fact professional actors, totally unrelated to each other, who had met for the first time minutes before the photo was taken, we would still tend to read the signs they are giving out as overwhelmingly those of 'familyness'.

Reading the photo, we may have no idea whether these people actually form a family or not; but we *are* certain that it is a very clear *coded representation* of a family. In the terms we used in Chapter 1, we can say that the *addressers* this photo constructs are a family, regardless of who the people who posed for the photo might be. We can read more than that, too.

This is just as obviously a *happy* family, and their happiness is coded in just the same ways. The *addressers*, that is, are a *happy family* (regardless of what the actual people who posed for the photo think of each other). This addresser-family is all but independent of the actual Taylor family. It is something the picture constructs out of common social codes: proximity means close ties, a smile means pleasure, etc. In posing for their photograph, the Taylors are playing a certain set of (addresser) roles provided for them in these codes.

This means that the family depicted in (or rather constructed by) the photograph can mean something more than the Taylors alone. This is a public photograph, to be seen by an audience who for the most part have absolutely no personal knowledge of the Taylors at all. If it carries meaning for such an audience, it can only do so because it draws on aspects of 'familyness' which are public, not the particular property of the Taylors alone. (Compare this photograph with a photograph from a private family album. Even though album shots too are generally highly coded, they may require a detailed commentary in order to make full sense to someone not in the family.) In a sense, this photograph is also a photograph of *the family in general*, as it is imagined and coded within the particular society from which it comes.

This is *metonymy* at work. *This* family stands metonymically for *the* family, as an idealised type. It plays on all sorts of received ideas about how families are imagined to be. As the clothes and the setting make clear (about which, more later), it is a middle-class family. It is a family with both parents, not one split by divorce or death. It consists of a dominant father and a mother who submits to his authority: look at the protective position of the arms of the two men. The son defers to his father (he is somewhat less prominent in the picture), but is ready to take on that masculine role himself (his arm duplicates the protective gesture of his father's). What's more, their smiles and proximity say that they are content with these roles they play, and are proud to display them publicly. Whatever the Taylors who are the subjects of this photo may be like, the family which semiotically addresses us from the picture is one which is entirely without dissent or unhappiness.

Something quite remarkable is happening here, then. This picture has all the force of an exact and precise depiction of the real: it *is* a photograph, after all, and what it depicts is presumably exactly what was happening in front of the camera at the time. But through these processes of metonymy, it is also at exactly the same time a depiction of something almost entirely imaginary, which has never existed as such: the perfect family. What we can see here, in this perfectly banal photo, is something of the immense power of signs to *produce*, or *simulate*, the real.

Poster

We shall return to this. But now we turn to the next-largest group of signs, the **poster**. Like the picture as a whole, it is made up of both pictorial image and anchoring verbal text. The anchorage allows us to recognise it immediately as an electoral poster, even though it is in a situation in which we would not normally expect to see such a poster displayed. The essential anchoring information is in the three words in large type: the names of the candidate, the party and the electorate. Where the first grouping of figures says *family*, this set of elements says *politics*, and in just the same metonymic fashion. If this poster works, it is not because it imparts any information at all about Bill Taylor's expertise, abilities or policies, but because it metonymically represents him as *the politician* in abstract, the *ideal* politician.

This is done largely through camera angles. The camera is slightly above the level of the subject's face, so he is looking very slightly upwards: that is, this addresser is somewhat lower (or shorter) than the viewer, and hence does not dominate the addressee. The addresser is deferential (he is, after all, asking for votes). And the entire shot is taken in three-quarter face: the subject is facing slightly away from the camera his eyes are looking at, as if there is also an entire world beyond the frame of the photo, in which he has been engaged, and which he has torn himself from in order to meet the addressing gaze. It's as if the electorate calls, and he listens.

Bill Taylor, of course, is the common element in both the family grouping and the electoral poster, and that both strengthens and complicates the implied metaphoric equation of the two. He frames the picture on both left and right:

family grouping = electoral poster

We have also determined that each of these groups may metonymically also stand for more abstract qualities: this family for *the family*, and this man for *politics*. This now leaves us with the interesting equation:

family = politics

What this picture is doing, then, is using metaphor to explain something relatively unfamiliar (politics) in terms of something more familiar (the family). The nation and its governance are just like a big family. There needs to be a strong and effective head, and there also needs to be willing acceptance of his headship from the others, over whom he exercises his just and natural authority. If Bill Taylor knits the two groupings together, this is because:

Bill Taylor's role in the family = Bill Taylor's role in the electorate

As he is to the family, so is he to the electorate. The family and the electorate are made to appear as basically continuous: the rules and structures which govern one also govern the other. We can see that he is a successful father of a happy and approving family. Can there be any doubt (the photo asks) that he will go on to represent Groom with the same success?

Setting

This is also where the third group of elements, the setting, comes in. The photo is shot within a house, presumably the Taylors'. Though there is not much detail available, we can make out some significant features of its style which may help us fine-tune things a bit more. In particular, the jointed tongue-and-groove walls, high ceilings and picture railing all mark it as a distinctively Australian style of architecture: a high-set Queenslander, possibly from around the turn of the last century. Designed as spacious family homes, these houses are highly desirable properties, and a sign of nationality, class and tradition. This house signals those who live in it as authentically Australian, as continuing a tradition of Australianness, and as members of the middle classes. Metonymically, again, it thus comes to stand for *the traditional Australian family home*.

As the family home, it is a private space: in fact, the very seat of the private. Note that it is also an enclosed space, without visible windows: the outside world does not belong in here. But on the other hand, *the private* (the family) is only one side of the equation, where it is balanced by *the public* (the political). Looking again at the picture, we will find that this apparently enclosed space is indeed open to the outside in all sorts of ways. The photograph itself, after all, is eminently public: not the sort of thing one might expect to find in a family album, but exactly what one might expect to find in a newspaper. And the poster, to take another example, seems quite out of place in a house: surely it should be displayed on a front fence or on a telegraph pole, rather than on the candidate's wall. It is a bit of the outside public world which has intruded into this private space. Notice also where it is hanging. It appears to be on a door, either in a hallway or on the front door itself: that is, in that intermediate area of the house on the edge between the public and the private, the hallway that receives strangers on their way into the house, and holds the family's coats and umbrellas for their own excursions. Look at the clothes the people are wearing: the man's white long-sleeved shirt with tie and the woman's necklace are articles of apparel which belong to working or public life rather than in the home. They stand at the threshold of their own house in greeting, welcoming the addressee into that part of their private life which, with the advent of the photographer who has carefully arranged this scene, will now become public. At the same time, in greeting us only at the threshold, they withhold the privacy and sanctity of *the family*.

Caption

Finally, we should consider the fourth grouping, which comprises the caption and the brief story text. This acts as an **anchorage** for the picture as a whole: it serves to stabilise the possible meanings by metalingually cueing in relevant codes as a frame for interpretation. To point out what an essential part this cueing has already played in our interpretation, all we have to do is show what happens with different cues, as in Figure 3.5.

Connotation and denotation

Because the relationship between signifier and signified is an arbitrary one, there is nothing in the nature of the sign itself to tie a given signifier to one signified alone. We all know from our own experience as language users that words are capable of having more than one meaning, and even of changing their meaning with time. Instead of a signifier paired to a single definite signified, the sign can more accurately be pictured as having a *spread* of signifieds, which we will call its **connotations**.

The **connotations** of a sign are the set of its possible signifieds.

A warning!
Don't get the terms *connotation* or *connotative* confused with the *conative* function we discussed in Chapter 1. The two are quite different in meaning and use.

Used in this way, connotation emphasises the plurality of the signifieds.

This is by no means the only usage of the term you will come across if you continue work in semiotics. For a brief discussion of these, see the 'Note on usage' at the end of this chapter.

Metaphor and metonymy, as we've just been discussing them, are processes of connotation: they are ways of generating a spread of signifieds around a given signifier. Connotations need not be true in any sense: a cigarette advertisement which juxtaposes the name of the product with a group of happy, active young people makes 'health' into a connotation of tobacco.

Figure 3.5 Changing the anchorage

ALL GROOMED FOR VICTORY

SPITTING IMAGE

Mr Andrew MacLeod has a problem which won't be over until Saturday's by-election – and even then may stay to haunt him, if the polls are any indication. Mr MacLeod is an uncannily close double of the Liberal candidate, Bill Taylor, even though the two men are not in any way related. The resemblance is so close that Mr MacLeod is often mistaken for Mr Taylor in the street. 'It gets embarrassing,' he says. 'I've never even voted Liberal.'

BRAVE IN DEFEAT

BILL Taylor, one of the many sitting members likely to lose his seat in yesterday's land-slide election surprise, is philosophical about his future . . .

STANDING FOR WHAT SHE BELIEVES IN

Mrs Jan Taylor, wife of Mr Bill Taylor, the Liberal candidate for Groom, rose bravely from her wheelchair yesterday for the first time in six years to go to the polls and cast one of the votes she is sure will bring her husband victory.

Connotations of the same sign may even utterly contradict one another: after all, another connotation of tobacco is 'cancer'.

Connotations may be plural, but this does not mean that they are a matter of individual subjective preferences. Like all meanings, they arise through codes which are ultimately shared and social. Connotations are not simply what you personally make of a sign: they are what the codes to which you have access make of the sign. Connotation is highly structured, if in a very mobile and flexible way, and one which lets us see quite clearly some of the means through which the social and the sign interrelate. *Through connotation, the entire social world enters the systems of signification.*

The link between a signifier and its signified is effected by a code, *langue*: change the code in which a given signifier is to operate, and the signified alters too. As we know, codes are social formations, shared and contested by what we could think of as communities of sign users. Social positionings such as class, gender and ethnicity make it more or less likely that a given sign user will have access to a certain code, and thus to a certain range of connotations. (We say 'more or less likely' because this is not a relationship of simple determinism, as if any of the above factors consign the bearer of them to a permanent position within sign systems. We will elaborate on this in Chapter 9.) What's more, some codes are more prevalent than others, available to more and larger groups. Not surprisingly, the specific connotations such a code carries thus tend to become the dominant ones of the relevant signs, and to gain a sort of stability within the spread of connotations of that sign. To users of that particular code, those particular meanings will tend to appear obvious, or natural, or even as simply true.

We can picture the spread of connotations of a given sign as a set with somewhat fuzzy edges. They are fuzzy because it is in principle impossible to exclude totally the possibility that any given signified can function as a connotation of the sign. (Even though the probability of the situation ever arising may be small, it's possible to think of a situation where *calculus* is a connotation of *custard*. Advertising, after all, has exploited many stranger connotations. All it takes is a code in common, or the link provided by metaphor or metonymy.) Within that set, there will be certain large clumpings for the dominant connotations, and a number of smaller concentrations. The set of connotations has something like a gravitational field: some of those possible signifieds are likely to appear of more central significance than others, or to have other connotations clustered about them. Such clusterings of meanings indicate codes. At the centre of the field are the most stable meanings of the sign, which we will call its **denotations**.

The **denotations** of a sign are the most stable and objectively verifiable of its connotations.

Precisely how such denotations come to crystallise out of the mass of connotations is a process we shall begin to investigate in the next section on *myth*, and continue in Chapter 8, when we discuss ideology and hegemony. For the moment, we will simply suggest that the relative stability of a denotation may come about in a number of ways:

1 when a certain common range of meanings is *prevalent* – that is, attributed to the sign by a number of the codes in which it operates;
2 when any of the codes in which it functions is *dominant*; and, in particular,
3 when the sign works within certain *objective or scientific codes*.

It is important to emphasise that though denotations may be relatively stable meanings, they are not fixed. Like all meanings, they are produced in a differential play of values among signs and codes, not by a simple correspondence of signifier and signified. Denotation's stability is purely a relative matter, and for this reason there can be no clear and absolute distinction between denotation and connotation: the difference is quantitative rather than qualitative.

Like all connotations, denotations may and do alter with time. At various times in the past, for example, the sign *woman* has included such denotative meanings as 'frailty', 'irrationality' and 'deceitfulness'. These have been denotative rather than merely connotative, because they have fulfilled each of the criteria above: they are prevalent and dominant meanings, which have at times been supported by authoritative religious, moral, medical, psychological and even scientific codes. To take another example, Figure 3.6 shows some of the ways in which nineteenth-century science was able to assert European racial superiority: that is, to assert that a *denotative* meaning of *African* and *Asian* was 'inferiority-to-Caucasian-ness'.

As these two cases suggest, denotation is inevitably bound up with historical and social factors, even in the case of those most objective of discourses, the sciences. Denotations need not even be true in any simple sense, but nevertheless, by the very fact of being denotations they have certain **truth-effects**: they demand to be taken as true, and claim the privileges we reserve for the true. It is not surprising, then (and again, we shall return to this later, in Chapters 8 and 9), that denotation is something over which there may be intense struggle.

We must underline the distinction we are making. This is an argument about *denotation*, which is a matter of signs and the ways in which they work. It is not an argument about *the real*, which is what is assumed to pre-exist signs and the way they operate, even though it is known largely through those signs and operations. To say that denotation is historical is not to say that the real is just what a dominant consensus makes it out to be. It's rather

Figure 3.6 Powers of denotation: two examples of racism at work in nineteenth-century science

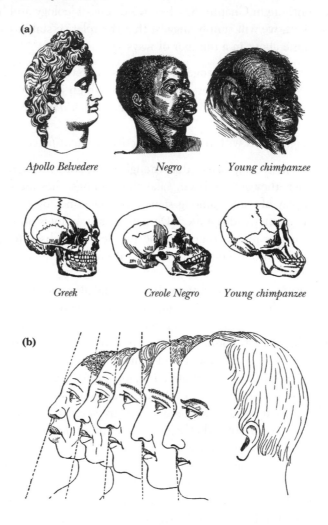

(a)

Apollo Belvedere *Negro* *Young chimpanzee*

Greek *Creole Negro* *Young chimpanzee*

(b)

to make the altogether more modest argument that the sciences, for example, can lay claim to unambiguous, objective meaning only because they build up a very elaborate and rigorous *semiotic apparatus* to ensure it. This apparatus – which includes not only scientific language, but all the signifying practices and situations which make science possible, from replicable laboratory procedures to questions of professionalisation, careers and funding – is historically variable, as the signs and explanations in Figure 3.6 exemplify. What such an apparatus does is *legitimise* certain denotations, by providing criteria for deciding which, amongst all the possible meanings of a term, are to be treated as valid. The very complexity of scientific language itself testifies to the difficulty of pinning signs down to single meanings. They have a constant tendency to escape from those meanings.

Denotation is what is often thought of as the 'literal meaning' of a sign, the obvious and true first-order signification which comes before and is independent of any secondary, later accretions like connotations. What we have been suggesting here is something rather different: that denotation is not so much the *natural* as the *naturalised* meaning of the sign. Denotation is a process of **naturalisation**. Denotation, as Roland Barthes put it, is the last connotation: it is the persistent shape which only gradually emerges in the space marked out by connotation. Recall the news photograph of Figure 3.3, which is denotative only through a screen of connotations.

There are some unexpected implications of all this. Since denotation is only one of the meanings of the sign, but one which comes to stand for all the others, *denotation is a form of metonymy* (an individual example substituted for the general case). As we shall now see, this means it is also aligned with myth. Far from being a non-figurative, absolutely literal sign use, denotation is always a figure of speech.

Myth

Denotation, too, is ordered. Let us return to that earlier example of race, and the diagrams of Figure 3.6. These come from nineteenth-century European and North American textbooks of anthropology. We must remember that they are drawn from the serious and respectable science of their time: they lay claim, as science must, to a strictly denotative meaning. What are these denotative meanings, and how are they ordered?

Each of these three sets of three diagrams sets up an implied continuum. At one end of the continuum is an ideal of human beauty or development: the Apollo Belvedere (a Greek statue from the third century BC); a European skull, its perfection signified by that suspiciously uncompromising right-angle of the jawline; and the apparently straight-up-and-down profile of a caucasian man. At the other end, we have in two cases an animal; in the third (the lower set of profiles), it would be easy to extrapolate this out to place a chimpanzee there on the far left, with the shallowest angle of facial declivity of all. Somewhere between those two extremes, grouped according to certain stereotypical and often just imaginary racial characteristics (look at the distortion of the Creole Negro skull in the second series, and the increments of alertness and intelligence in the faces of the third), lie all of us who are not affiliated with Greek statues or eagle-eyed fair-haired Europeans. In each case, the continuum can be read in two ways. In one direction, it tells the story of a progressive evolution towards the perfection of the European (and the European male at that). In the other, the story is of a degeneration towards the animal, which acts as a warning of the dangers of racial mixture: it is not accidental that the most monstrous single distortion of all the series belongs to the *Creole* Negro skull, that mixture of two races which is shown here as further from the European right-angle than even a chimpanzee.

It is clear, we hope, that what is informing all of this is a massive fantasy about race, and in particular about racial superiority and degeneration. This provides the framework into which all of the data will be placed. Everything finds a place between civilised and primitive, perfect and degenerate, human and animal, white and coloured. That framework orientates the project. What it looks for is data which fits it, or which is perceivable in the terms it offers. What it doesn't see – and perhaps cannot even conceive, as it has no framework which would make sense of it – is data which might suggest all sorts of other quite different relations. Data can even be distorted to fit the framework, if need be. Look at that Creole Negro skull: at work in this representation, surely, there is an overwhelming *desire to see things this way*, even at the cost of overriding the evidence of observation and measurement. At the apparent *centre* of this denotative field, the sun around which everything revolves, we have the caucasian (and specifically the male). As we move away from this luminous centre, and the angle of the profiles in the third series becomes more and more shallow, we move progressively through the southern European, then the Semite, to the Negro, and finally to the purely animal.

Everything is measured from the norm and peak of perfection which is the white man. The further an element is from this point, the less highly developed it is. All relationships are reduced to this distance. All sorts of undeniable *differences*, in all their cultural, historical and social complexity and richness, get reduced to *degrees* of that one single difference. No matter what it is that the nineteenth-century anthropologist is measuring – whether it is the angle of declivity, the size of the skull, the shape of the nose – feature after feature will be arranged to show the same relationship, a gradation in perfect towards whatever particular version of that feature the caucasian is presumed to have. The entire field is structured by a massive metonymy, which reads the same single story in whatever individual feature it examines. The white male becomes the type of human who best sums up everything from technological prowess and evolutionary development, to beauty and intelligence – in a word, the white man is *humanity* itself. The white man is the *most human* human. Everybody else is less human: less *than* human.

Look at what is happening semiotically in this move. A set of signs (*human beings*) has been ordered according to a single overriding principle of *race*. One particular term (*white*) has been made dominant over all others in the way its denotations are arranged: from now on, the denotations of *white* will be *most highly developed, most intelligent, most moral, most beautiful*, and so on. On the one hand, *white* is just a subset of *humanity*; but on the other, it lays exclusive claim to all those qualities which define the whole set.

Everywhere we turn in this system, the relationships are metonymic. One particular term (race) comes to stand for all terms (intelligence, beauty, etc); within *that*, one particular race comes to stand as the yardstick of all; and one particular possible relationship among terms (a scale of superiority or inferiority) comes to stand for all relationships (cultural and individual differences). We can give a name to this coding which is structured entirely by metonymy: **myth**.

Myth is a coding in which:
- a dominant *term* stands metonymically for all terms in the system; and
- a dominant metonymic *relationship* among terms stands metonymically for all relationships.

The effect of myth is a radical simplification of all the relationships within that system. Myth **overcodes** an entire system onto a single dominant element and a single relationship. Among the ways in which it can perform that simplification, two are very powerful and frequent:

- **Binary opposition**: all relationships are reduced to the single scale set up between two opposing terms.

Two terms are in **binary opposition** when they are related through a quality which is present in one term and absent in the other.

Thus *light* and *dark* form a binary opposition based on the presence or absence of light; *good* and *evil* form a binary opposition if evil is the absence of good. In our detailed example, *white* and *non-white* are the binary opposition which structures the scale on which everything can be arranged.

The figure of the 'dole bludger', often depicted in news media as exploiting the social security system, is mythic in precisely this sense. It simplifies an enormous range of social relations and possible reasons for unemployment to the presence or absence of a single and purely personal quality: some people have the initiative to get out there and look for a job, and others don't. The former are good, the latter are bad. Indeed, the latter even become the simple, single mythic *cause*: unemployment happens because people don't want to work.

' A woman's place is in the home' is a mythic statement because it metonymically represents a general category (women) by a specific example (the woman whose work is maintenance of a family home), and then arranges all other members of that category in relation to that dominant example, according to whether they are or are not *domestic*. The woman whose place is in the home becomes the *real* woman, the one against whom all others are measured; all other women are *less womanly* the further they are from her.

A warning: do not be too hasty to label any pairing of terms a binary opposition. There are other more complex relationships two terms may have. Two terms which work as a binary opposition in one framework (code) may not work that way in another. *Male* and *female* form a binary opposition only if one is seen as lacking what the other possesses (Freud, for example, argues that the child first experiences sexual difference as a binary opposition, because it sees that some people have a penis and others do not); much feminist work sees it far more useful to argue that the two sexes are irreducibly *different*, rather than positive and negative versions of the same thing.

- **Indifferentiation**, or the refusal of difference. Binary opposition might involve two poles, but they really only order things according to one quality anyway: it is present in one term, absent in the other. An even more direct way of simplifying relationships within a system is just to declare all terms equivalent with respect to this one quality, and to ignore any differences. Where binary opposition is mythic in that it divides the world up into two sorts of people, indifferentiation sees no differences at all. To argue that there should be no differential treatment of certain groups (such as indigenous people or gays and lesbians) on the grounds that 'we're all citizens of the same country' is mythic to the extent that it refuses to register the very real historical, social, cultural and political differences which often mark such groups, and the specific needs which go along with those.

Because myth is metonymic, it is not necessarily in itself either true or untrue: it may simply be highly selective. This is why myth is often difficult to dislodge: as evidence for the myth, one can always just point to the element which is being made to stand for the whole. To 'prove' that a woman's place is in the home, you simply point to a woman who is happy in that role; to 'prove' that migrants are in control of the trade in illegal drugs, you find a migrant with a drugs conviction; to 'prove' that the education system is a failure, you find a child who can't spell. The mythic quality on which such an assertion hinges is generally something quite common or obvious, like the signifiers of *race*, but that need not always be the case. This quality may conceivably be quite *un*typical, or even non-existent. The blond hair and blue eyes which characterised the Nazi myth of Aryanism, for example, are quite commonplace in northern Europe. But – so the story goes – when Japan entered the Second World War on the side of the Axis powers, the Japanese were granted honorary Aryan status: in this case, the mythic signifier of Aryanism had no actual referent. What this suggests is that even when it appears to be referring to the obvious and the commonplace, the mythic sign does not really depend on any accuracy of reference. It works not because it is true in any sense, but because it is metonymic. At the limit, the trait it takes to stand for the whole need not even exist.

Note that throughout this book we are using the word *myth* in the specific sense it has in semiotics. This is different from the senses it has in other areas, including everyday speech.

Mythic is not a synonym for *untrue, false, inaccurate, illusory, subjective, stereotype* or *belief*.

Myth is not something *represented* in a text, but a way texts have of *structuring* their representations.

In conclusion, we will simply point out that as myth overcodes an entire sign system onto a single denotation, it also takes over many of the properties of denotation. In particular, it is a powerful agent of the *naturalisation of meaning*, and is often *the site of struggles over meaning*. We shall examine these aspects in more detail in the next chapter, in which we can now turn to questions of analysing cultural texts.

A note on usage

The way we have used the terms *connotation* and *denotation* is not necessarily the one you will find in other textbooks, though we believe it is one which is both a logical outcome of the Saussurean model and a way of getting round a number of conceptual difficulties in other accounts. Though connotation and denotation are terms which are common to a number of areas in philosophy, linguistics and literary criticism, they are used in a variety of ways, without any necessary agreement among the various areas.

Here, we have used **connotation** to refer simply to the entire spread of possible signifieds of a given signifier, and **denotation** for the most stable of those connotations. Other writers (such as Fiske, Hall, Hartley, O'Sullivan) define connotation more narrowly as *a sign whose signifier is itself a sign*. This gives a two-tiered linkage of signs, like this:

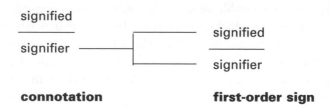

connotation   **first-order sign**

Hamlet, for example, is a complex sign capable of acting in this two-tiered way. Its signifiers are English words, and their (first-order) signified is a story of revenge and tragedy. But *Hamlet* – the entire complex sign – itself also functions as a signifier to evoke a whole series of connotations. On this second-order level, *Hamlet* signifies 'drama', or 'Literature' (and in particular, 'English drama' and 'English literature'). Through the figure of Shakespeare, it signifies 'genius'. Put these two together and it connotes 'great art' – and so on.

This way of defining connotation comes from the work of the Danish linguist Louis Hjelmslev; it is best known in English through Roland Barthes' adaptation of Hjelmslev in his *Elements of Semiology*. Barthes and Hjelmslev use the term **denotation** correspondingly to mean a sign whose signifier is *not* a sign in its own right. For them, a denotative sign is one which doesn't enter any further into the play whereby a sign's meaning is generated by its interrelationships with other signs. Follow the chain of connotative linkages back, and eventually you will always arrive at denotation. Denotation, in this view, is a 'first-order' sign, and connotation is 'second-order'. Denotation logically precedes connotation: first there must be denotations, and then there can be connotations. Denotations thus appear as something like the 'real meaning', the official or dictionary definitions, with their firm link between signifier and signified. Connotations will correspondingly seem somewhat 'less real', imaginary or illusory meanings.

The problem with this, as Barthes was to argue later in his career, is that, as we have just seen, this sort of fixity of meaning is just not possible in a Saussurean system. In this system, signs take on their meanings from their relationships to other signs, and this produces all the effects of signification. For denotation as Hjelmslev sees it, though, just the opposite is the case: the denotative sign doesn't gain its meaning from other surrounding signs, but purely from the vertical relationship of signification between signified and signifier. It is hard to see how this can be contained within a Saussurean system. Barthes' response to this later in his career was to reverse this model, in the way we have outlined in the main text. Rather than see meaning as starting from denotation, Barthes now gave priority to connotation, of which denotation would be nothing more than a special case.

Before we leave the subject, consider a variation on the diagram for connotation. Is there a second-order sign whose *signified* is a first-order sign (rather than the *signifier*, as is the case for connotation)? A sign whose signified is another sign is a sign 'about' another sign: that is, a **metalingual** sign. Most of the sentences in this book, for example, are metalingual. This sentence is metalingual.

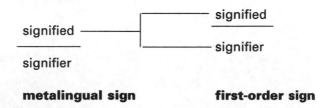

metalingual sign	**first-order sign**

The idea of a metalingual function is already familiar to us from the model we considered in Chapter 1. As you'll recall, there we suggested that *every* utterance has such a function to a greater or lesser degree. And here we run into a similar objection to that we found in the case of connotation and denotation. If the Hjelmslevian version of denotation implies a sign where signifier and signified are joined without the mediation of the entire system of *langue*, so too does the first-order non-metalingual sign. The Saussurean idea of system would lead us to expect that there are no signs which are not *both* connotative *and* metalingual in Hjelmslev's sense. If that is the case, then the distinctions named by each term are largely imaginary ones.

In short, rather than the hierarchy implied by Hjelmslev's schema of connotation and metalanguage, we wish to emphasise that:

1 all signs are plural and connotative; and
2 all codes are to some extent metalingual.

EXERCISES

1 Analyse how metaphor and metonymy combine to generate meaning in Figures 3.1, 3.2, 3.7 and 3.8. Use our analysis of the newspaper photo in Figure 3.3 as a guide. How do metaphor and metonymy work together to invest what is depicted with certain significations?

   Still using Figure 3.3 as a guide, investigate some other ways in which family and politics, or family and nationality, may be run together mythically. Events and cases which you might like to consider in this light include the roles of First Families (the Buckingham Palace, Downing Street and White House Web sites are a rich source of images here), the funeral of Princess Diana, or the emphasis on place and family connection in television soaps.

2 How do the meanings of a national flag differ according to the various myths which structure the connotations it invokes? What different connotations are invoked if it is flying over a government office, on a warship, at the

Figure 3.7 The funeral procession of Princess Diana, 1997

Source: http://www.time.com/time/daily/special/diana/dianafuneral/index.htm

Figure 3.8

Olympics, at the United Nations, or depicted on a postcard, a waistcoat at a football match, a coffee cup, the label of a commercial product, the cover of a school textbook, or in the corner of another country's flag (as with the Australian and New Zealand flags)? What different metonymic and metaphoric links are being made in these cases? In each case, what factors alter the ways in which the connotation set is configured? How would you characterise these semiotic myths which govern the connotation set in each case?

3 We have concentrated on two broad types of graphic sign: the news photograph and the print advertisement. What other signs and processes could be described in terms of metaphor and metonymy? How might the name of a designer work on a clothing label, for example, or that of an author on a bookcover? (Do all authors' names work the same way?)

4 Analyse the following as mythic statements in the sense we have defined that term earlier. What is the dominant term on which the myth focuses? What is the single relationship to which the myth reduces all relationships?

(i) The rise in crime is due to the breakdown of the family unit.
(ii) Foreigners are taking our jobs.
(iii) Americans (or the British, or Australians, or feminists, or environmentalists) have no sense of humour.
(iv) AIDS education condones a homosexual lifestyle.
(v) 'Greed is good.' (Gordon Gekko, the broker in Oliver Stone's 1987 film, *Wall Street*)

5 Certain activities are often represented mythically, through metonymy. The man with the guitar, for example, is often used to stand for popular music in general (rather than, say, a woman with a guitar, or someone behind a mixing desk, or an accountant). What are some of the effects of representing a highly complex social process such as popular music like this? Can you think of other cases where metonymy gives powerful mythic effects?

SOURCES AND FURTHER READING

Denotation and connotation are concepts which come primarily from Louis Hjelmslev, *Prolegomena to a Theory of Language* (Madison, Wisconsin: Wisconsin University Press, 1969), where they are grafted onto a basically Saussurean apparatus. Roland Barthes' *Elements of Semiology* (London: Cape, 1967) draws heavily on Hjelmslev, and is the main source of the use of this distinction in cultural studies. Both of these are difficult texts rather than introductory. Barthes' later, briefer and much more approachable reconsideration of these terms and the relationship between them is in 'Change the object itself', from *Image –Music–Text* (London: Fontana, 1977).

One of the classic texts on the semiotics of advertising, which is still very helpful, is Judith Williamson's *Decoding Advertisements: Ideology and Meaning in Advertising* (London: Marion Boyars, 1978). A more recent study of semiotics in the media is Jonathan Bignell's *Media Semiotics: An Introduction* (Manchester: Manchester University Press, 1997).

The concept of myth comes from Roland Barthes' *Mythologies* (New York: Hill & Wang, 1987), and in particular from that book's long final essay, 'Myth Today'. Our 'Note on usage' details some of the changes we have made to this concept. Helpful studies of Barthes' work include Michael Moriarty, *Roland Barthes* (Cambridge: Polity Press, 1991), and Philip Thody's *Introducing Barthes* (Trumpington: Icon, 1999).

PART II

Cultural texts

Texts and textualities

CONTENTS

Why a text?

To consider the different sorts of meanings that signs generate we emphasised the paradigmatic axis of meaning. Both signifiers and signifieds take their values and meanings from sets of possibilities. A signifier can always have more than one signified, and a signified may be linked to a number of signifiers. Because of these multiple possibilities, a sign's meaning results from its contrast to other meanings it might have.

The sign has various meanings according to contexts – the words 'herb' or 'weed' signify something quite different to weekend gardeners than to fans of reggae music. Of course, someone might be a gardener and a fan. In that case he or she would use the sign 'herb' in different ways depending on the situation (though it is not hard to imagine a sentence where both meanings would be used).

Signs link together to form texts, so the notion of text involves ideas of syntagmatic combination as well as paradigmatic choice.

> A **text** is a combination of signs.

Obvious types of texts are a sentence someone writes or a fashion outfit someone wears. Each of these texts has paradigmatic and syntagmatic features. The words and clothes can be thought of as signs, and they join together to form a *verbal* text and a *fashion* text.

In a sentence a number of choices are made: which words to include (there are always synonymous words or phrases that could be used, and choices that are made seem to be based on a number of factors such as convention, decorum, code and connotation as well as the writer's vocabulary); and what codes and rhetorical strategies to use (will something be said straight or ironically, flatly or persuasively, and so on). Paradigm choices of words will depend on which strategies are employed and which functions are dominant.

As these sorts of choices are being made, the words are also being joined into a sentence. Syntagmatic rules apply to how the signs can be combined. In the case of language, grammar is a key set of such rules. The sorts of choices and rules that are available change through time, as well as according to the social groups the writer belongs to or is addressing. Different groups use different grammars and different syntagmatic rules. A sentence like 'Good grammar is a sign of good character – not!' is an example of rhetorical strategy, word choice and combination working together to produce an unexpected meaning. The sentence invokes a traditional idea about language only to attack it, and the unconventional grammar registers the attack as much as the final word and punctuation choices. The choices and the rules of combination work together to produce the text's meanings.

We can see the same double process going on in producing a fashion text: choices of shirt, pants, socks, shoes, even (if absolutely necessary) a tie. All the items then have to be combined. The point would be not only to make sure that you don't put the socks on your ears, but that everything 'goes together'.

The syntagmatic rules and conventions for dress may be quite subtle. Questions of taste come up. We could think of fashion taste as a set of connotations, signified by certain clothes, that a group considers suitable for specific social events or occasions. Different groups will have different ideas of what is suitable, and members of one group might try to challenge the ideas and taste of another group. A great part of the impact of a Mardi Gras parade, for example, is the way that those on show might combine different styles of clothes, for instance, wearing masculine and feminine attire together. Part of the fun is to challenge the conventional combination of dress choices that many people would make. Their outfits rework more orthodox fashion texts.

What do we gain by calling the way someone is dressed a text? There is a series of advantages if we are trying to think about how culture works:

1 By rethinking fashion as a type of text we can apply semiotic concepts to it, to see what sorts of social meanings are involved in a particular outfit.
2 We can relate fashion to the ways that other kinds of social texts work to produce meanings. (As we will see, fashion is an important part of the way advertising and news work. It is not only advertised or newsworthy in

itself, but can signify many social meanings and values in relation to other issues.)

3 We can consider how different groups use certain styles of dressing and the meanings they connote in order to distinguish themselves phatically from other groups. Fashion is one of the main ways of producing group and personal identities.

Overall, then, the key effect of thinking of something like fashion as a text is that we break through any façade of naturalness it may have. We realise that fashion, like any text, is always *socially constructed* in its production of meanings and what it does with them (such as creating an identity or an impression). All textual construction occurs through the two processes of paradigm choice and syntagmatic combination.

Cultural studies suggests that we can learn a great deal about how a society functions by using semiotic concepts of textual analysis to examine its different customs, structures, institutions, as well as the verbal and visual texts it produces. By *textualising* these various cultural areas and events – that is, by thinking of them as comprising choices of signs that are combined into larger groups or patterns – we can start to uncover the attitudes and beliefs that they motivate and can then go on to think about their effects.

The textual approach to culture is not the only way of thinking about how it works. Other approaches have included seeing culture as a game (as we shall see), or as a drama; instead of using semiotic theories, different kinds of economic, political or religious schemes have been used. Often these sorts of approaches can be useful supplements to seeing culture as text. Yet as we hope to show in this and subsequent chapters, once we have taken on board the basic semiotic concepts we can start to analyse a vast range of cultural texts and activities. We can investigate our own habituation to the meanings that surround us and through which we live.

Practising analysis

Before we develop these ideas on texts and textuality further, let's try a little textual analysis. The aim is to see how the semiotic concepts that were introduced in the previous two chapters can help us uncover the processes of social meaning that go on in everyday texts. It is not only literary texts such as novels, plays and poems that express interesting and ofen complicated themes and ideas. As we saw in the last chapter, similar processes of meaning go on in all kinds of social texts – from films to ads to news stories – and semiotic theory provides a set of concepts through which these processes of meaning can be traced. We can start by looking at another magazine advertisement, Figure 4.1.

Figure 4.1

The ad is for Dunhill cigarettes. To analyse a text like this one, we have to move between the text's paradigmatic and syntagmatic axes, first considering the possible meanings of each of the chosen signs, and then noting how they combine and whether they reinforce one another's meanings. What are the key signifiers in this text? The colour gold, the open cigarette packet, the sheet music and clarinet, the gold lighter, and the phrases 'Dunhill De Luxe' and 'Always in good taste' seem to make up the important signifiers.

What are some of the possible signifieds? The colour gold, as well as signifying the malleable and ductile precious yellow metal of the dictionary definition, can signify wealth and status. The sheet music looks classical, and along with the word 'Always' seems to signify timeless taste and classiness. The open packet and lighter suggest accessibility.

All of these signifieds are already **connotations**. The signs are being related to certain *codes* of meaning over others. In these, wealth, taste and status come into play far more readily than health, mineral and music. An important reason for this is the *syntagmatic effect of combination*. When placed together, the different signs emphasise the codes they have in common. Codes that are not shared fade back into (but do not disappear from) the text. In our example, metallurgical meanings may be signified by the gold, but they do not seem to relate to classical music or cigarette codes. This syntagmatic cross referencing among signs and codes activates some meanings and sidelines others.

A second factor involved in considering which codes of meaning are active in the text is their *familiarity* to readers. The signs in the Dunhill ad are used in many other social texts to trigger off similar codes of taste and status. In the next chapter on genre we will consider that just as signs in the one text refer to one another, so they relate to each other across separate texts, and the texts themselves can also refer to each other. For the moment, however, the point to note about the familiarity and repetition of taste and status codes through signs such as gold, classical music and accessibility is that they transform these connotations into **denotations**. The semiotic link between gold and status or classical music and taste does not seem to be a possibility – a single connotation from one code – but the true, timeless meaning of the sign.

With these denotations operating, the text has a further semiotic effect. By being linked to gold and classical music, as signifier Dunhill no longer merely connotes cigarette. It metaphorically denotes lasting status and taste, and its apparent accessibility – the open pack, the handy lighter – seems to put these socially valued ideas within our grasp.

There are other things we might note about this text. Its spatial structure is important, with the cigarette packet centrally placed, the cigarettes leading our sight to the music, and the lighter guiding us to the slogan. There is also a kind of semiotic contest going on in the text: it includes an official warning that confronts the other signs but seems to be overshadowed by them. Furthermore, we could consider how the text's signs and codes are informed by valued social ideas, but at the same time signify those values and quite possibly reinforce their appeal to readers. *The text is both produced by and reproduces cultural attitudes*. In these various ways, our analysis would develop by continuing to explore the exchange of meanings between signifiers and signifieds, and the interaction between choice and combination, paradigm and syntagm.

Social texts, social meanings

In considering how this advertisement is working we followed a particular analytical procedure. It involved a sequence of steps:

1 We located the key signifiers in the text.
2 We proposed a range of possible signifieds for each of the signifiers.
3 We identified the connotations and social codes to which the signifieds were relating.
4 We noted which of these connotations seemed to become the naturalised, true meanings in the text, its denotations.
5 We considered that these denotations might reinforce familiar social structures of thought. We tried to derive the larger systems of cultural beliefs and attitudes which the text seemed to represent.

It is worth thinking a little more about this last step. When signs and conno-tations appear normal, this is because the text presents itself as *obviously* truth-ful. Such connotations disguise the particular social influences that underlie the relevant codes. When this occurs, we can recognise **myth** at work.

Myth implies extremely familiar and influential social structures of mean-ing. Frequently it has traditional, historical acceptance. Later on, in Chapter 8, we will link the notion of myth to that of ideology. At this point, however, it enables us to start to talk about the social functions and effects of textual meanings. As we saw in the last chapter, myth emerges in texts as an order-ing of connotations. It conceals its identity as one social meaning among many for a text's signs, and seems instead to be the only, natural meaning. It parallels and extends, on the level of texts, the ways in which, at the level of signs, denotation acts as the apparently truthful connotation.

The effect of myth is to naturalise social meanings and values. Its extreme effect is to *hide* the semiotic workings of a text's signs and codes. The deno-tations appear so true that the signs seem to be the things themselves. In Figure 4.1, myth guarantees that Dunhill cigarettes do not merely signify status and taste, they *are* status and taste. Myth turns social signs into 'facts'.

Since signs and codes are produced by and reproduce cultural myths, the processes of textual meaning must be seen as central to social thought. Texts should be seen as kinds of social activity. Semiotic analysis reveals the poten-tial effects of such activity. Another example (Figure 4.2) may clarify these points.

Textual analysis and production

The kind of analysis applied to these two advertisements comprises a basic

Figure 4.2

THE FRESHEST TASTING RANGE OF SOUPS HAS JUST SPROUTED THREE NEW VARIETIES.

Introducing All Natural French Onion, Creamy Cauliflower and Garden Tomato & Vegetable. Made from the freshest ingredients available. From Campbells. Naturally.

The key signifiers in this advertisement include the *colours,* the *vegetables,* the *cans of soup,* and the *words* 'natural', 'freshest tasting' and 'sprouted'. The dominant signified seems to be *nature.* Together, the vegetables form a metonym for nature. The colours and images of the vegetables are transferred to the labels, which also then signify nature. The tins of soup operate as *metaphorical* signifiers of nature and *metonymic* signifiers for the Campbell's company, and even for society itself.

The text sets up a *contrast* between the natural and the cultural: fresh vegetables versus tinned soup. But this opposition seems also to be dissolved through the soup, and by extension through Campbell's. Like the brand name, which sounds like a family and a company, the tinned soup is a double sign – of nature and culture. Its *denotative* value of 'soup' compresses and reconciles two supposedly opposed signifieds.

This reconciliation works in other ways through the text. First, there is the *arrangement* of signs. The abundant supply of vegetables and the rows of tins make up a neat picture, almost like a school photograph. Indeed, the tins organise the excess of the vegetables, seeming to impose some sort of order upon them. It is a benevolent order. The cans signify the best features of nature combining with the best aspects of culture. Campbell's all-natural soup harmonises nature and culture, by not manufacturing but 'sprouting' a new product.

There are some important *myths* about nature in this text. Nature and culture seem to be opposed. Culture, however, is able to control nature, reduce its excess and make it beneficial for people. This text picks up on a long tradition of social thought and texts concerned with the links between nature and culture. It represents a positive image of their rela-tionship – that culture brings nature to fruition. It is possible to see this myth determining the signs and codes of many other texts, particularly ones denoting social progress. Such texts, in turn, can work to justify and endorse programs of research, development and change. Textuality translates into social action.

set of steps which can be used to study many types of texts and their social meanings. A simple diagram shows how it works

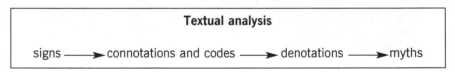

Textual analysis

signs ⟶ connotations and codes ⟶ denotations ⟶ myths

As can be seen, the analysis moves from locating specific signs, to examin-ing the structures of social myths. We can make several observations about this approach. It involves the following assumptions and makes these connections:

1 The basic premise of textual analysis is that *all signifiers have multiple signifieds*.
2 Signs' connotations are always related to *codes* of social meanings. (Remember that a code is a set of meanings shared by users, the produc-ers and the readers of the text.)
3 Each text is a syntagmatic *combination* of signs, with their related conno-tations.

4 The *connotations* likely to be emphasised by different readers vary with their social positions, that is, the class, gender, race, age, and other factors that influence the way they think about and interpret texts.
5 The most stable, central and socially preferred connotations become *denotations*, the apparently true meanings of the signs and the text for readers.
6 Denotations get their stability and centrality from the ways in which connotation sets are ordered by *myths*, which carry cultural values.

It is useful to think of this sort of analytical process as one that gradually *unpacks* the text. In a way the process reverses the structure through which social texts are produced or 'packed'. Texts are always produced in social contexts; they are always influenced by and reproduce the cultural values and myths of those contexts. The prevailing cultural myths determine what a text's key denotations, codes, connotations and signs will be. Even if a text contradicts those values and publicly announces its disagreement – as, for example, graffiti often do – it is still being influenced by them. So at this point, we can say that in many cases the process of textual production looks something like this:

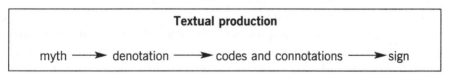

Textual production

myth ⟶ denotation ⟶ codes and connotations ⟶ sign

This process also has a couple of implications. On the one hand, the influential myths and cultural attitudes seem to affect the structure and meaning of texts. Myths underlie texts' meanings and values. On the other hand, because the myths do underlie the text and seem to be natural, they remain hidden within the text. They are not noticed because they invite acceptance as social truths. Take someone who is reading a magazine and sees one of the advertisements we analysed earlier. This person's understanding of the text would be influenced by the cultural myths that structure the signs, though he or she need not be conscious of that influence. The text addresses the reader as if its meanings were natural and normal, and invites the reader to read the text in these terms. As we shall see (particularly when we discuss ideology in Chapter 8), much of this process of **socialisation** takes place through texts and their functions of address.

Myths structure texts but, for many readings, they remain unrecognised. It is these naturalised, invisible myths that the analytical process we mapped out earlier tries to unpack. Hence there is a twofold relationship between text and myth:

1 Cultural myths structure the meanings and values of the text.
2 The text hides the myths which structure it.

It is this double process of the structuring and hiding of cultural values in texts that semiotic analysis aims to reveal.

The surface or literal meaning is only the tip of the textual iceberg. Its impression of finished meaning requires a lot of semiotic work to be done, in the exchange of signs, connotations and values. Yet that image can be so powerful and convincing that it conceals all the work and ends up looking real. There is more to semiotic reality than meets the eye.

Social readers, social reading

Texts never exist in abstraction. As we have seen, they work through semiotic processes such as metaphor and metonymy, where social meanings are exchanged and social codes interact. They don't make the real present, but *re-present* it through codes and signs.

Furthermore, texts are always to be read. The notion of text always implies an audience; there is always an addressee, a role usually filled by more than one reader or viewer. What we need to do now is to consider the various ways in which different texts produce social meanings for readers. What's going on when we read a text?

Let's begin to answer this question by having a closer look at some examples of the relationships between social attitudes and texts. Initially, we shall consider a couple of texts which seem to reproduce Western myths about African and Oriental cultures: see Figures 4.3 and 4.4.

The principal signs and codes in these texts pick up on a social grid of understanding which is founded on a basic cultural and mythic opposition – that between *us* and *them*. If the image *represents* a non-Western *them*, it *addresses* a Western *us*. We don't simply note the West–East contrast, we are addressed as being already on one side within it – as someone for whom this image is one of exoticness, unfamiliarity and fascination, rather than of a familiar and even banal day-to-day reality. This is how the text encourages readers to privilege one set of values and meanings over the other: simply, it sets up a *mythic opposition* and then addresses readers as if they *already* belong to one side rather than the other. Later, in Chapter 8, we shall spend a bit more time looking at the ways in which texts set up these sorts of contrasts as ideological default options for readers: us–them, West–East, culture–nature, masculine–feminine.

We can sum up; in the two examples we have been looking at:

1 There is a mythic opposition set up between *Western* and *non-Western*. The dominant term is *Western*, because everything revolves around that *difference* from Westernness: the exoticness, mystery and fascination of places and people which are very emphatically not Western.

Figure 4.3

This advertisement emphasises the exotic difference of the Orient. There is a blurring of Western time ('travel forward to the past'), as well as a blending of apparent contraries ('allow what is forbidden', 'obtain that which is elusive'). As a counterpart to this, the image presents a dreamlike superimposition. The fan also works metonymically in a myth of race and gender, to suggest the modesty and seclusion of Oriental women.

These verbal and visual signs come from codes that represent the Orient's cultural difference, but difference from what? The Western world, of course. In reverse, and as it represents the East, the text also works to stabilise the signs of Western culture as the known, the familiar, the everyday. Further, as the fan suggests, there is even a sexual contrast being hinted at – the feminised Orient and the masculinised West – and through the Revlon product this archetypal but exotic femininity can be transfered to Western women.

Figure 4.4

DECORATE YOUR EARDRUMS.

SONY.

This advertisement emphasises the exotic difference of the Orient. There is a blurring of Western time ('travel forward to the past'), as well as a blending of apparent contraries ('allow what is forbidden', 'obtain that which is elusive'). As a counterpart to this, the image presents a dreamlike superimposition. The fan also works metonymically in a myth of race and gender, to suggest the modesty and seclusion of Oriental women.

These verbal and visual signs come from codes that represent the Orient's cultural difference, but difference from what? The Western world, of course. In reverse, and as it represents the East, the text also works to stabilise the signs of Western culture as the known, the familiar, the everyday. Further, as the fan suggests, there is even a sexual contrast being hinted at – the feminised Orient and the masculinised West – and through the Revlon product this archetypal but exotic femininity can be transfered to Western women.

2 What is *represented* is the non-Western, but the *addressee* is Western.

From this, it is easy to see a common general mechanism by which texts **position** their readers to read them in certain ways rather than others:

---

1 The text sets up its meanings according to a *mythic opposition*. That is, it arranges everything in relationship to one dominant term.

2 The text *addresses* its meaning to an addressee on the side of the dominant term, and *represents* everything else *for* that addressee.

One consequence of this is that what is actually the dominant term need not be represented at all: even though the idea of Westernness dominates our examples, neither of them represents things Western. Because it remains out of sight, as it were, taken for granted as part of the functions of address, the dominant term *Western* is all the more effectively naturalised and made to appear obvious. The text simply offers an apparently obvious addresser role. It positions you *as if* you agree. Earlier, we suggested that texts hide the myths which structure them. This is how.

The Yves Saint Laurent advertisement considered in Figure 1.3 provides another variation on this, through an apparent reversal. In it, we have a clear mythic opposition of male and female. (Note the contrasts that run through the differing body positions and patterns of address of the two figures, the man and the woman. A set of male-related signs confronts a set of female-related signs.) At first, the expected opposition seems to be inverted. Instead of male control and female subordination, the ad *represents* a besotted man and a coolly knowing woman in control. But the reversal is only apparent, and that becomes clear when we consider its *address*. We are addressed *by* the product: YSL is promising to help us do the reversal. But to do that, it has to say that the normal, natural state of affairs without YSL is, after all, male dominance: otherwise, why buy it? The *addressee* is female: the woman in the picture addresses us in knowing complicity, as another woman. What they share is the pleasure of that reversal, *as* a reversal (it's not the occasion for a sly smile if it's the usual state of things): which is again to say that male dominance is the norm. If the ad addresses us as female, it also addresses us as taking the familiar mythic relationship of the sexes as obvious and natural. What the ad *represents* seems to run against the myth by turning it around; but the functions of *address* show it at work in the familiar uninverted way.

Let's return to another earlier text to examine a slightly different case: the Taylor family of Figure 3.3, still happy after Bill Taylor has won the by-election. On the surface, as you'll remember, the naturalised denotation is of a happy, middle-class family. The obvious myth which organises everything here is *family*: everything comes back to it.

If *family* is the dominant myth, the one whose signs take up most of the space of the picture, there is another apparently secondary myth riding on it. This is introduced by the poster: *politics*. We saw in Chapter 3 how Bill Taylor is a metonym for a traditionally patriarchal, political system; we also saw how the connotations with which the family codes surrounded him are transferred metaphorically to the political codes. Bill Taylor is a father *and* a politician, and the qualities of the father become those of the politician (the close, happy family becomes the contented electorate). There is an equation between the two Bill Taylors in the photograph, which synthesises the two myths: *family* becomes the model for *politics*.

The effect of this fused, doubly mythic sign of Bill Taylor is to *naturalise* patriarchal politics. If politics is modelled on the family, if we read it *through* the myth of *family*, then it is hard to reject the myth of politics we are being offered. To reject it would be to reject the ideals of the happy family – this family, the one we see in front of us. What seemed at first to be the secondary and less immediately striking myth – politics – turns out to be the dominant one, the one which is the point of the photo and governs all its meanings. It is represented less prominently, but it is what addresses us as if we were already in agreement with what is obvious and natural. What positions us to accept the way politics is being *represented* here is, again, the way we are *addressed*.

The family myth seems to bail out the politics myth, by making it more palatable or acceptable, and even by pressuring the reader not to reject the apparent denotations of family contentment. What is at stake in this process of using one myth to support another? What does it tell us about the way cultural myths work in texts?

Politics is not always embedded in positive myth. It often reverberates with connotations of impropriety and dishonesty. Political scandals bring a deep paradox in political mythology into the open: politics is both good and bad, respected and denounced; politicians are forthright leaders and shady schemers. These paradoxical meanings reveal an important aspect of the way all cultural myths are structured and function in texts. *No myth is unambiguous or singular*. Like signifiers and signifieds, myths are often multiple, quite possibly in contradictory ways. Look at the Campbell's soup advertisement in Figure 4.2: nature is depicted as providing for culture or needing to be controlled by culture. In the Sony ad, the female other is both desired and confronting. A myth is dominated by one term, and places everything else in one sort of relationship to that. Generally that relationship is a moral one: the mythic term is *good*, and everything else is more or (generally) less good in comparison with it. (Think of the clear moral lesson of that progression of faces from nineteenth-century anthropology in Figure 3.6.) This means mythic oppositions can easily invert themselves. For every mythic framework which sees nature as good and culture as bad, there is another which sees nature as chaos and culture as the order which saves us from it; for every myth in which the passing of time means progress and improvement, there is one which sees it as degeneration and fall; for every myth in which the child is an innocent who needs protection and nurturing, there is one in which it is an asocial figure who needs to be disciplined and educated. In the texts we have been examining just now, the family may be read as a restrictive patriarchal unit or a nest of support and contentment, and politics may be the basis of society or its corruption.

The myths that structure texts are often *oppositional*, and frequently split into conflicting versions of myth and counter-myth. If texts can be interpreted in different ways by different readers and groups of readers at different times, it is because they give rise to a number of possible meanings from the beginning. Texts are not containers for meanings which have already been fixed there, and to read them is not simply to passively receive their information. It is to *negotiate* these splits, along with the potentially very different set of values, meanings, myths and counter-myths which in turn make *us* the readers we are. Small wonder, then, that what reading produces in this collision can be quite unexpected, and even surprise us.

Dominant, negotiated and oppositional readings

A text like the photograph of the Taylor family thus works in a somewhat contradictory way. On the one hand, it is composed of codes of social meaning so conventional that they seem natural, and many readers who are familiar with these codes and signs are unlikely to interpret them in surprisingly different terms. To accept the addressee positions this text offers is to read it in accordance with a very prominent set of social myths about the family and politics which structure it.

On the other hand, readers don't always accept what is offered. Texts get interpreted in a variety of ways. Some readers may question the mythic images of family happiness and unity in the Taylor photograph, or dispute its political values, to a greater or lesser degree. It is possible, for example, to reject the particular political party or the approving middle-class connotations of the photograph, for example, but happily accept its patriarchal model of the family and politics.

An actual reading of any text can involve the acceptance, rejection or negotiated contestation of it, and in particular of the addressee positions it offers. These possibilities are often given the following names:

1 A **dominant** or **preferred reading**, in which readers take up the addressee role the text offers and the ways in which they are positioned with respect to its myths.
2 A **negotiated reading**, in which readers do not completely inhabit the addressee role, and question some of its myths.
3 An **oppositional reading**, in which readers reject the myths and addressee role completely.

The point of the model is not to prove that there are only three ways of reading. The most useful way to see it is as a further phase of the analytical procedure. Once we have moved through the basic steps of semiotic analysis and uncovered the complex play of meanings among the signs of a text, once we have identified the key social codes and related them to cultural grids of beliefs and attitudes or myths, we can then consider how its address works, and the ways in which it can be read and taken up by its readers.

There are undoubtedly many ways in which any given text could be interpreted by different groups of readers, according to age, gender, class, ethnicity, educational background and all sorts of other social factors. Moreover, no single factor will be completely determining. Texts do not contain fixed ideas but are involved in people's *negotiations* with and responses to social values and attitudes, connotations and myths. For this reason, the negotiated reading is probably the rule: reading is a perpetually re-enacted contest and reconsideration of social values.

A clear example of the way texts try to tie down their meaning can be seen in the way captions work in photographic texts. In Chapter 3, we called this function of the caption **anchorage**: it tries to tie down the connotations and codes that the visual signs are generating and orient them towards the underlying myths. Anchorage is a feature of news photographs, but we could also compare the effects of the title of a painting, especially a non-realistic painting, or a reporter's voice-over accompanying a piece of news footage. *Anchorage attempts to fix the addressee position of response to such texts.*

The effects of anchorage are, of course, not absolute. In the first place, in news texts the visual signs are often far more striking than the verbal ones – one of the main reasons for using them. Secondly, and more relevant to our understanding of textuality, *the anchorage itself constitutes another text*, with a complex interplay of signs, codes and readings. Anchorage may even increase rather than reduce textual interactions and interpretations; it rarely finalises them.

Consider some of the most famous social texts of recent times: the video of Rodney King being bashed by four Los Angeles policemen; live coverage of the funeral of Princess Diana; the Report of the Independent Counsel,

Kenneth Starr, into the relationship between American President Bill Clinton and White House aide, Monica Lewinsky. For many viewers and readers the meanings of these texts seemed clear. For example, in the King video it seemed that the unarmed man was the victim; yet as the legal defence and the jury finding in the initial trial showed, this text could be negotiated in unpredictable ways. As an amateur video, cameraman more or less unknown, there seemed to be no way of working out a stable preferred meaning. The connotations became complex as many codes were triggered by the video – law and order, police brutality, violence against blacks. Behind these were still more complex myths of justice, morality and racism.

The controversy over the verdict enacted an intense response to the signs' possible meanings. A single preferred reading was not possible. More and more texts were produced – film of other violent acts, interviews with experts, eye-witness accounts, recollections of social unrest in the 1960s, and, ultimately, a second trial. None of these texts reduced the complexities, for each drew on different codes and was open to conflicting interpretations.

Analogous proliferations of texts, codes and meanings were produced around the death and funeral of Princess Diana and the release on the Internet of the Starr Report. The funeral triggered numerous textual responses which explored and debated social values and codes including family relationships, the future of the monarchy, the nature of English society, and the functions of contemporary media. Poignant shots and photographs of the Princess's family, especially her sons, served to draw these issues together, as their personal vulnerability to political and national forces seemed to be highlighted. In related ways, the revelations of President Clinton's affair with Monica Lewinsky in the Starr Report set off a constant stream of texts, ranging from serious political and journalistic responses, to comments on talkback radio and opinion polls, to a vast number of World Wide Web sites which promised lurid but true pictures of what really went on.

The King video, the coverage of Princess Diana's funeral, and the publication of the Starr Report suggest that in social terms textual meanings cannot be fully understood by focussing purely on what seems to originate in the sender's mind or on what is understood by a single receiver. These texts' many meanings, their **polysemy**, were the condition of their circulation through the local, national and international communities. In each site, and for each group of readers, the significance was perceived very differently. These texts were then used to justify specific structures of social, legal, racial, moral and sexual attitudes and became the immediate pretext for a range of social actions from protest to law enforcement, public grieving to celebration, political support and condemnation. As noted earlier, not the least of their effects was to initiate a continuing cycle of other texts.

Texts are combinations of signs with multiple, social meanings. These meanings derive from cultural codes and myths. Because polysemy is basic to signs (as we have seen in Chapter 2), a text's meaning never has a single origin or final destination. It always in principle involves negotiation, and this is handled differently by different social groups of readers. What we have found is that textuality and reading are always social activities: meaning is not something that takes place in isolation, but in a world where meanings are already ways of doing things.

EXERCISES

1 Many types of social gatherings can be analysed as texts. Try to examine the structure and meanings of such events as a barbecue, a concert or a party by using the semiotic concepts introduced in the last three chapters. What are your text's key signs? Do they work metaphorically and metonymically? What are the different sorts of readings that people make of these texts?

2 Your university or college campus can also be analysed semiotically – from the overall layout to the design of individual lecture theatres and seminar rooms. Which cultural myths inform the oldest buildings on the campus? Do more recent buildings suggest changes to these myths? How could the lecture theatres or seminar rooms be analysed? What are the connotations of the students' seating arrangements in contrast to the position set up for the lecturer or tutor?

3 Collect a series of magazine advertisements that depict family groups. Note the key signifiers for the different family members. What are their connotations? Find some family advertisements from twenty or thiry years ago, and analyse any changes to myths of the family.

4 Like Figures 4.3 and 4.4, many magazine advertisements rely on drawing cultural contrasts to set social meanings in play. Collect some recent advertisements that depict characters and settings from African or Asian countries – analyse the key connotations and denotations of cultural identity that these texts set in play. Consider if they also imply notions of cultural difference. Difference to whom? How might negotiated or oppositional readings question or challenge the kinds of cultural relations and identities signified in the texts?

SOURCES AND FURTHER READING

For a general discussion of the different metaphors that have been used to discuss culture see Clifford Geertz's essay, 'Blurred Genres: The Refiguration of Social Thought' in his book *Local Knowledge: Further Essays in Interpretive Anthropology* (New York: Basic Books, 1983).

Barthes' *Mythologies* (New York: Hill & Wang, 1987) provides numerous examples of the concept of myth at work in cultural analysis. Other examples of this kind of analysis can be seen in John Fiske, Graeme Turner and Bob Hodge, *Myths of Oz: Readings in Australian Popular Culture* (Sydney: Allen & Unwin, 1987). Recent works that analyse advertising include Guy Cook's *The Discourse of Advertising* (London: Routledge, 1992), Jib Fowles's *Advertising and Popular Culture* (Newberry: Sage, 1996), and Greg Myers's *Ad Worlds: Brands, Media, Audiences* (London: Arnold, 1999). For a range of Internet links on advertising analysis see the related entry on Daniel Chandler's Media and Communication Studies site at www.aber.ac.uk/media/Functions/mcs.html.

There are numerous works which discuss the models of textuality and reading introduced in the chapter. For a clear summary, see Graeme Turner, *British Cultural Studies: An Introduction*, 2nd edn (London: Routledge, 1996). Stuart Hall's essay, 'Encoding and Decoding', in *Culture, Media, Language: Working Papers in Cultural Studies, 1972–79* (London: Unwin Hyman, 1980), provides a more complex account. David Morley's books, *The 'Nationwide' Audience: Structure and Decoding* (London: British Film Institute, 1980) and *Family Television: Cultural Power and Domestic Leisure* (London: Comedia, 1986) apply theories of reading to television viewing.

The concept of dominant, negotiated and oppositional readings comes from the work of the British sociologist Basil Bernstein, *Class, Codes and Control* (St Albans: Paladin, 1971). It is discussed and applied in many of the works noted above.

Genre and intertextuality

Textual relations

One of the key effects texts have is to provide a context in which other texts are read and experienced. Surrounding texts influence readers' responses to any particular text. They suggest *metalingual* cues through which a text's codes may be recognised, understood and often questioned. And they link up with the *contextual* function, through which a text indicates the context in which it is operating. These surrounding texts form an **intertext**.

> A text's relationship to other texts is its **intertextuality**. The specific texts it draws on for its meaning are its **intertext**.

To continue to examine the social meanings and effects of texts, we therefore need to expand the kind of close semiotic analysis practised in preceding chapters. That type of analysis can disclose the interplay of signs and cultural values at work within one text. It can also suggest the various readings of and attitudes to the subject matter that is depicted. These are important steps to take if we want to investigate how a culture functions and how it is represented. But these steps need to be supplemented by considering the contextual and metalingual interactions between texts that also affect the processes of textuality, address and reading.

Up to this point our focus on the possibilities of reading a single text has sought to explain one of the basic conditions of social communication: that every text is understood in different ways by different groups of people at different times. To understand this, we mapped out the general polysemic potential of signs and texts. Such a focus must, however, be broadened, since one text never functions in total independence from others. We could compare the way in which the relationships among individual signs are what give them their signification. Something similar is bound to happen with texts, too. We have already seen examples of this in the impact of anchorage on news photographs, where visual and verbal signs work together. Our analytical method needs to be able to address the effects of these connections.

Texts can interrelate in a wide range of ways, from imitation to confrontation. In general terms, these relations come into play when a text reproduces or refers to the paradigmatic selections and the syntagmatic combinations of signs from other texts. Reproductions may be more or less exact. At one extreme, the same signs can be used in the same order and elicit the same sort of interpretation or response from readers.

Take, for example, the movements and gestures of a military parade. Think of them in the semiotic terms we first suggested in Chapter 2, Figure 2.5. The actions of each soldier are selected from a restricted paradigm set of bodily signifiers and signifieds. A strictly defined code governs the sequence of their combination into the syntagm of the parade movements: these are in effect a *text*. As each soldier snaps to attention, the commanding officer sees a precise reproduction of connotations of authority and obedience. As more soldiers repeat the move, this authority and obedience are naturalised within the context of military life.

A complex set of interactions takes place among these soldier-texts: all reproduce the connotations separately, yet in doing so they construct a group effect. Each soldier signifies individually *and* contributes to establishing a cumulative meaning. In one sense, individual signification is dependent upon the group. The action of a single soldier – the snap of the salute, the click of heels – realises meaning through its resemblance to the actions of the others. Because it is similar, connotations of obedience and authority are immediately set up. In turn, the signification of the one text contributes to the overall effect and helps to enact a myth of *discipline*. Each successive salute seems to reinforce the truth of disciplinary values.

If a soldier trips or refuses to salute, the meaning of the act is underlined by its contrast to the others. This contrast may also serve to disrupt the meaning of the other salutes, of the parade as a whole, and of the myths which structure it. One text could change the meaning of the whole group by altering either the choice of signs or their combination. Even without making these paradigmatic or syntagmatic changes, a single text may always receive negotiated or oppositional readings which would question the seemingly settled body of connotations, meanings and values that it and the other texts have. The hundredth perfectly executed salute convinces a watching pacifist of the madness of military culture. Although this response is the opposite of the commander's, it is nonetheless the links *between* the soldier-texts that allow their apparent meaning to be challenged.

This example illustrates some of the key features of textual relations:

1 Most importantly, it suggests that the relationship between one text and others is always *reciprocal*. That is, the single text and the group affect each other's meanings.
2 The group provides the *context* within which the text is placed and read.
3 Some aspects of context may act as metalingual *cues*, though these cues need not be taken up.
4 A text can always be read *against* rather than within context, and the reader may always be able to connect it to a different set of texts – the tripping soldier could be removed from the set of parade-texts and linked to a set of anti-military texts, such as protest rallies and sit-ins.

This last point indicates a further feature of the reciprocal relations between one text and others. While the group of texts with similar codes does provide a context for the single text, it is one that remains dependent on the contribution of each individul text. The group codes are reinforced by every text which is structured by them. But instead of confirming the codes, an individual text may also disrupt or change them, and thereby affect the group meaning. To complicate things, some readers may see one text as enacting this kind of disruption even though other readers continue to view the text as reinforcing the usual codes.

These possibilities suggest that textual groupings and their social meanings are not static. They can change through a single text's reworking or adapting the conventions of sign choice and combination, as readers challenge the previously accepted meanings of texts like it.

Two elements are thus particularly important in thinking about the relationships between texts. These are:

1 The *texts* themselves: the selected signs, their combination, and their metalingual functions.
2 The *intertext* of references they set up amongst themselves.

In the rest of this chapter we will examine some of the different operations and effects of these interactions among texts.

Genre

A **genre** is a grouping of texts which are similar in structure or subject matter.

Genre has often been used simply as a means of categorising texts. If they are considered to share enough characteristics they can all be placed in the same genre – plays like *Hamlet*, in which a heroic character dies, are called tragedies. This use of the idea is fairly limited, and we will attempt to expand it.

Genre is not simply a cataloguing device, but instead names the ways in which texts can relate to each other. As emerged in the previous section, the relations between texts – what makes them seem 'similar' or not – are complex and variable. Furthermore, these relations do not only depend on a text's internal features. They are also constructed through the social readings that texts may be given by different groups.

As we recognised in our discussion of texts in Chapter 4, all elements of textuality are cultural activities, from the selection of signs to the options for reading and relating them to different social experiences. Genre is no exception. In fact, because a text's genre entails questions of sign choice, reader response and so on, genre is preeminently a cultural concept. Generic issues relate to all aspects of textuality as social process. They involve the conventions (and so also the exceptions) for thinking about texts in terms of:

1 *Textual production*, including semiotic factors such as sign choice and combination, as well as the technical and institutional features of a medium.
2 The *relations among texts* and whether they affect each other in terms of contrast or similarity;
3 The *cultural conditions and contexts* in which texts are used and the effects of their use.

In short, in dealing with the ways in which texts are read, interpreted and used, genre is a matter of the *social functions* of texts.

Because it presumes that different texts can actually be related through genre, a further implication of the generic approach is that neither a text nor a reading can be unique, or entirely original. Texts form part of a network of social meanings and values, in which each text builds on and makes variations on others. This is neither a defect nor a symptom of an unimaginative text or response: even the most innovative text owes something elsewhere. Texts come trailing signifieds and values from previous uses. As we will see, such repetitions and interplay add to the social meanings of encounters with texts.

One of the aims of the generic analysis of texts is to investigate this interplay. By tracing the relationships between texts, we can examine differing social responses towards the subjects being represented. This kind of textual comparison and contrast reveals that such variation has two dimensions:

1 It shows that the connotations and myths triggered by signs change over time. That is, generic considerations can uncover the *historical process* of social meaning.
2 By comparing texts and responses from the same time period (or, from a relatively restricted period, say of a couple of years), one can begin to gauge dominant and alternative ways of understanding a particular topic. In this case, generic analysis reveals the *contemporary structure* of social meaning.

These two dimensions may interact to produce further effects. For example, generic variation may also suggest conflicts or contradictions within a structure of meaning, and so point to the beginnings of change in attitudes and values. In that case, comparisons among texts can show a contemporary structure of meaning being transformed into historical process and change.

Hence there are a number of advantages in introducing the concept of genre into the analysis of social texts. In the first place, genre foregrounds the influence of surrounding texts and ways of reading on our response to any one text. More specifically, it confirms textuality and reading as functions rather than things and shows that they take place within two kinds of context. The first is the *intertext* of other texts, with the cultural values they represent and the myths which structure them; the second is the context of *social readings, interpretations and responses* to those values and myths. Just as a text's structure is influenced by similar texts, so readings are shaped by traditions and trends of response. Genre exemplifies the fact that reading and producing texts are social actions.

Finally, the concept of genre suggests that texts, readings and the myths they support and enact are historically placed. Analysis based on comparison and contrast is the premise of the generic approach to textual relations, and it enables us to measure against each other the changing representations of and responses to cultural values and beliefs. In considering effects of genre, our understanding of texts can move beyond the static analysis of single objects, and begin to see that textuality, representation and reading participate in unfolding processes of social and historical change.

Reading genre

These processes can best be studied by focusing on a particular genre and examining its textual and contextual effects along with the range of readings that confront it. As a genre, media news illustrates many of these important points. Let's begin by considering the way the opening sequence of television news works. Figure 5.1 give an idea of its choice of signs and the way it structures them.

Figure 5.1 The evening news

We hear the signature music, perhaps before we see any of the other signs. It is stirring music, a set of aural signs that connote urgency, importance and drama. While it sounds, we see computer-animated images of the globe, crisscrossed by lines of communication like those that are about to bring us the breaking stories. The network news logo moves along these meridians, sliding around and over from the other side of the globe. This world, like the coverage it will receive, is hi-tech, dynamic and up-to-the moment. The colours are perhaps those of the flag, so there is a double connotation: of a national perspective on international events, and of the importance of national events as news in themselves. A complex set of phatic functions is being set up here, involving not only nation and world but also – most importantly – the network without whose coverage we could not know ourselves to be part of this community.

The sequence cuts to a series of shots taken from the three leading stories of the bulletin, anchored by voiceovers from the two newsreaders, a man and a woman in alternation. They are the big stories of the day, and in their newsworthiness (see Figure 5.2) they again raise the phatic question of community, on an international or national level.

Only then do we see the two newsreaders behind the studio desk, the man on the left and the woman on the right. The wall behind them looks like a large window. On it, arcs and lines crisscross, echoing the opening animation. Behind the window, we can see what seems to be the newsroom, with people at desks, telephones and terminals, busy gathering the news for us. Every time we cut back to the newsreaders in the studio, this will quietly remind us of the network's role in this community of information we are invited to share. The woman tells us of a fourth story ('And also tonight . . .'), this time without footage. 'But first', says the man, launching us into the main story.

This opening segment of the news can be framed as a text in itself. Most of us would probably find it very familiar: that is, we identify it *generically*. The precise set and order of the signs may be different to those we have seen before: the headline stories are not the same every night; the newsreaders change every now and then; the graphics team might refashion the logo or update the images of the world and the soundtrack. Different networks have different signatures – different logos, themes and newsreaders. Nonetheless, as experienced TV viewers we easily identify the kind of text. Paradigmatic and syntagmatic variations do not disrupt the generic structure we recognise immediately as *the news*.

By responding to the text in terms of its genre, we are able to distinguish it from other aspects of the surrounding social and television intertext. We can easily see here how genre works to categorise texts, but we can also see a wide range of interpretive and cultural effects it has. In recognising a genre, readers are subject to an array of socialising factors.

One of the first steps involved in recognising the text as news is to acknowledge the significance of the reported events. Not everything that occurs in the world is considered newsworthy. Indeed, the media use a set of **news values** to decide which events will be covered as news (Figure 5.2). These criteria thus work as *generic markers* of the news.

In defining what makes news, news values also reinforce cultural values. The generic principles of news selection work socially at the same time. The subject matter is selected to match assumed social concerns. If events are given news coverage, their importance is emphasised, and they are transformed into *issues*. In being reported, issues are then reinforced as central social concerns. The process is circular – social concerns define the issues which reinforce the concerns. Each story then develops such concerns either by noting the general importance and relevance of the events or by offering specific judgements and interpretations of them.

As they recognise these events *as* news, viewers are being offered generic and social judgements of what is meaningful to them. This may have powerful socialising effects:

- *News tells us what is important.* Events which may be of the utmost interest to some social groups may simply not be included: they may not fit many of the criteria for newsworthiness, or be crowded out by stories which fulfil more of them.
- *News represents events in specific ways.* A recurrent structure of reporting is used. It has two key features:

  (1) First, the news relies on official figures or experts – government, administrative, professional and other appointed speakers – to set up the **primary definition** of the issue: what is the question, what framework should it be seen in?

> The **primary definition** of an issue is the framework within which it is placed. **Primary definers** are the figures used by the media to provide the primary definition of the issue.

Because news values tend to emphasise the familiar, the readily (and already) understood, *the primary definition tends to be mythic*: that is, it may simplify what may be a complex set of events down to a single set of values, and an opposition: freedom versus tyranny, greedy unions versus responsible management, government versus opposition, us versus them.

Figure 5.2 News values

Threshold: Big events such as wars, famines and disasters get noticed more than small ones.

Unambiguity: The clearer the meaning of the event, the more likely it is to be reported.

Negativity: Bad news is favoured over good.

Meaningfulness: Events which meet audience expectations are favoured over those which don't.

Consonance: A story tends to be favoured if the media have previously run a similar story: that is, if it meets media expectations.

Unexpectedness: Exceptional events will be favoured over the usual state of things.

Cultural proximity: Events tend to be noticed more when they occur in the audience's own country, to members of their own cultural groups.

Reference to élite nations: Stories about powerful or western nations are run more often than stories about less powerful nations.

Reference to élite persons: Celebrities get more press than unknowns.

Personalisation: Events which can be seen in terms of individuals and their actions get more coverage than those which can't.

Frequency: Events which fit into the schedule of publishing or broadcasting are favoured over those that don't.

Continuity: Running stories may be followed up over several days or more.

Availability of images: Stories with striking images tend to be favoured over those without.

(2) This primary definition sets the story up to have two sides. An initial viewpoint will be followed by one which opposes it. (The government minister will be followed by a spokesperson from the opposition, a manager will be followed by a union official.) This has several effects. Because it is the subject of conflict, the importance of the issue seems beyond question. Other views are excluded if they do not fit the opposition set up by the primary definition, in which one side or the other must be right. And this structure of **balance**, where every statement is followed by a counter-statement, gives the news the impression of scrupulous fairness and evenhandedness.

These two aspects of news reporting – *choice of subject matter* and *structure of representation* – make up the genre's key paradigmatic and syntagmatic features. These aspects do more than simply set up the conventional form and content of the news; they also work to position viewers in specific ways, in relation to the events. The selection of stories, along with their primary definitions and closed for-or-against structure, offers an interpretation of the world. In its repetition and predominance of images of the country, and of the flag and its colours, the opening of the TV news bulletin, as in Figure 5.1, suggests that this interpretation revolves strongly around the point of view of the *nation*.

Hence these generic features not only tell us *what* the news is, they also suggest *how* to read it, and what kind of perspective to adopt. At a general level, this viewpoint is structured as 'in the national interest'. In specific stories, however, it is also based on the perspective provided by the primary definitions, which is offered to the viewers as authoritative, reasonable and true. This may be a hard offer to refuse, even when the story is in fact none of these.

In instructing readers and viewers on what is newsworthy and how it is to be understood, the news genre fits them with a cultural identity. This identity is both conative and phatic, being based on a shared way of representing and viewing the world. The textual processes of connotation and myth set up a strong phatic identity of both addresser and addressee. They invite a preferred reading of the news, through which the audience may accept the selection and interpretation of material as their own, and the various national and social identities and positions implied in it. In doing this, these generic processes naturalise the news. The selection and representation which happens through primary definition and news values may go quite unnoticed, with the generic features reinforcing the truthful effects of its subject matter and its interpretations, and thus the objectivity of the news itself.

On the other hand, this address can of course be rejected, either totally or partially. Audience members might find that the social viewpoint of the news alienates or oppresses their perspective. In a few pages we will discuss some examples of this possibility. As ways of representing the world, genres can be contested and changed.

Generic change

Since it implies a kind of group identification, the notion of genre may suggest that textual relations are based on stability, and that genres exist because textual relations are constant. The discussion of news in the previous section seemed to suggest that in this case at least, generic effects realise cultural stability and reinforce enduring myths of the nation and of citizenship.

By examining a series of generically related texts, we can, however, start to see that genres do not only work to tie down social meaning. The choice and combination of key signs may also alter as one genre is affected by inter-actions with others, and as the responses of different groups of readers exert pressure to change key patterns of meaning. In short, we can think of a genre as a body of signs, texts, meanings and responses which are being constantly rewritten. Rather than denoting settled social meaning, the seeming stabil-ity of genre forms a launching pad for revisions and innovations.

By looking at generic effects in one medium we can observe recurring signs and codes and then start to trace the range of shifts that can occur. Look at Figure 5.3, a series of newspaper photographs of businessmen. (One of the features of this genre is its focus on men.) Most of the pictures are taken from the business sections of major metropolitan daily newspapers, although some are also from the main news section. They appear to quote and imitate each other. Their cross-referencing seems to stabilise the way they can be read, reinforcing preferred readings and social values.

What are the recurring signs and codes? In most cases the camera is pointing slightly upwards at the figure, who makes eye contact with the reader by gazing downwards. The figure is in the centre of the frame, and his face is well lit. He is usually dressed in the work uniform of dark suit, though sometimes more active gear such as an industrial coat and hard hat may be worn. The accompanying written texts, though not included here, are invari-ably about the figure's commercial successes.

Perhaps most striking is the figure's relaxed but controlled pose, leaning either backwards, at ease in the surrounds, or forwards in concentration. The background is also relevant. It seems to signify the business setting in which the figure is expert – an aeroplane or ship, a boardroom or desk with computer. Against this backdrop, the authoritative pose connotes mastery and expertise. We might also note the prominence of the hands throughout the pictures, connoting a readiness to work and an ability to seize opportu-nities and success.

These recurring signifiers and connotations suggest a set of positive codes of masculinity and commerce. They invoke and reinforce cultural myths about progress, individuality and masculinity, with the businessman as hero. Economic success is naturalised as the product of a poised, male individual. The genre is distinguished by a combination of visual style (pose, camera angle, lighting), the single figure featured against these back-grounds, and the news context in which the texts appear. (The context is important; if these pictures were presented in a satirical article on men's

Figure 5.3a

Figure 5.3b

Figure 5.3c

Figure 5.3d

Figure 5.3e

fashions, the connotations would change dramatically.) Again, the relationship between the individual photographs and the genre is reciprocal: each text is influenced by the generic conventions in the way it is put together, and in turn the conventions are reinforced by each text.

As we noted earlier, the conventions also affect the ways the texts can be read. Their repetition and familiarity mean it can be difficult *not* to see these texts and their connotations as simply and naturally true. They interact to establish a socially authoritative representation of the world and of people in it, and address the readers as part of this world.

There are various ways in which this particular genre can change. First of all, signs and codes are never separable from their *social context*, and are affected by changes within it. Such effects are also reciprocal: a genre develops according to prevailing social conditions, and transformations in genre

Figure 5.4

and texts can influence or reinforce social conditions. In both cases the transformations are part of a historical process of cultural change.

For example, the next photograph (Figure 5.4) is of a businesswoman. It was not placed in the business section, but framed as part of a human interest story. This location suggests that the image of woman as business hero tends to be an exceptional case within the genre. Nonetheless, the genre is flexible enough to represent and include such a figure.

Many of the same generic signs we noted earlier are reproduced here: the upward camera angle, the assured but comfortable stance, power dressing, the work environment, the connotations of being both literally and metaphorically on top of the world. A notable difference is that the woman does not meet our gaze. She looks up, connoting future prospects – her own, the company's, perhaps the future of other women in the corporate world. Such shifts within the genre register changing social conditions, with the entrance of more women into domains and activities that had previously been exclusively performed by men.

While the gender of the business figure may change, the other myths that link commercial success to heroism and individuality have not altered. If the gender code is emphasised, the text could be read as signifying a step forward for women in certain respects. If the business code is underlined, the text could be viewed as a sign of the flexibility of business practices, so that women as well as men can be successful in commerce. This augmenta-

Figure 5.5

Worth its wait

THE GOLD CARD · TO APPLY CALL TOLL FREE 008 23 0100 OR SYDNEY 886 0666

tion of the genre may signify the strengthening of the business ethos through the community rather than any revision of it. Generic change can itself be interpreted as symptomatic of different cultural trends.

A genre may also change by *interacting with other media and genres*. Paradoxically, one of the basic rules of genre seems to be that it is always breaking its own boundaries, with key signs and codes often cutting across to other contexts. As different kinds of texts interact with each other they recycle signs, codes and social values of different genres. These get transposed to different settings, and assume new references. Once again, the effects of such movements are hard to predict. Social myths may be more strongly reinforced and naturalised by being represented in a wider range of texts. On the other hand, the values that a genre tends to advocate can be disrupted or questioned through the contextual shift.

We can see an example of this in Figure 5.5. In part, its connotations derive from the genre of news photographs considered previously. Many of their features are recycled: the prominent hand, not ready to work but already grabbing the fruits of its labours (a celebratory gin and tonic, or perhaps a reinvigorating mineral water); individuality; business dress; black and white photography; a view, from on high, over the metropolis. The major change is that the businessman does not face the reader. Instead, we see what he sees: addresser and addressee all but coincide. We come close to sharing his successful identity. Yet the angle of our view is not quite his; the desired identity eludes us. Of course, the text insinuates, we can get a lot closer by obtaining an American Express card.

Despite the shift in the codes and signs from news to advertising texts, the ordering myths about masculinity and success continue to be emphasised. A set of intertextual effects may also be triggered by the shift. For it seems that both genres, advertising and news, are quoting from each other, moving signs from one setting to another. The effects of such moves are not always predictable and can, in fact, work in quite contradictory ways. For example, the advertisement may borrow something of the familiarity of the news images, to make the advantages of possessing a credit card seem equally familiar and obvious. At the same time, the repetition of the news images in the advertisement reveals that in addition to providing information, the news photographs are also selling something – a cultural system based on economic success and individuality.

This last point suggests that in addition to supplying signs and codes, thereby supplementing their social meanings, different genres may *react against* each other. The connections between texts need not lead to a synthesis of values and meanings, but to contests between them. This is the last outcome of generic interaction that we will consider: genres also participate in conflictual *dialogues*. In so doing they open up opportunities for readers and viewers to question and rewrite the myths and values they represent.

Dialogism

Just as signs interact within texts, and texts interact within genres, so genres interact with one another. At times, these interactions can be relatively harmonious, and the genres' meanings can combine or reinforce one another. It is also possible for there to be degrees of difference or contradiction among genres. When such differences emerge, a unity or synthesis of the genres' meanings is precluded.

These differences can occur in various ways. As we saw in the previous chapter a cigarette advertisement promising prestige and status can be challenged by a medical warning. Two genres clash within the one text. Here, the contradiction is quite obvious. In other cases, conflicts of meanings may not be so prominent. They will result from the interpretations of certain groups of readers who, in relating the text to their social values and attitudes, challenge meanings that other groups might immediately accept. In this instance, conflicts of meaning may arise as groups of readers struggle to maintain their interpretation.

Texts and readings interact as if in dialogue with each other. When a group of readers reads certain texts it fills them with meanings related to its social position. Their readings debate or agree with the texts. As part of their response, readers then produce their own texts, ranging from raised eyebrows to spoken comments to published articles and books. These readings and texts will be more or less different from those produced by other groups. A dialogue of social values commences between readers and texts and among different groups of readers.

Reading and texts are an important site for the expression of differing social viewpoints. This kind of **dialogism** is another of the basic conditions of textuality, and in particular of intertextuality. It is also a fundamental aspect of social action. Texts and readings impose and contest cultural dominance, and offer resistance. Genres play an important role in this dialogic process; in the interaction and conflicts among genres we can see the connections between textuality and power.

If we now turn to a particular set of genres and texts we can start to see these social processes at work. Let's consider all the texts and genres related to a specific social institution. They will tend to have a hierarchical organisation, with some genres being privileged as more important, more relevant and even more truthful than others. (Chapters 7 and 8 have a more detailed discussion of the cultural and ideological workings of institutions and the discourses that they produce.)

For example, running through the social institution of the *law* is an expansive set of genres and texts. At the top of this institution, certain genres are employed: political statutes and decrees; decisions by attorneys-general; court rulings; findings of commissions of inquiry; pronouncements by law societies; statements by police officials; academic research reports, and so on. Through a combination of subject matter, style, the addresser roles, and the contexts in which they are produced, these genres have the broadest social authority. The figures who produce these sorts of texts – politicians, judges, commissioners, and other official spokespersons – are the primary definers of the legal institution. They establish official definitions of the law.

These figures also establish which genres and texts are most important in running an institution. The genres they use exert great power in setting up the terms through which the rest of us can think about legal issues and texts. The more these genres are used, the more strongly the positions of the primary definers and others involved in the institution are entrenched. As we saw in an earlier section, the social impact of the definers of these genres is frequently intensified by the news media.

The hierarchy of legal genres and texts does not, however, stop at these levels. It moves from there to include media reports on the law; consultations between clients and lawyers; arrests and orders issued by police; courtroom dramas in books and on screen; two people chatting about the enforcement of drink-driving laws while they wait at a taxi rank; groups protesting about cuts to legal aid funding; people complaining on talkback radio about old-fashioned judges, and so on. Although each of these texts belongs to a different genre, all of them refer to the same social institution. Yet they do not all represent it in the same way, or with the same effects. The connotations of *the law* range from positive to negative, and the influence of the different genres on other people varies considerably.

There are also specific kinds of interaction going on among these genres. There is tendency for the official genres to represent a shared conception of the law as a 'pillar of society'. They might at times disagree on the best way to fortify the law – an official inquiry or commission might challenge the views of politicians – but none of these genres questions the necessity of supporting the law.

In contrast, we might note that the last few genres mentioned above – private conversations, public protests and comments – contest the primary definitions of the official texts. They question the authoritative versions of the legal institution, and propose their own rival definitions of what the law is and how it operates.

Although genres are often organised hierarchically, the hierarchy is never totally fixed or accepted. Instead, the official genres are continually liable to active re-reading and response, with other texts offering alternative definitions. These interactions among genres reflect and programme the changing balances of power relationships within the wider social system which are continuously being worked out. They take place over the ways that social institutions operate, but also over the ways they are represented and who is entitled to speak about them.

Hence the interaction of social genres is like a dialogue in which speakers are always negotiating their positions and identities. A clear example of this process can be seen in Figure 5.6, an exchange between a patient and a

Figure 5.6 In the doctor's surgery

Doctor:	Good morning Mrs Johnson. I'm Doctor Spencer.
Patient:	Good morning Doctor. I've come as I'm sure I have a, um, hormonal imbalance. I seem to have symptoms of [...]
Doctor:	So many women think they have hormonal troubles nowadays. Describe the problem. I'll do the diagnosis.

The exchange sets up a relationship of social power between the two speakers. The doctor initiates the dialogue, asserting both speakers' social identities by using titles ('Dr' and 'Mrs'), and is more likely than the patient to call the other by their first name. The doctor imposes two roles in the exchange: one who knows and one who doesn't. In this scheme only the doctor has legitimate knowledge. He or she reacts sharply sharply when sensing that the patient has usurped some specialised language. The implication of this reaction seems to be that in starting to use the doctor's speech genre, the patient threatens the power hierarchy ofo the exchange, which is that of the medical institution. She is rapidly silenced as the doctor seeks to restrict the sort of speech she can use and thereby control the situation.

doctor. It reveals much about the genre contests that construct the social institution of medicine. It shows that dialogues between genres do not merely reflect relationships that pre-exist in the community. Rather, they are one of the key avenues through which these relationships are founded, reinforced or challenged. In the interaction and contests between genres, questions of social power are worked through.

We can see how genres and power interact in more detail by looking at the ways in which economic matters are often presented on television news. In itself, economics may appear a dry and undramatic topic ill-suited to television. The solution is to embed it in a number of *televisual* rather than economic genre conventions:

- As we have seen in Figure 5.1, the framing of the news has already set up a *national identity* for viewers, and foregrounded supposedly shared viewpoints and experiences. Before it begins, the story is already embedded in a srongly phatic effect. In the story itself, collective nouns may help to further realise these effects: 'the nation has ...', we are now closer to living within our means'.
- The story may employ the *specialised vocabulary* of economics ('monthly surplus on goods and services', 'seasonally adjusted balance of payments', 'All-Ordinaries') but in a way which is significantly more *metalingual and phatic* than referential. The codes it invokes are those we can recognise as

belonging to a specialist knowledge, even if we do not understand their referential content. It invites us to accept expertise.

- This is emphasised by *primary definition*. The story is defined from the outset as one about economics, the management of money (rather than, say, welfare or education). This agenda will be embodied in a *primary definer* (the Treasurer, a senior minister in the government, an independent analyst), against whose statements all others are implicitly measured. What has now been underlined is the legitimacy of the specialised vocabulary of economics as a description of *our* world. Primary definition is often, but far from always, vested in the public figure and the specialist knowledge; but a story may, for example, set up public opinion rather than expertise as its reference point, and then measure up various experts and public figures according to the extent to which they are in touch with this.

One of the most significant means through which genres and texts register the exchange of social values is the way in which they refer to or depict each other. Through analysing these kinds of *intertextual* links, echoes and repetitions – the way one text uses other texts to make its own points – we can trace the shifts in social values that are taking place. As we have seen, texts constantly cite and quote other texts, and in removing their generic norms to new contexts they adapt their meanings and implications.

This dialogic, intertextual process is exemplified by *parody* and *satire*. In parodying the style of another text – be it the jargon of specialists or the uniform of officials – the new text criticises the other's social perspective. The practice of graffiti is a revealing example of the way texts re-use other texts in articulating their ideas. Graffiti rework and reclaim public places, turning them into spaces for private performances and interpersonal conversations. They challenge social institutions by rewriting their codes and connotations, using satire and irony to transform their meanings. Graffiti on advertising billboards are perhaps the clearest example of this kind of intertextual challenge. They re-evaluate the text's generic structure to uncover the absurdity of a product's link to paradise or the violence of its attitude towards women. Graffiti set billboard ads against themselves, and in so doing reveal that the interactions between texts and genres are always a form of social action.

EXERCISES

1 Genre can often work as a compact form of communication, relying on a few recurring signs to enable readers or viewers to recognise a text. By examining the opening sequence of three or four TV soaps, try to identify the key

signs that distinguish the genre. What sorts of social values and myths do these signs signify? Write a parody of the openings that questions those values.

2 Identify and analyse some examples of teenage sub-cultures that adapt the fashion genres or uniforms of official social groups.

3 Sketch out the hierarchical organisation of a social institution such as a university department you study in or a place where you work. What kinds of genres and texts are produced at the different levels?

4 Collect a series of recent newspaper photographs that depict national sports champions. Do they constitute a genre? If so, what are the genre's key textual signs and meanings? How might these meanings reinforce cultural values and attitudes not only towards sport but also towards myths of competition, the nation, moral virtue, and so on? In what ways are cultural values regarding gender roles and relationships reinforced or challenged by this genre? Do these cultural values have political implications?

SOURCES AND FURTHER READING

Many works on genre discuss the concept in relation to literature and film. One of the clearest introductions to traditional literary genres is Heather Dubrow's *Genre* (London: Methuen, 1982). A more complex but important discussion of genre, especially in relation to film, is Stephen Neale's *Genre* (London: British Film Institute, 1980). If Dubrow tends to assume that genres are relatively stable things, there is also a growing body of work which concentrates precisely on their instabilities. See Anne Freadman and Amanda Macdonald's *What is this Thing Called 'Genre'?* (Mt Nebo, Queensland: Boombana, 1992), and Freadman's 'Untitled: (On Genre)', *Cultural Studies*, 2(1), 1988.

Some of the key ideas in this chapter derive from the work of the Russian literary critic M.M. Bakhtin. Bakhtin's work is quite complex, but the essay 'Speech Genres' in the collection *Speech Genres and Other Essays* (Austin: University of Texas Press, 1986) is accessible. An overview of the topic is provided by Graham Allen's *Intertextuality* (New York: Routledge, 2000). A collection of very useful resources on genre theory and intertextuality is available at Daniel Chandler's Media and Communications Studies Site at www.aber.ac.uk/media/Functions/mcs.html.

Two studies applying many of the key notions of genre and intertextuality to examining popular television, film and fiction are John Fiske, *Television Culture* (New York: Methuen, 1987), and Tony Bennett and Janet Woollacott's more complex *Bond and Beyond: The Political Career of a Popular Hero* (London: Macmillan – now Palgrave, 1987). Some more recent works in this area are Rick Altman's *Film Genre* (London: British Film Institute, 1999), Wheeler Windston Dixon's *Film Genre 2000: New Critical Essays* (Albany: State

University of New York Press, 2000), and Marjorie Garber, Jann Matlock and Rebecca L. Walkowitz's collection, *Media Spectacles* (New York: Routledge, 1993).

For detailed analysis of the news media, see Stan Cohen and Jock Young's collection of essays, *The Manufacture of News* (London: Constable, 1981), John Hartley's *Understanding News* (London: Methuen, 1982), John Eldridge's collection, *Getting the Message: News, Truth, and Power* (London: Routledge, 1993), and Justin Lewis's *The Ideological Octopus: An Exploration of Television and Its Audience* (New York: Routledge, 1991). Two important studies of theories of representation in the media are Robert Ferguson's *Representing Race: Ideology, Identity, and the Media* (Oxford : Oxford University Press, 1998) and Stuart Hall's *Representation: Cultural Representations and Signifying Practices* (Newbury Park: Sage, 1997).

The classic work on news values, on which we drew in Figure 5.2, is Johan Galtung and Marie Holmboe Ruge's essay, 'Structuring and Selecting News', in *The Manufacture of News*, edited by Stan Cohen and Jock Young (London: Constable, 1973). The idea of primary definition comes from Stuart Hall, *Policing the Crisis: Mugging, the State, and Law and Order* (London: Macmillan – now Palgrave, 1978). Mick Underwood's Cultsock site has an excellent discussion of how news values work, with linked examples (www.cultsock.ndirect.co.uk/MUHome/cshtml: use the index to find the pages on *news values* and *agenda setting*).

Narrative

CONTENTS

Texts and time

One of the key points that our study of textual relations has revealed is that texts are not static structures of social meanings. By looking at genres of texts we can see the ways in which signs, connotations and myths develop over time. Texts are what carry changing cultural beliefs, and especially in the case of popular mass-media texts, these changes are fed back into wide sectors of the community. They are responded to in various ways by different groups, who not only interpret the texts but produce new texts about them. In this ongoing process of textual reading and production, the history, or histories, of a society unfold.

Genres and texts, then, are located in time. We can use this diachronic angle to supplement our analysis of their synchronic structures. But there is also another way in which the notion of time is central to textual and generic processes. Texts and genres are not only situated in social time; they *depict* the passing of time. Time is a key semiotic element in many genres. It works paradigmatically and syntagmatically, being used as sign as well as a means of structuring signs.

Consider a simple 'time text' – a before-and-after advertisement. Time itself is not the signified product, but a metonym that indicates the product's effects. In addition, time is what arranges and structures the other signs in the text – the straggly, bleached split ends of *before*, say, are transformed into *after*'s bouncy, shiny coiff. The way time operates here confirms that the paradigmatic and syntagmatic axes of texts always work in tandem. Time is a structural and meaningful component of many texts.

The process and effects of representing time in texts are called **narration**. A **narrative** is a text structured by the time sequence of the events it reprsents.

Narratives are everywhere in the social texts that surround us, and we are all very competent in the cultural skills of producing and analysing them. This makes narrative an important topic for the study of texts and textuality. As we did with genre, in this chapter we will try to slow down familiar, everyday narrative processes in order to examine the ways in which they set up certain patterns of meaning to which readers and viewers respond.

Because narrative occurs in many different kinds of genres and social contexts, it cannot properly be said to be a genre itself. We can think of it as a textual *mode* rather than a genre: one that depicts events and ideas by foregrounding their movement through time. Narration is just as much a feature of nonfictional genres as it is of fictional genres. Think of the host of stories offered by news, documentaries, histories and biographies. It also occurs across many different kinds of media – from language in a novel, to visual images in a film. Even the contrast of old and new building designs in a city centre may tell stories of the community's development.

Narration is not specific to one type of text over others. Indeed, one of the most interesting effects of narrative processes is that they cut across distinctions between genres, or between fiction and nonfiction. The concept of narrative is one of the main textual strategies used by seemingly very different texts to represent reality. Further, by studying the stories that social groups produce, we can gain insight into the way culture functions. Narrative is a way cultural signs are organised.

All sorts of important aspects of narrative arise from that time dimension. As we shall see, there are many variations in narrative structures, different ways of telling and retelling events, all producing distinctive effects and possibilities of response. Because of these possibilities and their widespread use, the study of narrative offers numerous insights into the social interactions which occur when texts are produced and read.

Narrative movement

Some texts, like novels and films, unfold over a certain timespan. Others,

Figure 6.1

This advertisement has a number of links with the genre of business photos we were analysing in the previous chapter. Recurring features include the use of black and white photography, eye contact between viewer and the male figure, and a specialised vocabulary with terms such as 'superannuation' and 'Balanced Pool Super Fund'. These signs combine to portray the modern 'businesskid', and adult-child, who seems to be both vulnerable and in control. His hybrid nature triggers the cute humour that is often generically central to advertising.

As well as being a portrait, the text also sets a narrative in motion.

It tries to tell a story by taking a number of specific steps.

- It proposes a *chronological and causal chain of events* that moves from the past into the future. It envisages the progression of time and calls for action to be taken: 'You must provide now for your later years.'
- It introduces *characters*: the businesskid Rex, who is to take action, and his future partner on whose behalf he is to act. It foresees the course of a person's life, suggesting the genre of novel or biography, and the narrative effects which they use (flash forward).
- It even establishes a goal or climax for this life: 'a decent lifestyle.'
- In the light of this goal, it passes judgement on the quality and personality of its central character: Rex is potentially a heroic figure, a decision-maker who will respond actively to the social imperative to 'Make a decision,' and thereby ensure a *happy ending*.

like magazine advertisements, photographs and pictures, seem to give up their meaning much more rapidly, perhaps at a glance. Nevertheless, even these allude to and are structured by the passing of time and events. By tuning into the way such texts may incorporate narrative elements, we may gain a fuller understanding of the meanings they represent. Narrative structures often intensify the generic and textual effects we have been considering.

In Figure 6.1, for example, we can see that the oppositions set up by its cultural myths are reinforced by its narrative structure. The opposition of childhood potential and adult achievement takes on a timeline, a progression from one to the other: it becomes a story. Economic issues are translated into an optimistic tale of individual success, financial and moral. And if stories are about actions, and activity is mythically masculine, then perhaps its very *being* a story tends to suggest mythical gender defaults. When myth is given the extra dimension of narrative movement, we have a particularly rich and culturally suggestive text. Its progression from past to future is not only a representation of the world: it invites imitation.

We can suggest that narrative structure accentuates and complements other textual and semiotic features in three main ways:

1 It introduces a **time dimension** to the connotations and myths.
2 It reinforces a network of social meanings by transforming events into **actions performed by characters**.
3 It adds the **pleasures** which go along with story.

The narrative gets us in. We like stories.

Narrative pleasure and desire

By alluding to news and biographical genres, Figure 6.1 can address readers with a network of positive connotations. It depicts economic and personal values in a rosy light, and encourages us to read them in that way. (The functions of address are particularly complex in this case: you might like to unravel them.) The narrative elements intensify these effects of address, inviting readers to join the story and foresee its outcome. Of course, many readers will also refuse the narrative's invitation and turn the page or criticise the connoted values. But for those who read the text affirmatively, Rex's story offers a certain degree of pleasure. The question of whether he will make the right decision seems happily anticipated by hints of his success.

One of the most powerful signifying effects narrative often has is to offer different kinds of **pleasure** to readers and viewers. These pleasures may arise in number of ways, and we have already seen some of them at work: the chance to identify with a particular character through the text's forms of address, watching or sharing their prospects and experiences; the satisfaction of seeing events and situations resolved. We will return to these particular aspects a little later when we consider narrative structure and point of view in more detail.

Readers enjoy and anticipate narratives. There are two pleasures involved, a kind of double desire: the motivation to follow a narrative, and the satisfaction from doing so. Readers both desire narratives and respond to them with desire. This may range from curiosity, to yearning, to lust. Even where readers might, as we will also see, reject one ending and seek to replace it with others, the enjoyment derived from narrative may still be at work. In fact, the desire for narrative pleasure seems to stimulate readers' efforts to re-tell and rework stories.

The advertisement in Figure 6.2 is a good example of a text provoking various kinds of desires. It has an enigmatic quality and seems to raise questions rather than give information. Who is she? Who is she waiting for? Whose car is it? Where is this scene? What does her expression suggest? It puts readers to work, forcing them to weigh up contrasting possibilities: she is alone, she waits for somebody; she surveys the scene, she is looking for someone; she squats with relaxed authority, she crouches submissively; she leans on the car possessively, she leans on the car for support; and so on.

The text does not resolve these alternatives, but rather triggers a desire to know the answers. Our path to knowledge is routed through contesting cultural myths about gender and women. For the moment, these seem to concentrate around the woman in the picture. Is she a powerful or a dependent figure?

The desire to know the answer motivates our engagement with the text. But how does the text stimulate this desire? The ambiguity seems to arise

Figure 6.2

because it looks as if the picture has been taken from a larger syntagm. We try to imagine a framing context that will help us to interpret these signs. And we mainly develop this context out of other texts that we know. Our previous reading of narrative genres comes into play, and we search for metalingual cues through which we may comprehend this one.

The signs here seem to constitute one episode from a narrative, perhaps a movie. In that case, answers to our questions might or might not be resolved by what takes place in the next scene (if there is a next scene – this could be the last shot), or by what has happened in an earlier one (we might just have seen her companion hop into a truck with some-one else).

These possibilities inspire our interest. Our familiarity with road movies and love stories provides interpretive options, but the text seems to suspend them. The verbal anchorage does little to diminish curiosity. Instead it may increase our uncertainty. It offers a name – the product's, of course, but might it also be hers? Is she the answer we are looking for? Our wishes to know her and to know the answer to the narrative seem to be fused. (In an effect that many narratives construct, the female charac-ter becomes the *object* of our reading. We will return to this effect in the final section of this chapter.)

The story stays up in the air. The narrative provokes multiple desires as it draws us into the signified world. It interweaves our reading with questions that concern the narrative (What's happening? What's going to happen?), or sexual undertones (Who is she? Who is she with? Or is she alone?), or our own possible roles in it all (Where do I, the reader, fit in? Am I part of this story? Is she waiting for me?). The questions remain open, and because of this the address to us is all the more powerful.

In structuring traces of character and plot into this allusive form, the text triggers a complex kind of cultural desire. (Since it is an advertise-ment the preferred goal of these desires is, at one level, the product: we ask all these desiring questions about the clothes that it promotes.) What provokes readers is the range of intertextual references the signs set in process. The structure of stories and the ways of telling them is a key aspect of the narrative process, and helps orchestrate readers' responses.

The two texts we have been considering have quite different structures. The first one implies a happy ending, with the transformation of Rex into an active, successful man. The second defers, perhaps rejects, any neat conclu-sion. As we saw, both kinds of structure offer readers different kinds of plea-sure. Variation of endings is only one possible variation in narrative structure. Let's now examine these possibilities more closely.

Narrative events

Recall the basic description of narrative we gave at the beginning of this chapter: a narrative is a text structured by the time sequence of the *events* it represents.

> **Events** are the basic units of a story. They constitute the paradigm choices that are combined into the narrative syntagm.

For the sake of analysis, the textual frame can be elastic. In a movie, a single event can be bracketed off from the rest and examined in detail. All the techniques of textual, generic and narrative analysis can be applied: we can consider this event as a text, study it, and then relate it to other events in the movie. The availability of movies on video makes it possible to analyse one event frame-by-frame, each frame constituting, as it were, a complex text in itself.

We can think of an event as a *dynamic* part of the story; it changes a situation. Events combine into **sequences** to build up the story, which may include several sequences. There are two main kinds of events:

1 Some events *advance* the action by opening up alternatives: a stranger walks into a room, a telephone rings, there is a knock on the door.
2 Other events do not open up alternative actions but *expand* or *delay* their results: two people turn around at once, a character has to unlock the door to get to the phone or has just fallen asleep.

The way in which both kinds of events are combined affects the *tempo* of the narrative, the pace at which situations are introduced and resolved. Alternating these types of events builds up *suspense*, which invites you to use your familiarity with the genre – the sorts of things that happen and characters who appear in it – to predict what will take place.

Disruption and closure

One particular broad sequence of events is used by many narratives. It has three phases: starting from a point of stability or equilibrium, the story moves into a phase of disruption before stability is renewed:

equilibrium ─────➤───── disruption ─────➤───── equilibrium

Another way of saying it is that a story has a beginning, a middle, and an end.

The final stage is one of **closure**, resolving the possibilities that have been opened up in the middle phase of disruption, to restore narrative equilibrium. The classic closure: 'they all lived happily ever after'. The narrative's resolution may pass judgement on the preceding events, deciding who was really guilty and innocent, or who was truly in love, or that things are better now, or that they have returned to normal.

Accordingly, it is with narrative closure that the greatest pressure for the text's preferred reading may be activated. This pressure applies not only, say, to nineteenth-century novels or Hollywood romances where, after many scenes of nefarious doings, hero and heroine are united in a marriage that promises contentment and children, and seems to suggest broad cultural renewal. It is also seen in the human-interest story which ends the news bulletin reassuringly after stories of violence, wars and disasters, in the assurances of technological progress which frame a science documentary, or in the closing ceremonies of the Olympic Games and their reaffirmation of friendship over competition. In such celebratory endings, narrative closure works as a powerful means of expressing positive cultural myths and an attractive invitation to accept them.

News stories are based on an occurrence or event that breaks through or stands out from a background of the everyday and the ordinary. The reported event corresponds to the disruption phase of the narrative pattern: it is generally some kind of crisis or dispute. (Remember from the last chapter how news values favour negative events.) In contrasting such events with the everyday background, news reinforces the norms of daily life. News events are the exceptions, the unexpected, and once they are seen as such, they no longer threaten the background. The act of reporting an event signifies that it has been recognised and fitted into the usual routine. In this way the news restores equilibrium to the narrative of everyday life.

Specific news stories also have a narrative structure. Two characters may be pitted against each other, with their contest narrated to us by the news-reader or reporter, as in the exchange between a government minister and a community representative which we examined in Chapter 5. In some cases, a story will run for several days, as if having a number of chapters.

One of the most popular cultural texts also using the three-part structure is the TV situation comedy. Usually these programmes are set within a family home, or use a quasi-family group in settings like a workplace, school, even a desert island or spacecraft. They regularly commence with things going along smoothly until one of two kinds of disruption occurs: either one of the family members threatens to leave or reorganise the group, or an outsider jeopardises the group's integrity and unity. (Often there will also be a sub-plot in which a mini-version of the disruption also arises.) Through the course of the narrative the threat is contained. The episode closes with the narrative and the group once more in happy stability. The same pattern then emerges in the next episode. Sitcom characters are nothing if not consistent in their behaviour.

This narrative pattern changes when we turn to the TV soap opera. The difference suggests one of the central generic contrasts between a TV *series* and a *serial*. In a series (such as the sitcom), the narrative pattern is reproduced from episode to episode, and each episode is relatively self-contained. In the serial (such as the soap), each episode follows on from the last, and there are multiple storylines, perhaps each involving different characters in different settings. British, American and Australian soaps tend to be about community rather than family, as the titles suggest: *EastEnders, Brookside, Coronation Street, Neighbours, Home and Away, The Young and the Restless, Days of Our Lives, Santa Barbara*. As a result, they tend to have larger casts than sitcoms.

The soap opera defers closure. Its multiple storylines cut across the episode boundaries. Each episode ends not with closure but with at least one storyline nudged away from equilibrium. For every storyline resolved, another starts up or reaches crisis. This usually gives the soap a slower over-all narrative rhythm than the sitcom, but a faster rhythm of intercutting among stories.

The three genres we have surveyed all use very deliberate narrative structuring. While news stories and sitcoms follow the three-part pattern quite directly, soap operas draw out the disruption phase and defer resolution. Each genre regularly contains narratives within narratives. Even a news or current affairs show can be considered as a number of different narratives, all told by one narrator (the newsreader or presenter) and bound together by the familiar recurrent generic and mythic story patterns we examined in the last chapter. In all three cases, the narrative is usually located in the present, although flashbacks are sometimes used. These genres rely on a stable relationship among the events they depict (chronological order), and between the time when the events occur and the time when they are narrated.

Such relationships can, however, vary, producing different effects. The basic three-part structure we have considered so far can be complicated by changing connections between the order and timing of events and the way they are told. This is what we shall now turn to.

Story and plot

The distinction between *what* is told and *how* it is told is an important aspect of narrative structure. There are parallels here to the structure we earlier saw in the sign. Just as a sign comprises a signifier and signified, so narrative comprises two elements: **story** and **plot**.

Plot is the sequence in which the *narrative* tells the events.
Story is the logical and chronological sequence of the *events* being told.

Plot is what does the signifying; story is what is signified by plot. (Other terms are sometimes used to name these same elements; for example, plot is sometimes called *discourse*, which is a term we have reserved for another quite different meaning in Chapter 8. The point is not so much which term we use, but what the distinction can tell us about the way narratives work.)

The order of events in the plot and the story can be quite different. In a flashback, for example, two successive events in the plot (that is, narrated one after the other) may actually be widely separated in the story (with the second one a memory of something which happened years before). The logical and chronological sequence of the events in the *story* may be cut up and rearranged in all sorts of ways in the *plot*.

By making the distinction between story and plot we are able to analyse many of the narrative strategies used to create effects for readers or viewers. A flashback may show us a current situation and then move us back to see how it developed. A narrative may flash forward too, to drop hints about the consequences of present events ('Little did I guess then . . .'). A narrative will usually devote a lot of the plot to important events in the story, and little of the plot to the long stretches of story time in which nothing of significance happens. On the other hand, a plot may refuse to reveal key events in the story, or teasingly withhold them: this is a generic marker of the mystery tale, or the narrative of detection or suspense, which often sets story and plot against each other. The plot may omit an early event, such as a crucial rendezvous between two characters, before revealing it at the end. A murder may occur just before the plot commences; the story has begun before we read page one or see the opening shot, and the aim of the plot will be to recapture what happened in this lost scene. In all these cases, the alternating plot-story relationships are used to intrigue, frustrate and flatter readers' knowledge. In this context, the pleasures of narrative derive from that gap between story and plot and the comparisons they let us make between, say, what we (think we) know about what's going on and what various characters do or don't know.

The plot-story connection is one of the main ways in which narrative knowledge – who knows what – is linked to social power. Narratives frequently show us that the one who knows the full story remains in control of the situation, in spite of the false leads that the plot may throw up.

Characters and characterisation

The events which take place in narrative happen to characters. It is important not to think of characters as real people. Recall Bill Taylor from the by-election news photograph in Chapter 3: whether we know anything or not about the real Bill Taylor is quite irrelevant to this narrative's intelligibility. He functions as a character in a small mythic story about success. Similarly, the woman in the Simona advertisement is a syntagm of signs which work to connote certain culturally familiar meanings: woman, fashion, enigma.

Like everything else in narrative, whether it be fictional or nonfictional, characters are the effects of signs. Personality traits are signified through actions and events, speech and external appearance. Where most of this signification takes place early in the narrative, and doesn't change as it progresses, we have the effect of a flat character. The traits which make them up tend to be repeated in the course of the narrative, or at most undergo simple reversals. The virginal heroine of a Victorian melodrama sustains her innocence despite the schemes of the moustache-twirling villain. Characters appear more complex if they develop new traits as the narrative goes on, and even more so if these traits do not immediately seem to fit together (suggesting some sort of depth or capacity to surprise). Ripley in the *Alien* movies calls on previously unknown qualities to overcome the monsters; Samuel L. Jackson's hitman Jules in *Pulp Fiction* undergoes an on-the-job religious conversion. A character's *proper name* works as a metonymic sign for the potentially never-complete set of these attributes.

Different characters have various *functions* in events and sequences of events, and can be identified and analysed according to these. One ready distinction is between *active* and *passive* characters, doer and recipient. Conventional characterisation tends to depict male characters as doers and female characters as recipients. Consider our Victorian virgin – she is on the receiving end first of the villain's misdeeds and then of the hero's brave feats. One of the interesting features of Ripley's characterisation in the *Alien* films is the way she develops as a female doer. She becomes an increasingly complex character as her function in the narrative becomes more active. As her macho companions in *Aliens* all succumb to the creatures, their apparent active role contrasts ironically with her ultimate effectiveness.

Like other aspects of narrative, such as plot and closure, characterisation often illustrates the ways in which narrative works through conventions. The various genres of narrative, from news and documentaries to novels and films, tend to rely on long-established semiotic codes to represent characters. We have just seen one obvious coding, with the passive female character and the active male. Other examples are easy to find: the scientist in the white lab coat, the well-dressed smooth-talking politician, the hippie in beads and caftan, the mafioso in pin-striped suit, the doctor with stethoscope and the dog-collared priest.

These clusters of conventional character attributes are **stereotypes**. Stereotypes are neither true nor false, but *mythic*. They are mythic because they are metonymic (they represent an entire grouping through a small number of conventionally-selected characteristics) and generally ordered according to simple oppositions (they offer themselves to us as ready objects for approval or disapproval). Particular stereotypes may belong to particular genres, where they can be cued in by only a few details – clothes and make-

Figure 6.3

This 30-second TV advertisement is notable for the speed with which it establishes situation and characters. It has all the narrative interest of a soap. A man sits up blearily out of sleep, looking somewhat hungover from the night before. We see a shot of him from behind as he staggers towards the door, pulling on a T-shirt as he goes. In the kitchen, he fills an electric jug and finds a pack of Liptons tea bags; we get a close-up of a tea bag brewing in what looks like a jam jar of hot water. He smiles as he raises the jar to his lips and inhales the aroma.

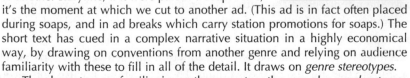

As the tea wakes him up, he suddenly seems to remember something, and looks back half-incredulously towards the bedroom door. At this point we can see, just a moment before he does, that the T-shirt he is wearing is a woman's, with the word 'Foxy' on the front.

Delighted and eager, he hurriedly makes a second tea (in a mug this time), and knocks in anticipation at the bedroom door. A woman is sitting up in the bed he has just left, the quilt nervously up around her neck. A shot from her point of view (which we now see was that of the earlier shot of the man staggering towards the kitchen) shows the man at the door, wearing her T-shirt and solicitously offering her the mug of tea. A flash to the slogan 'Switch on', which morphs into the Liptons logo, and then we get a last shot of the woman's face, still nervous but with her hands now cradling the steaming mug as she wonders just what she's got herself into.

This is exactly the point at which we would cut to another storyline, if it were part of a soap. Here, it's the moment at which we cut to another ad. (This ad is in fact often placed during soaps, and in ad breaks which carry station promotions for soaps.) The short text has cued in a complex narrative situation in a highly economical way, by drawing on conventions from another genre and relying on audience familiarity with these to fill in all of the detail. It draws on *genre stereotypes*.

The characters are familiar in another way, too: they are also *gender stereotypes*, set up quickly and simply. The untidiness of the bicycle in the hallway and the basic but crowded kitchen suggest this is the man's house. He is delighted when he realises what seems to have happened the night before; the woman is not so sure. The encounter is casual and uncomplicated for him, a matter of potential anxiety for her.

The storyline moves rapidly from its initial situation, to a dilemma when the events of the previous night are remembered. At this point of dilemma, it momentarily raises and flirts with the possibilities of moral disapproval (has this all been an awkward mistake?), or even blurring of sexual identity (why *is* this man wearing women's clothing?), but then rapidly pulls everything back to potential resolution in that gesture of sharing a tea. Indeed, the product offers itself as familiar, in just the same way as the storyline and the characters offer themselves as familiar – and comforting because of that familiarity. Tea is the first thing the man searches for when he wakes up, a routine grip on the day. And it's his way of negotiating the situation, by offering that same familiarity and comfort to his companion.

up, a certain speech style or ethnicity. Stereotypes seem to have a wholly denotative meaning. We shall consider some of the further ideological effects of stereotypes in the next two chapters.

Narrative address and point of view

So far, we have looked mainly at the various functions of signification in narrative: what it represents, the codes it draws on, and the form of what it shows. Yet narrative also has quite specific and complex functions of address. In particular, narratives have addressers and addressees, which are usually given specific terms:

> The **narrator** is the narrative's *addresser*.
> The **narratee** is the narrative's *addressee*.

Keep in mind that like addresser and addressee, narrator and narratee are roles constructed in a text. They do not pre-exist the text, and in particular they should not be confused with actual authors or readers. (Of course, we can always speculate on what a real-life author might have meant and what actual readers might be thinking. Studies of literary narratives have often been preoccupied with such questions. But as we have seen throughout this book, the intentions of the author or sender may account for very little in a text, and in the possibilities of cultural meaning and response which texts open up.)

As a textual effect, the narrator can function through various sorts of relationships to the story he or she is telling. These variations involve both events and other characters. The narrator might tell the story during or after the events, even conceivably before them. S/he may or may not be a character in the story. If the narrator is not a character, s/he may tell the story by surveying all the events and characters from an external viewpoint. S/he may use a single character's perspective on events or introduce a number of characters' perspectives. These multiple viewpoints may be synthesised, working to confirm each other and leading to a united closure, as at the end of an episode of a sitcom. On the other hand, the narrator may contrast different characters' viewpoints with one another, precluding that kind of resolution.

All of these structural possibilities and variations affect the narratee positions offered to readers by the text. For example, if the narrator is a character in the story, we might expect the narrative to be partisan, to have its own interests, or perhaps even be strongly loaded. A character, even if that character does narrate, cannot necessarily be expected to have a full knowledge of events and other characters. A narrator who is not a character might be expected to give a more accurate and reliable account; so might a narrative which uses multiple character-narrators. These responses are further complicated by the relation between the time of telling and the occurrence of the events. Reports from the thick of the action may have a different sort of reliability from recollections after the event.

These different effects in the narrator's relationship to other characters and events can come to work as generic conventions. Factual narrative genres such as news and history use narrators who survey a range of characters' views and tell the story after the event, offering it with all of the powerful effects of authorisation and naturalisation. Yet for all their possible truth, these effects are no less conventional or constructed than the hazy ripples on the screen and the violins on the soundtrack which signify the start of a narrative flashback when a character in a movie has lost consciousness.

Narrative negotiations

Narrative is no exception to the social process of reading through which all texts and genres are open to negotiated and oppositional responses. In the news, protesters may force their views into a story, not only by disagreeing with either of the parties, but also by disrupting the debate itself and the terms of its primary definition. The official white narrative of Australia's settlement – the brave actions and resourcefulness of the founding fathers – has been strongly and successfully contested by Aboriginal readers, in various ways: criticising the portrayal of white figures as heroic and of Aboriginals as savage or aimless; rejecting a storyline that begins in 1788 and has highpoints such as federation and the bicentenary and a closure that implies continued social progress; rewriting that as a continuing tale of the survival of their cultures despite deadly oppression. The pleasure and desire that narrative triggers thus arise as much from the powers of readers and viewers to re-tell and re-narrate the stories that surround them as it does from responding to circuits of identification and suspense that texts set up.

Some of the strongest examples of the re-telling of narratives are the responses of women to patriarchal narrative structures. The responses comprise a wide range of textual genres and activities. They include feminist film and literary criticism that questions and attacks the way conventional plots use female characters to indulge the desire for sexual power of male characters and readers; and narratives in which these conventions are revised, rejected, rewritten and refilmed to foreground women's perspectives.

Feminist criticism has re-read the 'married and lived happily ever after' finale of narrative fiction, film and much journalism as signifying female characters' re-enclosure in patriarchal systems. Film and art theory has especially paid attention to the way women's bodies are dissected and depersonalised for the gratification of male visual desire. In contrast to conventional depictions of women, films like *Thelma and Louise* or *Boys on the Side* adapt standard 'buddy' and road-movie motifs to represent women's experience. The journey of the two main characters allows them to evade and invert many of the constraints of patriarchal culture and develop a strong personal relationship. Much critical attention has also been paid to the ways many women read popular romance fiction. They rework the apparently sexist narratives into stories that not only provide such pleasures as seeing a man come fully to appreciate the heroine's personality, but also offer imaginative and intellectual support for the day-to-day domestic routines and family lives that the readers lead.

These various strands of feminist analysis have been prominent in underlining the point that narrative genres have a central role in social experience. Narrative texts constantly represent a wide range of cultural myths and meanings to readers. But perhaps the more significant effect is the opportunities narrative gives for readers to tell and retell their own versions of social stories.

EXERCISES

1 Collect a number of strip cartoons or jokes. Identify the plot–story distinction within them. How is this related to the humour? For a challenge, consider a narrative in a plot which effects a complex rearrangement of the time scheme of the story, such as *Pulp Fiction*, and make a detailed comparison of the plot and story. For yet more of a challenge, analyse what happens in a time-travel narrative, such as *Peggy-Sue Got Married*, or the *Back to the Future* movies.

2 Choose one magazine and one TV advertisement, each with a narrative dimension. Reconstruct the story of each. From whose perspective are they told, if anyone's? How do these perspectives (or their absence) relate to any narrative closure they ads might realise?

3 Retell a sitcom episode from the viewpoint of one of the minor characters. Do different social values come into play? Does narrative closure have to be rewritten or reconsidered? What different responses are invited?

4 'Reality TV' is now a very common genre. Is this a 'new' genre or does it feed off other television genres – which ones? What relationships does it have to other media genres in the way it constructs its characters and storyline? Analyse the ways in which Reality TV uses and develops narrative suspense – does it subvert or consolidate narrative closure? How are the desire and pleasure of viewers triggered in these programmes? Consider

whether they rely on sexual and gender norms in representing the narratives – are feminine and masculine stereotypes reinforced or questioned by the trials and tribulations of Reality TV?

SOURCES AND FURTHER READING

There are many studies of narrative processes and structure available. Some of the more helpful ones are Seymour Chatman, *Story and Discourse: Narrative Structure in Fiction and Film* (Ithaca: Cornell University Press, 1978); Shlomith Rimmon-Kenan, *Narrative Fiction: Contemporary Poetics* (London: Methuen, 1983); Michael J. Toolan, *Narrative: A Critical Linguistic Introduction* (London: Routledge, 1988); Steven Cohan and Linda M. Shires, *Telling Stories: A Theoretical Analysis of Narrative* (New York: Routledge, 1988); Patrick O'Neill, *Fictions of Discourse: Reading Narrative Theory* (Toronto: University of Toronto Press, 1994); and Ronald Sukenick, *Narralogues: Truth in Fiction* (Albany: State University of New York Press, 2000).

For accounts of narrative structures in television and film see John Ellis, *Visible Fictions* (London: Routledge & Kegan Paul, 1982); Robert C. Allen (ed.), *Channels of Discourse, Reassembled: Television and Contemporary Criticism* 2nd edn (Chapel Hill: University of North Carolina Press, 1992); Steve Neale and Frank Krutnick, *Popular Film and Television Comedy* (London: Routledge, 1990); and Chris Gregory, *Star Trek: Parallel Narratives* (New York: St Martin's, 2000).

There are also many studies of women's re-readings and rewritings of narrative and other textual conventions. Some of these include: M. E. Brown, *Television and Women's Culture: The Politics of the Popular* (London: Sage, 1990); Rosalind Coward, *Female Desire* (London: Granada, 1984); Tania Modleski, *Loving with a Vengeance: Mass Produced Fantasies for Women* (New York: Methuen, 1984); Janice Radway, *Reading the Romance: Feminism and the Representation of Women in Popular Culture* (Chapel Hill: University of North Carolina Press, 1984); and Judith Williamson, *Consuming Passions: The Dynamics of Popular Culture* (London: Marion Boyars, 1986). Gender issues in the media are also examined in Steven Cohan and Ina Rae Hark's *Screening the Male* (London: Routledge, 1992), Barrie Gunter's *Television and Gender Representation* (London: John Libbey, 1995), and Myra McDonald's *Representing Women* (London: Arnold, 1995).

PART III

Cultural practices

Discourse and medium

CONTENTS

Signs and texts, genres and narratives, all involve people in social settings, who recognise and use them for different purposes. We now need to consider in more specific detail the various ways in which signs and their intertextual links connect with social and institutional contexts.

Institutions

All forms of sign activity are regulated and conditioned by social organisations and language structures. For instance, any act of speaking takes place within a context which defines certain **rules**: what can most properly be said, by whom and how. Adults may rarely speak frankly to children about a range of topics, such as sex, money and politics. This has a lot to do with the way family roles are structured and played out. The structures and interrelations of these roles can be examined by considering the family as an **institution**.

> An **institution** is a relatively stable set of social arrangements and relationships, which provides a structure of roles, relationships and functions for those who inhabit it.

The institution of the family consists of a number of social identities (roles), such as mother, father, children, uncle, aunt, etc. The relationships between these identities are played out according to rules of varying formality. The parent-child relationship is constantly reinforced and revised through the full range of daily routines and interaction: when a child is to go to bed, when homework is to be done, when television is to be watched.

But the parent–child relationship is far from merely interpersonal. Some aspects are formally legislated by the state, such as the parents' responsibility for the child's education, health and moral well-being. The state also offers less rigorous guidelines to the parent. These include censorship and the classification of films and television programmes, pre-schooling and immunisation programmes. Further, there are the many informal but influential rules of etiquette, dress and demeanour, involving things as disparate as the available styles of children's clothes, magazine advice on child rearing, advertising, and conversations between neighbours and friends. All these affect the seemingly natural, personal bond between parent and child. Other bonds within the family institution also work in this way.   One way of making the institutional, social and conventional nature of all these relations stand out is to take an example which is slightly unfamiliar: from a slightly different culture, or from several decades ago. Figure 7.1, for example, is a magazine advertisement from the early 1960s. Its codings are no longer as naturalised for us as those we live in; they stand out now with an effect which now looks thoroughly conventional, and can even look slightly comic or naive.

Institutions are not self-enclosed. They are always open to each other and to the social world in which the exist and to which they respond. Furthermore, every individual relates to others through a network of intersecting rules and values. The child who disagrees with her parents about whether she is to do her homework or watch television is not simply being disagreeable, but probably negotiating about the intersection of social roles and their respective values: the dutiful or recalcitrant daughter in the family, the pleasure-seeking television audience member in popular culture, and the conscientious scholar or student in the education system. All three roles are played out or *negotiated* by the child in the family situation.

Discourse

Institutions are made up not only of intersections among people but also *practices of producing texts*. The negotiations between child and parent involve certain kinds of talk which signify attitudes and feelings about the issues under discussion. Talk is about positioning speakers with respect to each other, in order to control or effect a situation. Talking conveys not only feelings and attitudes, but *power*. Even the noisiest family table-talk is not

Figure 7.1

sheer chaos, but a contest for speaking positions, in which family members test and redefine their roles, obligations and duties. *All institutional identities can be defined in relations of power.*

Talk is one of the many forms of textuality that are produced institutionally. Government departments are administered through issuing and exchanging many kinds of oral and written texts (directives, memos, etc.) which contain information, requests, commands and so on. The main textual work of media institutions may seem to be newspapers, magazines, radio and television programmes for mass audiences. But they also produce a host of other, administrative texts, along with the entire range of routine talk between their workers. All these texts serve various purposes. Some define, limit or reinforce people's positions and courses of action. Others clarify the way jobs are to be done. Still others communicate information to the outside world.

Institutions, then, are not just groups of people who live or work together, interacting according to rules and conventions. They also include all the texts and genres through which interactions take place, and whereby the rules and conventions are written down or recorded in some way. An institution takes on different characteristics through the different texts and genres it uses. The way a customer speaks to a shop assistant in purchasing a product will be different from the way the same person, as, say, a student, speaks to a teacher. Different interactions and hence different power relations are involved. The institutions of retailing involve speech genres distinct from those in education, even though the same person can participate in both institutions.

And here we connect right back to the functions of address we first examined in Chapter 1. These roles are none other than addresser and addressee roles, which we can now see in all the concreteness of their real existence in the social world. *Institutions operate by setting up addresser and addressee positions. These tend to place individuals in foreseeable power relations with each other, with the institution, and with the social world.* This is a tendency, a default option rather than a rigid determination. As we shall see in the next two chapters, there is a great deal of flexibility in these roles and the ways they can be played, even against themselves.

A **discourse** is the particular mode of textuality of an institution. It is a set of textual arrangements which work to organise and co-ordinate the actions, positions and identities of the people who inhabit them.

Discourse has four principal characteristics:

- concrete social **sites** at and within which it circulates (institutions);
- **roles** for those who participate in it (functions of address);
- **power relations** carried in those roles; and
- certain **topics** which tend to be spoken about there (themes).

Institutions **reproduce** themselves through discourse. They do this through the repeated production of texts (talk, written, visual), each of which provides addresser and addressee roles through which people relate to and interact with one another. For example, we all know that when people play the social roles of a customer they speak quite differently from when they are playing the roles of a student. These ways of talking are not the spontaneous expressions of the individuals involved. They are discursive and institutional, and use a range of generic conventions.

Above all, discourse is a matter of the way in which things said are *embedded* in the social world. Even before it is concerned with *what* is said, it may be concerned with *where* things are said, *by* whom, and *in* what relationships of power. That is, a theme or topic is not enough to specify a discourse, because any given topic is likely to be talked about at a number of different social sites and institutions, in different ways, with different roles for the speakers, and in different relations of power. Nationality, for example, is not a discourse but a topic for a number of very different discourses. We can see them as soon as we think in terms of the institutional sites in which nationality is an issue: political, governmental and legal discourses on nationality, economic discourse, sports discourses, media discourses, news discourses, military discourse, and so on. Some discourses may have a very complex spread, across a number of very different but interconnected sites, in each of which the basic topic is spoken of in very different ways, with quite different roles and relations of power set up among the participants. What we could broadly call medical discourse, for example, is actually spread out over a large number of institutional sites, in each of which the discursive ways of going about things are quite different. The GP's surgery, the university, the research laboratory, the pharmaceutical industry, the insurance office, the legal profession and the forensics laboratory all might be speaking *about* medicine, but they are distinct *sites*, they set up different roles *for* those involved (the doctor's role is different from the research scientist's, the patient's from the pharmacy customer's), and different effects of *power* are carried in those roles (the doctor has an authority quite different from the insurance broker's).

Not surprisingly, all sorts of aspects of everyday life can be analysed in terms of discourse (see Figure 7.2).

Embodiment

The ways in which people interact with one another in everyday life may appear to be instinctive and natural. But this ease is actually the outcome of a process of learning, acquisition and habituation. One of the key paradoxes explored by cultural studies is that in many, if not all, cases the 'natural' is repeatedly revealed to be the culturally learnt. Let's try to unravel this paradox in a little detail, beginning with a simple analysis.

In driving a car, the competent driver does not consciously invoke and weigh up the rules of the road (which side of the road to drive on, who to give way to, which lane to drive in, when to turn lights on or indicate), or the

Figure 7.2 The shout

The drinking ritual of 'shouting', in which each member of a group takes a turn at buying the drinks, can be seen in terms of discourse. What makes it discursive?

- First of all, it is found in a particular *institutional setting*: the pub. The pub is more intimate than the workplace, more public than the home, with some features of both. It is a commercial business site, but its business is group sociality.
- Second, it involves a complex set of *roles*. By being in the shout, individuals may feel free to speak to each other in ways they might not in other social and institutional settings, such as at home or at work. It's as if the shout gives a license for men to be together, sharing the same ideas, and sense of camaraderie despite any differences in social background, providing a common basis for male bonding. It involves a recognition of group identity (mateship) which is at the same time a competitive mode of friendship (keeping up with the shout – slow drinkers are often excluded from the group). It phatically defines common values and interests, and sets up the rules for that belonging: buy when it's your turn, and keep up.
- And third, these roles involve *power relations*. Most obviously, the shout is predominantly male, part of the everyday routines of patriarchy.

These various effects are illuminating because shouting is such an ordinary kind of activity. The accumulation and repetition of everyday talk and practices in various contexts – in the workplace, at the pub, or at home – construct a network of discursive positions and cultural values which are *embodied* in the daily lives of those who take part in them.

specific techniques of driving (such as clutch and brake manipulation, use of mirrors, cornering). She simply drives. In other words, the driver has **embodied** a discourse: she applies a technique and a set of knowledges which allow things to be done in interaction with others. She can get from one place to another through the shared network of roads because she automatically reproduces the skills and practices involved in driving a car.

Embodiment is the learning and acquiring of a set of knowledges and competences which can be routinely reproduced as a practice.

Embodiment produces a certain identity or a set of multiple, intersecting identities. The driver becomes recognised as a driver by the state when she passes her driving test and is licensed to drive. There are then many possible variants of this identity. The 'good driver' displays the requisite courtesies to others, such as giving way and allowing adequate space to other vehicles. The 'bad driver' tends to ignore or flout these driving conventions. Furthermore, the same person already embodies many other quite different competences (as worker, parent, etc). All forms of social identity depend upon the embodiment of discourse and its display in public interactions.

The exchanges among the natural, the institutional and the discursive that we see in the process of embodiment occur across all social activities and operations. One of the most significant areas of these exchanges is the mass media. We will now turn to examine their institutional processes and their cultural effects on social identity.

Medium

We saw in Chapter 1 how the *material support* of a text gives rise to many of its formal functions: paper favours written language and static images, the television screen gives relatively small moving images with sound, and so on. But paper, television screens, movie screens, computers and so on have another dimension, which we can now see. They are also part of massive social *institutions*: the publishing industry, the film and television industries, the hardware and software industries, with all of their complex relationships to each other and to other institutions (law, government, education).

So rather than just naming which sense is linked to particular kinds of texts – as in the phrase, 'TV is a visual medium' – the notion of medium is much more important for our understanding of social and textual practices. The term **medium** names the institutional and social dimension of the material contexts in which texts are produced and read.

> The **medium** of a text is its material *institutional* support.

Every text has its medium. Just as every text has its material support, so too is that material support involved in perhaps a number of institutions. Even *voice*, the support of *speech* and apparently the most personal and individual of all supports, has this institutional and social dimension to it. Just think of the ways in which the situations where we do and don't use speech are discursive and institutional: some genres and situations will never use it (company reports, government legislations, business contracts, bills and spreadsheets); others will use it in a highly coded and ritualised way (parliamentary debate, speeches at annual general meetings); in others, of course, it predominates (in the home, and in many aspects of the workplace).

The term *the media* is often used as a shorthand for the **mass media**, those institutions whose business is precisely the widespread dissemination of texts: print, television, film, radio, the internet, and particularly journalism and advertising in all of their various forms.

Mediation

One of the ways in which media discourses work is to *mediate* between different social domains. **Mediation** occurs when one party acts between two others, bringing them into a recognisable relationship. For example, in a court case a barrister or lawyer mediates between her client and the judiciary, arguing a case by using appropriate language, thereby bringing them into a legal relationship where outcomes can be achieved. Mediation involves discourse. In nineteenth-century Europe, young middle-class men and women could not become romantically involved unless chaperoned (mediated) by an older person with certain social credentials. Mediation *produces* a relationship between parties based on social identity and cultural values.

Media mediate. That is, they *link* social institutions, their discourses, the events surrounding them, and the audiences who read, view and listen to media texts. For example, news reports about political events are broadcast to an audience by the agency of television and radio news programmes and newspaper stories. One institution and its discourse (politics) is thus mediated by another (news broadcasting). This makes certain knowledges and information available to yet another institution – the public.

In general, the public does not have direct access to the daily decision-making which goes on in government. Through the mediation of the media, however, the public is provided with stories on government and parliamentary activity. Audience members can pick up knowledge of political events and decisions from newspapers and television programmes. They can construct ideas about the influence and effects of party politics and governmental attitudes about society and the way it operates. Indeed, it is mainly through the media that people become politically 'informed': capable of forming opinions about political attitudes and courses of action which become part of their own everyday lives. Through mediation, individual audience members become part of the social domain, capable of reproducing knowledge about political programmes and their effects in society.

While they are readers or viewers of media news, audience members are also citizens, who are subject to the administration of the state. This second relationship intertwines with the first. Being a citizen is mediated by being an audience member, and vice versa. Media news provides information which has been selected for newsworthiness, and much of this information will be the basis for ways in which people think of their relationship to the state. Media news also mediates the way individual audience members *imagine* their relationship to other institutions, such as the local community, family, the nation and the world in general.

In this sense, the imaginary is the capacity of an individual to feel that she belongs to a larger group of people whose presence is not immediately apparent in everyday life.

An **imagined community** is one made up of individuals who do not interact face-to-face, but who nevertheless identify as a community.

Nations are imagined communities. There is no way in which individual members of a nation could ever hope to know and interact with anything but a small minority of the rest of the members. Nevertheless, they share a strongly felt sense of that national community, and its coherent values and common interests.

Media play a significant role in reproducing the imagined communities of nation, as well as those of the more local kind, such as neighbourhood, region, city and town. Media *mediate* between individual audience members to create a sense of communal belonging in terms of national, city, regional, local or neighbourhood interests. The community is imagined as having certain values (unity, strength, purpose, moral fibre) not because of any essential quality it might have, but because of the circulation of these values in media stories and representations.

Because of their mediating capacity, the media have the power not only to represent but *actively to maintain* the relationship between audiences and social institutions. This takes place in the routine reporting of events and occurrences which are worked up into news stories, loaded with particular values. Stories about the Olympic Games held in Sydney in September 2000 and published in the Australian press often included words and images designed to create a sense of national purpose and pride.

For instance, Australian athlete Cathy Freeman's win in the 400 metres track final was portrayed in the Australian media in terms of how it contributed to national pride and honour, made all the more emphatic through emphasis on her indigeneity, providing at least one powerful image of a new kind of racially unified Australia. Competitiveness between individuals and teams was also played up, often with the co-operation of the athletes themselves. In the swimming pool, the rivalry between the USA and Australia was occasionally embodied in the different characteristics of individual swimmers. The supposed 'brashness' of America's Gary J. Hall was contrasted with the 'quietly determined' demeanour of Australia's Ian Thorpe. These characteristics came to typify different national attitudes, leading to the metonymic identification of individual competitors not only with their national team but also with a more abstract set of values and meanings, already circulating in the public culture.

The coverage of the Olympic Games thus helped to reproduce an imagined community amongst its audiences, based on patriotism. Yet further coverage by the international media reproduced other imagined communities in which national interests intermingled with a more global sensibility, as part of the 'Olympic spirit'. By watching the games on television, the audience members could feel part of a vast international community of viewers, all sharing the same experience and values.

By allowing certain kinds of stories and images to be published or broadcast, while excluding or repressing others, the media often privilege one aspect of an event, making it look like the only aspect that can be taken, or the natural or normal way of seeing things. We have already seen how this works in the case of the Olympics. Personality clashes between competitors are highlighted to emphasise nation-against-nation competitiveness, while more cooperative actions between individual athletes are either sidelined or excluded altogether.

When it takes place on a routine basis, this metonymic selectivity of media coverage can feed into and maintain a sense of belonging amongst the audience by framing events with conventional values, thereby making it difficult to understand them in alternative ways. It becomes difficult to see the Olympics in terms other than extreme international competitiveness, where one team or one individual triumphs over all others. Officially, the Olympic Games are about international cooperation and the promotion of peace, but media reportage seems to say the opposite: that the fruits of achievement should only go to the winners, and that national pride should be based on victory over rivals.

Another instance of this kind of selectivity in the media can be noted in the way that industrial unrest is often reported in terms of irrational and aggressive attitudes adopted by union leaders who do not have the 'ordinary worker's' interests at heart. On the other hand, management attitudes are often characterised as willing and cooperative. By repeated reportage along these lines, political attitudes are maintained in a consistent manner, but at the expense of one group – unions – who are cast in the mould of unpatriotic spoilers, or self-serving propagandists. The reality may be quite different.

Media also have the power to *change* the relationship between audiences and social institutions. By allowing certain stories and images to appear, the media can trigger a desire for change. For instance, by exposing state or corporate corruption, investigative journalism has sometimes been able to change the political climate of a nation. A good example here is the exposure by journalists in the USA of the cover-up of scientific information on the ill-effects of cigarette smoking, as portrayed in the film *The Insider*. In the film, a television station refuses at the last minute to broadcast revealing information about the tobacco industry by an ex-employee (played by Russell Crowe) because it might compromise its relationship with big business. Although the film mythologises the quest for truth in terms of the heroic individual fighting overwhelming forces – the Russell Crowe character risks his career and marriage in order to make the information public – it nevertheless indicates the contradiction at the heart of media and their mediating practices. On one hand the media speak on behalf of the media public, but on the other, they speak (or in this instance stay silent) on behalf of powerful capital interests.

The ability of media discourse to alter the way an audience relates to social institutions is not confined to the realms of news and politics. All media texts reproduce social institutions and discourses in ways which may run counter to audiences' everyday lives. We considered some of these ways in our discussions of genre and narrative. *Narrative closure* is one of the most significant. Its apparent commonsense function in ending a story may conceal the kinds of institutional pressures it is exerting.

For example, despite their widespread use, happy-ending devices in a TV sitcom like *Friends* – with domestic order restored through consensus – need not reflect the audiences' own situations and experiences. Rarely are such experiences neatly solved in half an hour. They are nearly always more complex, involving a wider range of factors and influences. Thus situation comedies often involve a paradox: the representation of everyday life on television may contradict the viewer's situation at the moment it proposes itself as a perfect match. Because of this contradictory relation, the mediating process is marked not by a union, but by a disjuncture between social institutions and their audience. The audience may have to try and resolve contradictory values and accommodate the media discourses into other aspects of their everyday life. Most viewers watching a popular show such as *Ally McBeal*, *Party of Five* or *90210* need to resolve an enormous contrast between the metonyms of seemingly ordinary life portrayed in the text, and their own circumstances. It may be that because of this disjuncture the predominant mode of watching television is not at all one of passive belief, but of a knowing response, perhaps even a cynical distance. These responses all combine to produce 'enjoying TV' as quite a complex kind of pleasure.

Mediation and self-effacement

We suggested earlier that mediation involves one party bringing other parties into a relationship with one another. In most cases, this relationship is recognised and accepted by the institution in which it is practised. Further, it occurs across a wide range of social activities, from those generally considered to be morally proper – a priest mediating between a lay person and God, a general practitioner between patient and specialist – to those which many might think of as improper – a pimp mediating between a sex-worker and client, or a dealer as a middle-man between heroin importer and user. Mediation sets up relationships between parties whose interests may not be coincidental, or where there is considerable risk (financial, spiritual, legal) involved in negotiation.

For mediation to take place, the mediator cannot be seen to act on the basis of self-interest. Mediators must act on behalf of all parties brought together by mediation. But mediators always have some interest in the process. This is often financial, but it could also be based on such things as parental authority (a parent mediating a squabble between two children), and state authority (a social worker mediating a dispute between neighbours). Thus a real estate agent engaged to sell a house often talks up its value to a potential buyer. The agent's stake in the sale of the house is played down, in order to secure the buyer's confidence and clinch the sale. The accountant preparing a tax return will usually encourage the client to claim deductions, but must take care that they will be accepted by the tax office.

Media discourse is also subject to this kind of **self-effacement**. To gain the confidence and co-operation of the parties brought together (social and commercial institutions on the one hand, and audiences on the other), the media must offer certain guarantees that their texts do not misrepresent the way things are, and do not simply serve their own interests. Otherwise they risk losing the respect of both audiences and institutions.

This self-effacing function is one of the central features of media discourse. Media discourse includes an array of techniques and modes of signification that seek to erase the self-interest of the media in the stories that it tells about the world. These include claims to objectivity and truth, or claims to know the audiences' feelings or attitudes about certain issues. The point here is not whether these claims are true in any objective sense, but that they are routinely used by the media to justify their practice, and hence to efface their own interest in the process of news gathering and the representation of events.

Media self-interest and community

The professional techniques of the media involve, amongst other things, representing news stories through the recurring use of narrative schemes and denotative categories of representation. These generic conventions are intertwined with assumptions about objectivity, truthfulness and knowledge of the audience, to reproduce certain versions of the world. For instance, stories about migrants often play up their ethnic origins, casting individuals into stereotypical moulds. Vietnamese schoolchildren are represented as 'hardworking', while African migrants are cast as poverty-stricken refugees, lucky to be free from oppression back home. Certain aspects of their stories are selected as appropriate, while others excluded simply because they don't fit the predefined scheme. This, as you'll recall from Chapter 3, is exactly what **myth** does.

Myth attempts to make the world look familiar to the audience or reader, by creating a coherent view of the world based on narrative schemes and categorical types. Stories about political events, crimes and show business personalities are generally made to fit these schemes (politicians are in conflict with each other, crimes are against the community, media personalities are privately suffering, and so on). To tell a story in this way is to give consistency, and to offer values which the media presume the audiences will accept. It is to create the phatic conditions for a **media public**. A powerful sense of community can become established through the media's mythical representation of the world in the interests of the public, brought together by the media in the constant stream of stories and visual images which flood through everyday life.

The *Realpolitik* of media institutions is not about providing a public service to the community, but involves survival and profitability in the marketplace. Media success is not defined by an ability to please audience taste or to be united with audience views. This is more or less guaranteed anyway, by the routine marketing techniques of audience monitoring (ratings, surveys) which have been developed over many years and are used by all media. Rather, success results from engaging with other institutions in the market economy, by forging strong links with other media outlets as protection from predatory take-overs, in securing market share, and providing sufficient capital for regular technological upgrades necessary to maintain circulation and broadcasting capacity.

The forging of these links creates a powerful allegiance to the investment driven imperatives of capital, and the values associated with the free market, individual effort and the pursuit of free choice. At the same time, media discourse must create a media public whose values it claims to represent. These values may not be equivalent to those related to investment capital – not all readers and audience members are investors. And indeed, many of them may be hostile to the ideals of large-scale investment and its indifference to the ordinary worker, pensioner or small business operator. Thus, media discourse is contradictory at its heart. By trying to represent the interests of the whole public (its readership and audience imagined as a community, or large-scale collective), it must make these interests appear to coincide with those of the groups to whom it is allied in a capital investment sense. (This process is what we shall call *hegemony* in the next chapter.)

To realise this contradictory, ambiguous representation, media texts use certain strategies and devices, which we will now consider in more detail.

Media presence and direct address

So far we have been considering the institutional structure of the media. We have looked at their internal structure (mediation, disjuncture and contradiction), their relations with other social institutions, and the effects of media discourse in forming media publics. We now want to develop this last aspect, to examine how the media construct presence, or a sense of 'being there', through technology.

Media discourse is bound up with print and electronic technologies. It depends upon huge investment in equipment capable of reproducing texts of all sorts (type, images and sound) over vast social spaces. The means of circulating media texts are far removed from those used by individuals to produce the ordinary, private discourses of everyday life. Nevertheless, what they produce is the effect of direct and even intimate address.

Television is a prime example of the direct address of the media. News presenters always speak directly to the camera, taking on some of the aspects of a private conversation with the viewer. This is often reinforced by news presenters adopting a personal style of address, calling each other by nicknames and inserting personal comments in between news stories. It's as if they were right there in our living room.

Human presence can be affirmed in the media through visual imagery. Newspaper photographs are able to suggest the presence of an event, and its sheer actuality as an experienced reality. Because of their innate capacity to capture light reflected from real objects, photographs offer themselves as more real, more authentic than other forms of representation, and are thus an important part of media discourse. However, like all media texts, newspaper photographs are mediated. They are often edited and manipulated, and are always accompanied by written text which anchors the way we are able to read them. As we saw in Figure 3.5, the meaning of a photograph varies with its anchorage, thereby redefining the event. Newspaper and magazine photographs do not simply *reflect* real life: they *produce the effect of* reality. The effect of this is to play down the *constructedness* of newspaper texts and to reinforce their denotative, referential functions. The photographs seem to neutralise any signs of the institutional factors that might peep through the media's production of social and cultural values.

The effects of presence achieved through visual images are even more pronounced in television. In this case, audio-visual imagery transmitted from a live event takes on all the attributes of the event itself. The televised image offers itself as more immediate, accurate and intimately affective than the event from which the image is drawn. In televised sports, for example, close-up camera work and instant replays mean that television audiences are able to see the action more clearly than the spectators at the ground. As a result, real events start to take on the characteristics of the televised event. The style of play in many sports has become intensified for the immediate impact of the small screen, while the rules and formats of games such as American football or one-day cricket have been developed and refined to accommodate the interrupted rhythm of television's advertising breaks.

The effect of liveness can also be seen in programmes such as *Saturday Night Live*, screened in the USA and on pay-TV throughout the world. In this show, interviews with celebrities are characterised by overly candid questioning, while the various hosts often engage in mock scandalous behaviour. The aim of this programme is to give the effect of the intimacy of live, unrehearsed dialogue with all of its accidents, and uncontrollable elements allowed full reign, as if all quite unmediated. In Australia, the popular television programme *Good News Week* started as a studio-bound pseudo-quiz show, in which media personalities were given the opportunity to display their wit by answering a series of soft questions about recent news events to a small studio audience. The appeal of the show was not so much in the ability of the contestants to answer the questions correctly, but in their playful dialogue and often outrageous on-stage behaviour. Interestingly, *Good News Week* became so successful that it moved out of the television studio and into large concert and civic halls of towns and cities across Australia, as a kind of travelling TV show, attracting large audiences everywhere it went. Here we see a reversal of the usual process of live telecasting. Instead of a live event being covered by television, we have television becoming a live concert hall event.

In its lifelikeness and immediacy, television imagery makes it look as if things were simply happening of their own accord. Like news photography, it claims to reproduce things and processes with perfect technological objectivity and accuracy. Its effects seem to surpass ordinary human sight, yet they maintain the condition of presence necessary to invoke a community shared by both the media and its audiences. The technology seems to efface itself as it is used.

In summary, a key effect of media technology is to define the audience as a homogeneous group of people – a media public – present to each other and sharing a common identity through visualised speech. The media efface their own interest in the circulation of their discourse, by offering it to readers and audiences as direct and unmediated, in a phatic relationship where audiences and media seem to be part of the same community.

Popular idiom, gossip and personalities

Another way in which the media simulate presence is through the use of vernacular *language styles*. Listen to the different accents of the various presenters on television, and how they are distributed. The main news bulletins will generally be in the authoritative accent of the educated middle classes. Regional or class differences tend to occur elsewhere, in local news bulletins, the weather report and sport, for example. On British television, the regional accent of the chat-show host can act as a marker of conversationality rather than authority: Michael Parkinson's Yorkshire voice, Terry Wogan's Irishness and Clive James's Australianness are not qualities one hears delivering the main BBC evening news bulletin. Colloquial language is also often used in newspapers to suggest the presence and personalisation associated with speech rather than the impersonal distance of print.

Personalisation can also take the form of gossip. Gossip is usually about certain kinds of scandals and disgraces, uncommon events which seem to threaten the order of everyday life. Exposing scandal can strengthen social bonds by reconfirming mutual values. Media make use of gossip as a kind of phatic cement. Unusual stories such as 'Car kills salon client' (Figure 7.3) reproduce the effects of everyday gossip by showing how ordinary life is sometimes threatened by uncontrollable forces and events. Stories about the private lives of élite figures reassure us that no one escapes.

Figure 7.3

> IN BRIEF
>
> **Car kills salon client**
>
> ADELAIDE—A 63-year-old woman having her hair done was crushed to death by an out-of-control car which smashed through the front window of a hairdressing salon here yesterday. A witness said a green Mazda 626 careered on to the footpath and through the window at Fringes Hair Salon at Seaford in Adelaide's southern suburbs. Police said initial investigations showed the driver's foot had slipped off the brake on to the accelerator.

Stereotypes

As we saw in our discussion on narrative, stereotypes are a conventional form of characterisation. They encourage the reading of character in terms of fixed values, predetermined by social convention.

The representation of social identity in terms of stereotypes is a very common signifying practice in the media. Women and men are portrayed in terms of a set of fixed values, often determined by oppositions such as indoors/outdoors, domestic/public, worker/boss, passive/active, rational/irrational. For instance women are often portrayed as flightly and irrational as opposed to clear-thinking rational men. Stereotyping is a form of mediation which translates the complexity of individual character into a set of simple, socially defined distinctions. Woman are continually depicted in domestic or family situations playing nurturing roles, or in seductive scenes, as alluring objects of the male gaze. Men are seen in terms of work and career, or outdoor activities such as sport. TV soap operas, situation comedies and popular movies may all exhibit this kind of coding.

By the sheer weight of repetition, media texts endorse certain sets of social values as inevitable and natural, and certain beliefs and myths about social identities and cultural norms as universally applicable. These may become entrenched in society, and take on an authority which eludes the pressure of change. A good example of this is the way in which contemporary fashion and

Figure 7.4

are you a Quartz woman?

A Quartz woman knows what she wants. She says what she means. She expects her fragrance to be playful, vibrant, swinging and cool.

Quartz by Molyneux, the daring eau de parfum.

Available from selected pharmacies & department stores.

Even in women's magazines, images of women are dominated by scenes of flirtation or seduction. To whom is this woman's gaze addressed. Whose is this desire?

advertising imagery persist in portraying women as passive objects of male desire and control, despite current awareness of sexism in the media (see Figure 7.4).

The familiarity of this repetition is an important feature of media discourse in general, with powerful socialising effects. Its **redundancy** cues in the familiar, and thus confirms a common world view and invites readers and viewers into the phatic bond of a media public. But the media also work under the imperative to produce the new, day in and day out. This tendency towards the novel or unfamiliar exists in a perpetual tension with redundancy. We see this in that form which perhaps more than any other characterises television – the series. Each new series defines itself against others of the genre, marking off its similarities to what is already familiar and the differences which signal it as unique.

The long-running British series *The Bill*, for example, marks off its differences from current police dramas by importing techniques from the documentary: in particular, by the extensive use of mobile Steadicam cameras, following the characters through the labyrinth of corridors and rooms of the purpose-built police station which is its main set. Within the series, too, each episode performs a similar set of variations on the series' basic premise. This imperative to produce the new also means that television does not simply provide fixed stereotypes, but tends instead towards a loose liberality. Soaps such as the British *EastEnders* and the now-defunct Australian *A Country Practice* have always explored issues such as ethnicity and sexual preferences, in an atmosphere of emphatically liberal acceptance of differences. If, on television, new elements tend by and large to be absorbed into what's already said and known, the opposite process takes place too, as familiar forms cast new and often unexpected variations. What this produces is quite paradoxical, the effect of a world of endless novelty which nevertheless behaves in familiar ways.

Through this liberal tone, media institutions appear to disown their particular interests in favour of a community which is one of both plurality and consensus. They code texts as if all who read them share a common set of values and beliefs, and experience the same things in much the same way, and in this are able to suggest the phatic relationship of an imagined community. This sense of imagined community which we all carry around as part of our social awareness is one of the most powerful effects of the media in contemporary society, and the most important single effect of mediation. It creates within us all that strong feeling of interconnectedness despite vast distances and dissimilarities, which belongs to what we have called a media public. In the next chapter we will examine further the disjunctures and contradictions of these social relations.

EXERCISES

1 We spoke of discourse as having four characteristics: sites (where it circulates and is used), roles (for those who take part in it), relations of power (among those roles, and institutionally defined), and topics (what is spoken about). Take as an example a topic which is spoken about in a large and

complex network of discourses, such as medicine, education, nationality, sport, entertainment, money, or the family. Plot out graphically the various sites involved in this set of discourses, and their interrelationships. For each of them, look also at the roles and power relations set up, and the differences from one site to another (or even within the same site). (You will need a large sheet of paper for this, or a board. It works well as a group exercise.)

2 Stereotypes change over time. Compare various examples of advertisements drawing on stereotypes, such as Figure 7.1 ('Are you a good wife?' from the early 1960s) and Figure 7.4 ('Are you a Quartz woman?' from the late 1980s). What values have changed? What values have remained the same? What kinds of changes in the institutional discourses of the family do they register? Find an advertisement which draws on contemporary and quite naturalised ideas of family, or femininity, or masculinity. Imagine looking back on it from 40 years in the future, as we are doing with Figure 7.1: which of its codings do you think will now appear stereotypical and de-familiarised? Why?

SOURCES AND FURTHER READING

For a basic working through of the concept of institution, see Peter Berger and Thomas Luckmann, *The Social Construction of Reality: A Treatise on the Sociology of Knowledge* (London: Penguin, 1991, particularly pp. 65–109). The concept of discourse, as presented here, is derived from the work of Michel Foucault. You can go to his *The Archaeology of Knowledge* (London: Tavistock, 1972) for a detailed discussion. For introductions to Foucault's work, see Alec McHoul and Wendy Grace, *A Foucault Primer: Discourse, Power and the Subject* (Carlton: Melbourne University Press, 1993), Geoff Danaher, Tony Schirato and Jen Webb, *Understanding Foucault* (St Leonards: Allen & Unwin, 2000), and Gary Cutting (ed.), *The Cambridge Companion to Foucault* (Cambridge: Cambridge University Press, 1994).

For a definition and summary of discourse as applied to media and cultural studies, see John Fiske's *Television Culture*. Also see Tim O'Sullivan *et al.*, *Key Concepts in Communication and Cultural Studies*, 2nd edn (London: Methuen, 1994). John Hartley's *Understanding News* (London: Methuen, 1983) looks at the discourse of print media news. Norman Fairclough in *Language and Power* (London: Longman, 1989) and Roger Fowler in *Language and the News* (London: Routledge, 1991), analyse print media discourse from a linguistic perspective. For a seminal study of the media's treatment of crime along the lines of mediation, see Stuart Hall *et al.*, *Policing the Crisis: Mugging, the State, and Law and Order* (London: Macmillan – now Palgrave, 1978). More recent studies that analyse media discourse include William L. Nothstine, Carole Blair and Gary A. Copeland (eds), *Critical Questions:*

Invention, Creativity, and the Criticism of Discourse and Media (New York: St Martin's, 1994), Norman Fairclough, *Media Discourse* (London: Edward Arnold, 1995), and Allan Bell and Peter Garrett (eds), *Media Discourse* (Oxford: Blackwell, 1998). Norman Fairclough's *Critical Discourse Analysis* (London: Longman, 1996) provides a very useful introduction to the field of discourse analysis in general, as do the two volumes of Teun A. van Dijk (ed.), *Discourse Analysis: A Multidisciplinary Introduction* (London: Sage, 1997).

The concept of the imagined community can be found in Benedict Anderson, *Imagined Communities: Reflections on the Origin and Spread of Nationalism*, 2nd edn (London: Verso, 1991).

Ideology

Deriving from Marxist theories of society based on class conflict, the concept of ideology has always been a key analytical tool in cultural studies. In recent times, cultural theorists have redeveloped it in terms of discourse. Throughout this chapter we will deal with ideology as a *product of discourse*, that is, as a particular mode of knowing the world through signs and texts.

Broadly speaking, *ideo*logy is about the 'ideas' held in common by social groups in their everyday lives. It also suggests that these ideas are organised in certain ways. An ideo*logy* is a 'logic' of ideas, indicating that the groups who hold various ideologies perceive and understand the world in a certain consistent way.

In this sense, ideas are not simply mental events happening in the privacy of individual minds. Rather, they are public *meanings*, produced and circulating in everyday life and its processes of signification. Ideas about such things as democracy, justice, ethics and nationality obviously belong to this public arena – the big ideas about who we are and what our relationships to the (social) world around us might be. But so do more personal things, such as what we look for in our personal relationships, or our tastes in music, food, clothing or entertainment: the lyrics to songs, TV ads, radio, or just a glance at the racks of magazines in a newsagency give a glimpse of the ways in which these apparently personal choices are embedded in a vast and incessant hum of public discourse. (We shall be looking at some aspects of this in the next chapter.) Even the most personal and idiosyncratic ideas have this dimension of public meaning, in that they are in principle at least partially explainable to or understandable by others.

These circulating and social meanings tell us something about how we relate to the social world, and what our places in it might be. They *represent* the material, social domain in which we live. The problem however, is that they may not represent everyone's interests in the same way. Material differences and social conflicts are often smoothed over or represented in a way that appears to reconcile them. This process is called **ideology**.

Ideology is the process of representing material social relations, and of attempting to reconcile them in discourse.

As a matter of representation, ideology is a semiotic process like all the others we have discussed in this book. In particular, it is related to those concepts we looked at in the previous chapter: discourse, institution and mediation. There, we considered texts in terms of larger systems of cultural beliefs, especially through the process of mediation whereby institutions efface their own interests in favour of an apparently commonsensical and consensual stance. Now we turn to the ways in which those mediating processes work.

Power and address

Let us begin with the way in which newspapers tend to represent world events in terms of economic crisis and warfare. Where these crises are resolved, it is generally through the decisions of authorities (business, leaders, politicians) or through the actions of powerful individuals and elite groups (army generals, 'heroes', crack police units), all of whom are, for the most part, male.

The continual representation of the world in terms of conflicts resolved through male action and decisiveness enacts a *patriarchal ideology*. To represent the world in this way is to propose that social order is a matter of male authority. And to read these kinds of news texts is also to be addressed in a specific manner: to be oriented to the world as if it were *by nature* patriarchal. Think of the functions of address they offer to the reader: an authoritative, knowing addresser, a phatic consensus of common sense, an addressee who is *already* part of this consensus. They add up to a powerful invitation to accept and endorse the discourse of the media institution, as if it were the voice of society itself. Indeed, you are addressed as if you *already* agree, whether or not you do, and whether or not your actual reading is dominant, negotiated or oppositional.

So even before we get to the actual referential content, the media's *functions of address* are the site of ideological effects. This suggests that ideology may not be so much a matter of *what* is represented, but a name for *the social implications of the phatic effects of discourse*.

In this light we could say that ideology is *the way in which those roles within discourse get inhabited*. It is what binds us more or less closely into imagined communities of shared values, beliefs and identifications. In the particular case of media discourse, as we have seen, this imagined community takes the form of a media public. The phatic functioning of ideology is that it addresses individuals as *already* members of groups and communities.

Like other phatic effects, ideology works both to include and exclude, and with all degrees of belonging. We are already familiar with some of these effects from Chapter 4, where we discussed ways in which texts may set up a mythic opposition of terms, one side of which is *addressed* (as an *us*, who share a given set of values and identifications) and the other *represented* (as a *them*, who do not (Figure 8.1)). On the other hand, ideology can generate quite complex phatic relationships. It may also produce all sorts of subtle differentiations within such a group: we all belong to that same *us* in rather different ways.

Gender is one of the prime ways in which such differentiations get made: women and men belong to that larger social *us* in sometimes strikingly different ways. When those differences are inegalitarian and weighted towards masculinity, we speak of a patriarchal ideology. In such an ideology, social and personal success tends to be defined differently for each sex. For men, success is most obviously and frequently seen in terms of jobs and careers, and for women in terms of domesticity and family. But what then of the person who doesn't fit that pattern – the woman who is successful in business, for example? Even though western societies today have certain legal safeguards against sex discrimination, and even though the figure of the independent and successful woman is prominent, admired and offered as a role model, there is still some anxiety about it. We can see this residual worry in one of the standard questions put to successful women in media interviews: 'How do you do it? How do you juggle all this with home life and the family?' It's not a question that's often asked of men when talking about their success. It suggests a worry that to be successful in terms which are ideologically masculine may have a cost – to fail in ways which are essentially feminine, to be 'less of a woman'.

Note what is happening here: when the entire field of gender difference becomes represented by one term, the masculine, and the only forms of relationship are comparisons to the masculine, we have *myth* at work, in the sense of metonymy in which we used that term in Chapter 3. Patriarchy is mythic, in this precise semiotic sense. It functions ideologically through and as myth.

So ideology is something rather more concrete than ideas and values. It is a matter of the signs we exchange, and their phatic effects. Ideology has material effects in the world. Television, for example, addresses individual

Figure 8.1 How to spot a villain

As Figure 3.6 suggested, it was common practice in nineteenth-century Western anthropology to consider human character in terms of essential types. Thus, the working class looks and behaves differently from the aristocracy and the middle classes because of innate breeding, and members of non-European societies belong to a separate category of human existence altogether. Commonly held notions of criminality and justice are in turn defined by the ways various groups fit into these class and racial stereotypes. There were more than beliefs: they were complex systems of discourse, scientific, legal and medical. As with all discourse, they were ways of knowing and managing the world. These particular ones were put into practice by institutions in the west throughout the nineteenth and well into the twentieth century, as ways of managing criminality, class frictions, and a large colonial underclass.

Although these values are no longer held in any official scientific or governmental sense, they nevertheless survive and continue to flourish in other domains, where they provide an instantly recognisable metalingual framework. For instance, many movies and television crime dramas readily characterise villains according to exactly those stereotypes of criminality. To make it instantly obvious that a character is a villain, give them a certain facial complexion (generally swarthy and dark) or an obvious physical defect (obesity, say, or a limp). They sometimes have a foreign accent, a markedly campy voice (like Jeremy Irons in *The Lion King*), or a taste for indulgence and sensuous pleasures. American films and television programs often portray their villains as English, as if re-fighting the American War of Independence: recall Peter Cushing's plummy accents in the 1977 *Star Wars*. That film, along with the two sequels made during the Reagan presidency and the tensions of the final stages of the Cold War, gave its Imperial Officers the fur caps which have long been a stereotype of Russianness; in the 1999 prequel, The *Phantom Menace*, made after the collapse of the Soviet Union and with rising concerns about the potential international effects of an economic downturn in the Asian region, the villains speak instead with what sound very much like Japanese accents.

All of this establishes what might be called a fictionalised criminal class, recognisable through physical characteristics, an effect similar to that produced by nineteenth-century discourses on criminality. This fictionalised criminality divides society into two immediately and visible recognisable groups – just as certain ideologies of race divide it into those who are white and those who are not. It equates race and criminality, without ever having to *say* that non-whites are criminal. In its fantasy, crime has nothing to do with the way a society works (its inegalities, corruptions, or exploitations), but with those aliens, foreigners, loners and misfits whose nature places them outside it. The crime drama repeatedly plays out this fantasy of protecting a way of life from those who threaten it.

viewers as being *already* connected to many others, in the simple act of viewing. Part of the powerful appeal and fascination of watching a huge national or international live telecast – the turning of the millennium, or the Olympic Games – is knowing that so many millions of people around the globe will be doing exactly the same thing at exactly the same time. Ideology is precisely this enactment of common identity, through the sharing of signs.

Now we can see another reason for that separation of role and person suggested in Chapter 1 – for thinking in terms of addresser and addressee rather than sender and receiver. What texts do is *offer* roles, and offer them to you as if you *already* fill them. They cannot *make* you fill those roles. Thay have no control over whether you accept them or not, or to what degree, or over what you do in your life with these texts and their roles. Something always remains a bit indeterminate about that relationship between roles and the ways they are inhabited: falling into a role in a text is not like falling out of a window, where only one thing can possibly happen. Bernstein's model of dominant, oppositional and negotiated readings, which we discussed in Chapter 4, is already an attempt to describe this indetermination at the heart of texts; much of the next chapter will investigate some more of its implications.

Some texts seek to restrict this inherent flexibility with force. These texts tend to be the ones which carry and are supported by some of the main structural relationships of power in a society, and they are backed up by some of its more obviously powerful institutions and apparatuses. A road sign, for example, asks that you take your foot off the accelerator, and the police and the courts are there because the sign in itself is quite unable to guarantee what its actual readers will do. Once it has quite visibly and unambiguously stated the speed limit, the sign still leaves you free to drive very fast: all it can do after that is remind you of what may be the unpleasant consequences of that choice.

Other texts, though – most texts – don't have recourse to force. No matter how good it is, an advertisement cannot simply *make* you go out and buy the product, and it certainly can't call in the police for help. What it *can* do, though, is make a very attractive offer. Texts can offer roles that seem so commonsensical it may seem hard to conceive of doing otherwise. They can be seductive, so that it may seem odd to *want* things any other way. They can offer positions from which a number of difficult things suddenly seem simple, or conflicting things are reconciled. They can even offer you what seems to have been your own desire all along, reflected back to you. This is much more subtle a procedure than the use of force, because rather than impose coercion it asks for your consent. This *invitation* – this form of address – is ideology itself.

Interpellation

The ideological work performed by the functions of address is best known through the work of the French political theorist Louis Althusser. We will elaborate freely on the story he uses as an illustration.

Imagine you are walking down a street when you hear someone calling, 'Hey, you there!' It's not the voice of anyone you recognise, and your name certainly isn't spoken, so there is no reason to believe you're the one meant. Nevertheless, you turn around, just as you might have if you had been the one meant. So too (you notice as you turn) do a number of others on the street: they stop and look back, or hesitate momentarily in their step, or hunch their shoulders and go on, all of these in different ways responses to that call. In reacting, all of these concrete individuals here in the street are taking on that role of addressee provided for them, and in all sorts of different ways. They are recognising themselves, even if just for a moment, in that 'you there!' which may very well have been meant for none of them.

This process of **interpellation** (hailing) is a powerful model for thinking through the ways in which ideology works. It all hinges on that moment of recognition where, simply by turning round, or hesitating, or however it is you have reacted, you take on the role offered you – that of the one who is addressed. It doesn't rely on any particular way of taking on that role, but simply on your responding to the call *as if* you were the one meant all along: recognising yourself in it.

Althusser puts this in a particularly compact form:

Ideology **interpellates** individuals as subjects.

Think about what this implies. That word 'subject' has two common meanings, both of which are present here:

- The first is in a sense like that of the subject of a sentence: the active principle, the thing which does the acting. If *The cat ate my lunch*, the cat, not the lunch, is the active principle. In this sense, the subject is the source of an action, the thing that has made the decision and is responsible for it.
- The second sense is that in which we talk of someone as being *subject to the laws of the land*, or (in some cases) *a subject of the Queen*. This is something quite different: to be subjected *to* the cat's appetite, to have no choice in it, but to take what comes to you from elsewhere.

Interpellation makes me a subject in this doubled sense. What that moment of recognition does is pull together, simultaneously, both of those apparently opposed meanings. I recognise myself as the one hailed, and make the decision to turn round (or whatever it is I do); but at the same time, I do it because my strings have been pulled from elsewhere, by this voice I don't even know but nevertheless seem to be obeying. I am a free agent, and I momentarily give up my freedom to an anonymous call. Paradoxically, this happens all at the one time. I desire this product whose advertisement addresses me; at the very moment I respond to its call to turn around, it is a consent I freely give, a choice I freely make. I am a free agent *in the very moment* I give up my freedom to this other, *in the very act* of giving it up. Interpellation is essentially paradoxical: it addresses me as I already know I am, even if I didn't realise it before I was addressed.

Interpellation is a matter of address. We have seen the conative function of address and the ways in which it produces an addressee, but what of the expressive function, and the addres*ser*? Who – or what – is it that hails me in this way and makes me turn round?

Again, we must pay attention to that basic split, and be careful not to confuse addresser with sender. It is not the sender who has this effect on me. We have established that I don't even have to know this voice for it to work: a stranger's voice will do it just as well. What is the addresser of this brief text, 'Hey, you there!' which stops me in my tracks? Though the call does not appear to know me personally (it doesn't seem to know my name, and just refers to me as 'you there'), it certainly seems to be assuming a *right* to call on me, and a certain superiority. It is brusque and doesn't show any need for manners: one doesn't address people one respects or likes in this way.

Superior to me, and with a right to tell me what to do: what else could we call the addresser, this fictitious role within the text to which the call lays claim, but the Law? Not any particular law, or even the laws of a particular country or place, but just Law in general. I am driving in my car, and from somewhere behind me I hear a police siren: I don't for a moment think it's actually for me, but immediately I am ever so slightly more alert to the way I am driving, the state of my car and its tyres, the behaviour of the traffic around me. (I'm also so slightly more studiously *nonchalant* about my alertness, as if I'm oddly covering up for something like a guilt, which wasn't there a moment ago.) What makes this change in me is not any particular law (I'm obeying that speed sign after all), but just the general and abstract scrutiny of the Law. It works this way even if the actual speaker should have nothing to do with the real law, or have any real authorisation to stop and query me. Walking along the street I hear the call and turn round, and only then do I see by the smile on the stranger's face that it has all been a big joke; but by then, it's too late, I'd have already turned round in just the same way if the caller had been a police officer.

And I am not alone. Other people on the street here with me also react to the call, in ways which may be quite different from mine. Watch them carefully: the signs are slight. Some seem surprised, some mildly offended at this lapse of protocol; some give out the smallest but most legible signs saying they will not even give this hailing the courtesy of noticing it; some others look around, amused, for the possible entertainment that's about to begin. All of us are strangers, going about our own paths through the city, without the slightest coordination or knowledge of each other and our separate doings, but we all react to the call. This hailing is the only thing we have in common, but it is enough to make us, just for a moment, into a tenuous and diffuse group, even if that group vanishes again almost as soon as the call does: there may be the tiny raising of an eyebrow to nobody in particular, in recognition of that common interpellation; the flicker of a smile or a disapproving shake of the head, maybe even eye contact or a word in passing. Interpellation is doubly phatic. If only for the duration of the hailing, it produces a community: first of all *between* the one who is interpellated and the one who does the interpellating, between the Law and its subject; and then *among* those who are interpellated, through their common recognition of themselves in the interpellation.

We can sum up: in its address, interpellation produces two asymmetric positions and a relationship linking them:

- The **subject** who is interpellated. This is the addressee position, the one which the individual who turns at the call in the street is offered, the role she or he is invited to recognise her- or himself in. It is associated with the conative function.
- The **Subject** which interpellates. This is the addresser position, the position of the Law, and is associated with the expressive function. As a role, it should be carefully distinguished from any actual person who might do the calling.
- The phatic relationship which links subject and Subject. This relationship is that of a **community** of interpellation. It binds all interpellated subjects together by their common relationship to the interpellating Subject or Law.

Figure 8.2 shows some of the ways in which these work.

Hegemony

Interpellation invites you to recognise yourself as *already there* in the role the call offers you. This brings us to one of the most powerful ways of conceiving ideology – *hegemony*. In contemporary Western societies, power relations

Figure 8.2 Wearing the flag I

An image from an election campaign: set against or even draped in the flag, a politician solicits your approval.

There is an obvious but quite complex process of interpellation going on here. The poster addresses us, offers us a role as a certain sort of person, and invites us to perform certain actions on the basis of that: to vote for this candidate.

For a start, we should note just how clearly the picture is separating addresser and sender, the role and the one who fills it: it is even depicting that separation. The flag enfolds the politician in just the way a role enfolds the person who plays it. It is like clothing: someone in a diver's suit is taking on the role of a diver, someone wearing a business suit is playing a business person, someone wearing their nation's flag is *taking on the role of the nation*. To distinguish this role from the geographical place or the political entity, we will use italics for it here: the addresser of the poster – the imagined community which seeks to interpellate us, the voice calling 'Hey, you there' – is nothing less than this *nation*.

Now this is somewhat stronger than saying that the politician is taking on the role of, speaking as, a *citizen* of that nation. The relationship is closer and more direct than that. The claim being made here is to speak *as* the *nation*. It is a particularly powerful gesture when it is made in the name of independent or populist politics, because then this *nation* becomes the *true nation* which governments of either streak have forgotten, which has been suffering under this neglect, and which now returns to punish those political masters. It is as if the role of *nation* had been left empty, ready for the candidate to take it up. Here we see the mantle falling on the candidate's shoulders in a quite literal way.

There are three things we can say immediately about this *nation* in the light of our previous discussions:

- First of all, this *nation* is a highly **metonymic,** or selective, representation of the actual nation. From the diversity of things which make up that country, it selects a relatively homogeneous range of things, and these alone come to stand for the *nation*. The populist Australian politician Pauline Hanson, for example (whose electoral posters emphasise an image like this one), began her career – and lost her endorsement from one of the country's main political parties – by saying that she definitely did not represent indigenous or migrant people.

- As this nation is thus homogeneous and consensual, it is also quite **mythic**, in the sense in which we defined it in Chapter 3. It simplifies a vastly complex set of social and cultural relationships to one particular relationship: the degree to which anything is or is not part of that *nation*. As members of that *nation*, our relationships amongst ourselves take on their meaning by the relationship we all share to the *nation*. And because by definition that *nation* is homogeneous, this would have to be the same relationship for all of us: any differences would simply be the mark of *not* really belonging to it. Thus it would be simply unfair to give funding to some groups rather than others on the grounds of their special needs, because there can be no special needs in a *nation* where all are by definition equal. Simply to claim inequity is to place yourself outside that mythic consensus which structures everything. Not surprisingly, for Hanson's maiden speech the most un*Australian* group of all were thus Aborigines (www.onenation.com.au/maiden_speech.html).

- And finally, this *nation* is also utterly **ideological**, in the sense in which we defined it at the beginning of this chapter. It attempts to reconcile complex social relationships in terms of simple discursive relations – in this case, simply by excluding them from the metonymic selection. What this produces is a series of scapegoats, whereby problems are perceived – indeed, it is the only way they *can* be perceived within this framework – in terms of *theft*: what rightfully belongs to the *nation* is being taken by forces which are outside that consensus. If there is unemployment, it is because migrants are taking jobs which belong to its citizens; if there are ever-fewer funds for social welfare, it is because what there is is all going to those who do not deserve it; if industries are in trouble, it is because cheap imports are taking over the market; if there is racial tension, it is because there are too many foreigners in the country; . . .

These three factors – metonymic selection, mythic centralising and ideological simplification – are what gives this *nation* its coherence as addresser. It does not depend for its effect on its empirical or factual accuracy, but this does not mean that it is unreal. On the contrary, we should be very wary of making that judgement: this *nation* is real precisely because it is ideological. What our image does is actively produce that ideological *nation, into* the real, as the source of that voice which turns the heads of concrete individuals in the street. Interpellation produces not only the subject who is interpellated, but also the Subject who interpellates.

This is why it is so important to separate person and role: what addresses us in this poster is not an actual person so much as an entire imaginary nation, a *nation* which pulls together all sorts of myths and ideologies and integrates all of their contradictions into the one simple set of universal solutions. It also sheds light on why *demystification* is often so singularly ineffective a tactic. The populist politician who is inarticulate, easily caught out or factually mistaken may be demonstrating a strength rather than a weakness. All of these are qualities of the *person*, not of the role, the *addresser* which interpellates us in what she says. That mythical *nation* is not endangered by the fact that a particular person stumbles in a press conference or makes a false statement, but on the contrary, may even be strengthened by it. It is, after all, politicians who always have a word for everything, experts and bureaucrats who confound us with figures. What addresses us in the populist politician is that *nation* which has been brought to its knees by politicians and bureaucrats but is now fighting back, and whose best champion may be someone who couldn't be a bureaucrat or politician if she or he tried. To point out the *in*competence of such a politician may simply be to underline the very reason for their appeal. It may be that in such a case, a more effective counter-strategy is the paradoxical one: to insist on what a *good and effective* politician she or he is, in all of the usual ways, including those which make 'politician' such an easily pejorative term. In the day-to-day dodges and manoeuvres of politics, the populist may be quite indistinguishable from the politicians they invoke as a foil.

There is another aspect of the way this picture addresses us which we have not mentioned yet, but which is very important for its effect. Strangely, it takes the form of a certain reticence. Our politician is not looking at us. We already know that the gaze is a form of address (remember Figure 1.3), but here he refuses us that address, looking away from us at an angle. Why?

Here again, and in another form, the picture is emphasising that it is not the person who is addressing us, but the role in which the person is draped. Imagine the very different effect the photograph would have if we were to turn the head slightly and make its eyes meet ours. A photo like that would run two risks. The first would be the danger of collapsing that distance between addresser and sender, person and role – of saying in effect something megalomaniac (and strictly impossible), like *I am the State*. Look at Figure 8.4, for example, and see how an awareness of that danger has turned the gaze into an uneasy defiance. The second risk in the direct gaze would be to produce a corresponding distance between addresser and addressee: *I am not one of you*. The averted gaze heads off both of these, in a gesture of humility. It suggests that while we, as the photograph's viewers, are being addressed by the *nation, so too is the politician*. She is addressing us only because she in turn has already been addressed by this *nation*, which speaks through her. It says, in effect, *I am one of you*. The <u>nation</u> *calls me, just as it calls you. We all love our country. Because our politicians do not listen, the mantle of the <u>nation</u> falls to us: you and me. I am like you, because we are all children of the one <u>nation</u>. I am you*.

This, then, is the role of the addressee the poster sets out: the addressee is *one who has already been interpellated*. It invites you to place yourself in a double, layered role: as one who recognises herself or himself in what this *nation* offers, certainly, but more than that, as one who now, from this moment, recognises himself or herself as having *already* been interpellated *by* the *nation*. It asks for recognition: *Yes, that's what I've known all along*. All three functions of address – the expressive, which is what calls to you, the conative, which is the role you are offered; and the phatic, which is the community of the previous two – collapse into that one ideological *nation*, where there is nothing but perfect agreement because nothing but perfect agreement is admitted to the kingdom.

between groups and institutions tend to emerge through processes of consent rather than coercion or force. The authority of a dominant group is gained by the consent of subordinate groups and formations. Hegemony is a particularly subtle form of this, because it works in the ways we have just seen. In hegemony, ideology is not imposed on individuals, but *offered* them. But what is offered is not just an assertion of another set of values. It is not even another set of values offered as a reasonable proposition, and asking for your consideration. The twist is that the hegemonic is offered as something you *already* agree with, as a reflection of your own desires and wants, in which you can already and effortlessly recognise yourself. Hegemony seems to offer you what you already want anyway, even though it may in fact be a matter of the values and interests of a dominant social group which is not your own. This is why it is such a subtle and stable form of power and cultural leadership: if oppression and refusal are all the more likely to breed resistance, hegemony seems already to have given you what you want, in advance.

> **Hegemony** is the form of ideology in which the values and interests of the hegemonic group are experienced by others as already their own, and thus already consented to.

And all this works through those familiar functions of address, which do the offering.

In a hegemonic relation, the power between the dominant group and the others is not based on force, like that of a medieval king or a modern dictator. It needs to be maintained by a continual courting. Hegemony treats particular values as though they were universal, and as if consensus were simply a matter of following one's feelings or agreeing to the obvious. It says, *We all want the same way of life, we all feel about things in much the same way, don't we?* The flawlessly-complexioned model in the cosmetics ad, the happiness of the retirees who wisely invested in a superannuation fund, the four-wheel-drive on the cliff-top, all say *How could you not want this?* To resist hegemony can seem like resisting one's own desires. This is how it is so resilient.

Conflict and contradiction

Society is not a single, homogeneous structure. It is made up of different groups and classes of people, in sometimes highly unequal power relations. Conflicts occur because the interests of each group do not necessarily coincide. It is in the interests of an employer group, for example, to keep wages down and working hours up. For an employee group such as a trade union, however, the reverse is the case: wages need to be kept up, and working hours reduced. The relationship between employee and employer is thus marked by potential conflict.

In its phatic address, though, ideology proposes that all social groups and classes are governed by universal values, common ideas and commonsense principles. But ideology is itself the product of institutional discourses which arise precisely to serve the interests of a particular group. In claiming to be universal, what ideology is actually doing is *universalising* the discourses of that group. For instance, a national ideology might propose that there is a

Figure 8.3

Global Warring

AUSTRALIAN troops are keeping the peace in 10 of the world's trouble spots as we increasingly take on the role of the world's 'policemen'.

Aussie diggers are stationed in Syria, Cyprus, Afghanistan, the Persian Gulf, Western Sahara, Cambodia, former Yugo-slavia, Sinai, Iraq and most recently, Somalia, where these pictures were taken.

They show Queensland-based soldiers in action in the UN peacekeeping force in Somalia.

Colonel Bill Mellor commander of the Australian forces there, talks with children orphaned by the nation's four-year civil war and famine.

Above, Cpl Luke Entink of the 3/4 Cavalry based in Townsville, mans his .50 calibre machine gun on an armoured patrol in the streets of Baidoa.

(*Sunday Mail*, 14 February 1993)

Here, readers are offered the collective 'us', an identity that elides the many different group and individual interests of the large readership of a daily newspaper into a single, homogeneous national community. This 'us' is part of an opposition between 'us' and 'them': the technologically advanced First World over the impoverished and strife-torn Third World. There is nothing natural or essential about this ascendancy. It is a consequence of two centuries of European colonialism in Africa, but the ideological address here wipes out the traces of this historical residue, as if the conflict were somehow entirely of 'their', the Somali people's, own making. The address also effaces class and social divisions, as if the 'us' refers to a single unified group. The interests of a dominant military and government groups are given as the interests of all Australians, a benign and compassionate 'us'.

single national type, made up of certain values and sentiments dearly held as part of a national myth. Although there may be many different races, ethnicities and classes within the nation, the national ideology sees them all as sharing some aspects of the type, transcending local, class, ethnic and racial differences.

But this form of representation can mask the *differences* between the diverse groups which make up a nation, thereby appearing to resolve contradictions and conflicts into a false or pseudo-unity. For instance, the apartheid policy which segregated South African society by race simply refused power to the black majority and created a national sovereignty based on white rule; though its wealth relied on cheap black labour, it represented itself as essentially a white nation. Inevitably, the inherent contradictions led to conflict and the eventual collapse of the white regime in the late twentieth century.

An ideological analysis of *The Patriot*

When this ideological resolution of social conflict and contradictions is worked out in *narrative*, we have the process of **fabulation**. Fabulation tells stories about how conflict comes about, and how it is resolved; it tells moral stories about the good of a society. It does this by enacting or performing social ideas and values through a particular dilemma, and resolving them in specifically *narrative* ways, such as through the actions of characters. That is, it invites us to take the sort of resolution which is possible in a storyline to stand for a resolution of social relations which actually remain conflictual and contradictory. We can best see how this works in an example.

The Patriot is a film set in Carolina in colonial America at the time of the American War of Independence (1775–83). It tells the story of a colonial plantation owner and war hero from the earlier Indian Wars, Benjamin Martin (played by Mel Gibson), who refuses to fight on the side of the colonists against the British despite the fact that his neighbours and sons are passionately committed to the cause of the revolution. As the fighting draws closer to home, Martin and his family tend wounded soldiers from both sides of the conflict on the verandah of their house. At one point, a British officer (Colonel Tavington) leading a squadron of cavalry, callously shoots Martin's young son in the back. As a consequence, Martin abandons his pacifist objections and begins a guerrilla campaign against the British army by organising a militia group made up of local farmers and villagers, including his eldest son Gabriel.

The militia's hit-and-run tactics are at first tremendously successful, but eventually they cause the British to take reprisals. Led by the cruel Colonel

Tavington, British troops lock a group of villagers sympathetic to the militia into a church and set it alight, killing everyone inside, including Gabriel's fiancée. In a fit of anger, Gabriel rushes off seeking revenge, but is himself killed by Tavington. After further adventures, Martin and his militia eventually rejoin the main colonial army, which defeats the British army in a setpiece battle. In it, Martin satisfies his desire for revenge by killing Tavington in hand-to-hand combat.

The Patriot fabulates ideas about family, nation, duty and right action. Through narrative and characterisation, the film acts out in melodramatic form the birth of a new nation through the overthrow of an older, repressive order. The values associated with this new nation concern the rights of individuals over property, the primacy of the family, a love of freedom, and the commitment to an ideal. These are opposed to the born-to-rule attitudes of the British officer class, the over-sophistication of British culture, and the cruelty and deceitfulness of the administrative regime (as exemplified by Tavington), which governs by decree rather than consent. All of the actions and conflicts work inexorably to show how an older, morally decayed regime must inevitably give way to the new.

The United States is seen here as a potential, waiting to be brought into existence through a fortuitous historical mixture of decent colonial characters and justifiable action against a repressive regime. The problem however, concerns the violent nature of this birth, and the question this places over the legitimacy of the modern nation state. The film deals with the *social* dimensions of this contradiction through the *personal* dilemma in which the main character is caught, and the *narrative* resolution it gives to that dilemma.

During the Indian Wars some 20 years earlier, Martin was involved in an act of murderous revenge which he has since bitterly regretted. As a member of a scout detachment of the British army, he tortured and murdered a small group of native Americans who had previously attacked and killed white settlers. Martin has thus been part of the repressive tactics of the colonising power, a fact that he tries to disown. By turning to plantation farming and raising a family, Martin tries to blot out this stain on his character.

In helping the colonists' cause against the British, then, Martin is not motivated by the ideal of a free society, but by his earlier misdeed, which he both tries to exonerate *and* repeats (this is what *revenge* does). His old crime resurfaces, but this time in a just cause. The film thus resolves the contradiction between the birth of a new nation based on good principles, and the violence involved in making it happen, by displacing it onto the main character, whose acts of revenge are *both* the cause of his 'fall' *and* the means of his redemption. Revenge is one of the prime motivations in the style of fabulation known as melodrama.

In **melodrama**, individuals are faced with an oppressive force beyond their control, which at first causes them to suffer, but which is eventually allayed or overthrown through their morally charged actions. Melodrama forms the basis of much of the fabulation of contemporary popular culture. It sets up an instantly recognisable moral order of good versus evil. In melodrama, revenge is not necessarily immoral if it achieves the downfall of the original source of repression. By framing the violence in terms of the revenge of a wronged man, the film refocusses the question of legitimacy away from the founding of the nation state and onto a framework of conventional melodrama. A particular convention of narrative resolution (melodrama's ready acceptance of violence as a legitimate counter-force to oppression) stands for and legitimises social and political events (the colonists' revolutionary cause). It makes the latter appear to be a natural aspect of the former, a relatively simple and familiar resolution to a complex and contradictory set of events.

The ideology of the nation state is thus compromised right from the start. If the violent birth of a nation should always be in a just cause, here it is indistinguishable from and indeed a repetition of the violence already used by the older repressive regime. In order to show how the formation of a new nation can redeem the past, the fabulation of *The Patriot* repeats the very violence which needs redeeming. The narrative resolution doesn't so much do away with the dilemma as tie it into a knot: the new nation can come into being, it says, only by taking on the very aspects of the old order it most detests, and by reproducing these as the basis of its own power and legitimacy.

As a fabulation, *The Patriot* enacts an ideology of national origins seen in many Hollywood films, especially Westerns, where America is founded on patriarchal order secured through violent acts. What function does this kind of fabulation have in today's globalised world? It legitimises the nation state as a safe haven for ideals such as the sanctity of the family, the time for right action, and the role of the good citizen. By returning to the embryo-history of the most powerful nation on earth, the film provides a scenario of the birth of democracy, where the viewer can contemplate values currently under threat in the globalised world. We are invited to see the kinds of people and events which make a nation strong in a simple, melodramatic form. But at the same time, the fabulation places these ideals under question by showing how they are always intertwined in the old, and how the threat of violence is foundational to even the democratic nation state. The fabulation of *The Patriot* is a good example of how ideology can never deliver its ideals (a good society, a peaceful nation) without at the same time displaying their basis in the very values which it claims to renounce.

Reading ideology

As this suggests, ideology works by orienting people in social contexts towards accepting certain values about the world as natural, obvious, self-evident, or inevitable. In *The Patriot's* fabulation, the legitimacy of America as a nation is clearly seen in the obvious wickedness and cruelty of the British army, which overwhelmingly demands to be overthrown by the colonists and their just cause. Social identity is reinforced through the continual replaying of the ideological fabulations which structure films, television programmes and the media. In offering a narrative resolution to a social conflict or contradiction, fabulation promises something comforting and reassuring. And because the pleasures it offers in doing this are largely those which come from narrative, they can be taken up by readers and viewers who do not share the ideological interests at work in the fabulation: to enjoy *The Patriot*, we do not have to accept the values of the nation state as a patriarchal order, as the characters do.

Textual analysis reveals the ways the discourses and texts position readers to *embody* ideology. In this process of embodiment, people resolve contradictions and accommodate values which do not necessarily equate with their own day-to-day life. The values become built into their understandings of their own desires, identities and expectations of future situations.

Of course, there are many ways of reading *The Patriot*, and no single audience will read it homogeneously. Many British reviewers found it difficult to accept Tavington as anything but a caricature, and hence an unconvincing motivator for the kind of revolutionary action that the film shows. The final reconciliation between a white farmer and a black slave, both fighting in Martin's militia, can easily be seen as unconvincing, conveniently covering over the complex issue of slavery. Women may feel uncomfortable with the story of nations as things men build, and with the legitimation of violence as a political act.

The reading of mass media texts is not a passive exercise in which readers are duped into accepting dominant ideological values. Readers and viewers all the time construct, reinforce, modify, and even reject the social identities offered them, as a matter of course. They work to define, modify or contest their place in the world as it is determined by group and class interests. The analysis of ideology reveals the *constructedness* of the social contexts in which readers and texts interact, and in doing that suggests the possibilities of changing them. In the next chapter, we look at how the ways in which we inhabit ideology are always active and complex process of strategy and negotiation.

Figure 8.4 Wearing the flag, II

The Weekend Australian, 12–13 April 1997, p. 6.

EXERCISES

1 What ideologies seem to be at work in Figure 7.5? Consider the relation between the photographic image and supplementary written commentary. Can you see any intertextual associations?
2 Analyse the lead story of your local newspaper. In what way does it construct a sense of an imagined community? What kinds of ideologies are set to work in order to achieve this? What values are included, and what values excluded in so doing?
3 Tape an episode of a television situation comedy, soap opera or crime drama. Spend some time in class or at home analysing the text in terms of ideology. In what way is ideology fabulated through melodrama?
4 (i) Figure 8.4 is a news photograph of Pauline Hanson with the flag. Unlike Figure 8.2, here Hanson actually does address you with her gaze. Analyse this photograph as we did with Figure 8.2, this time focusing on the differences. Pay attention to the ways in which all three functions of address are now quite different. Why would this photograph not have worked on an election poster?
   (ii) Figure 8.5 shows some rather different ways of wearing a national flag. The first picture shows Australian Aboriginal athlete Cathy Freeman in the Aboriginal flag. The second was taken after she

Figure 8.5 Wearing the flag III

Indigenous Australian athlete Catherine Freeman wearing the Australian flag after competing at the Atlanta Olympics, 1996 . . .
Pic by Craig Golding

competed at the Olympic Games in Atlanta, 1996, and shows her wearing both the Australian and the Aboriginal flags. Analyse these photographs in semiotic and ideological terms, and compare them to Figures 8.2 and 8.4.

SOURCES AND FURTHER READING

A good starting point for overviews of ideology is Terry Eagleton's *Ideology: An Introduction* (London: Verso, 1991). The concept of ideology as interpellation and the story of the hailing in the street come from Althusser's essay on 'Ideology and Ideological State Apparatuses (Notes towards an Investigation)', in his *Lenin and Philosophy and Other Essays* (London: Unwin Hyman, 1980).

. . .and wearing the Aboriginal flag in a different setting.

Slavoj Žižek's collection, *Mapping Ideology* (London: Verso, 1994) is a valuable collection of some of the best-known work on the topic from the last three decades. The notion of hegemony introduced in this chapter comes from the Italian political philosopher Antonio Gramsci: see *A Gramsci Reader: Selected Writings 1916–34* (London: Lawrence & Wishart, 1988). The Resources on Antonio Gramsci site at www.soc.qc.edu/gramsci/ offers a helpful introduction to this important figure.

For a general treatment of media, discourse, power and ideology, the essays in *Culture, Media, Language: Working Papers in Cultural Studies, 1972–79*, edited by Stuart Hall *et al.* (London: Unwin Hyman, 1980), are an excellent introduction offering seminal work from the influential Birmingham school of cultural and media studies. In *Channels of Discourse Reassembled: Television and Contemporary Criticism* (London: Routledge, 1992), there is also a useful essay on ideology by Mimi White titled, 'Ideological Analysis and Television'. Chapter 4 of Dominic Strinati's *An Introduction to Theories of Popular Culture* (London: Routledge, 1995) provides a helpful discussion of politics, economics and ideology. The material on ideological analysis on Daniel Chandler's Media and Communication Studies site is also very useful(www.aber.ac.uk/media/Functions/mcs.html).

More advanced recent studies that apply ideological analysis to various media include Philip Green, *Cracks in the Pedestal: Ideology and Gender in Hollywood* (Amherst: University of Massachusetts Press, 1998), J.M. Balkin, *Cultural Software: A Theory of Ideology* (New Haven: Yale University Press, 1998), and Tom Cohen, *Ideology and Inscription: 'Cultural Studies' after*

Benjamin, de Man and Bakhtin (Cambridge: Cambridge University Press, 1998).

On connections between ideology culture and identity see Stuart Hall and Paul du Gay (eds), *Questions of Cultural Identity* (Newbury Park: Sage, 1996), and Tamar Liebes and James Curran (eds), *Media, Ritual, and Identity* (London: Routledge, 1998).

For a detailed discussion of ideology from a linguistic and social semiotic point of view, refer to Robert Hodge and Gunther Kress, *Social Semiotics* (Cambridge: Polity Press, 1988). Ideology is also discussed at some length in Norman Fairclough, *Language and Power* (London: Longman, 1989), Roger Fowler, *Language in the News: Discourse and Ideology in the Press* (London: Routledge, 1991), and Paul Simpson's *Language, Ideology and Point of View* (London: Routledge, 1993). For a discussion of melodrama and story-telling or fabulation, see Christine Gledhill's essay, 'The Melodramatic Field: An Investigation' in the collection which Gledhill has edited, *Home Is Where the Heart Is: Studies in Melodrama and the Women's Film* (London: BFI, 1987).

Systems and strategies

So far, one of the major attractions Saussurean semiotics has held for us has been the way in which it insists that meaning is not primarily a quality contained within or possessed by, an individual sign, but something which exists outside the sign, in its various relationships with other things and signs.

We have examined some of the implications of this in earlier chapters. In Chapters 2 and 3, we looked at some of the ways in which meaning results from relationships which are internal to a sign system – that is, from relationships among signs themselves. Chapters 5 and 6 were concerned largely with ways in which this sort of systematic structuring could be generalised to some of the larger unities signs display, such as genre and narrative structures.

We have also tried to emphasise that even though there might be very distinct regularities in the ways signs are used, they are never just the mechanical product of rules. Signs are never produced in a vacuum, but in specific contexts, and with certain concrete (if not entirely foreseeable) effects. In Chapter 4, we developed some ideas of textuality as a series of social practices, and kept these considerations in mind when discussing genre and narrative. Genre's interest and enormous flexibility, after all, comes from the fact that meaning can come from transgressing, combining and playing with conventions, rather than just blindly following them. In Chapters 7 and 8, we found that there are all sorts of different ways of inhabiting discourses: the offer ideology makes may be attractive, but it is never the only possibility. It is now time to examine in a bit more detail that flexibility between rules and practices – between the overall regularities and the sometimes surprising practices they give rise to.

Contexts and citation

Let's recapitulate briefly. A sign system (*langue*) is capable of producing an almost infinitely large number of possible utterances. All of these are intelligible because they are constructed according to the rules of the system (such as a grammar). If you know the rules of the system, you can construct, and make sense out of, utterances you've never come across before. Saussurean semiotics takes this governing sign *system* as its object of study.

The emphasis is on system. When Saussure relates signs to what is outside them, he is primarily interested in their relationships to *other signs*, *within* the system as a whole, and not to things which aren't signs. He's not denying that signs really do have relationships with other things outside the sign system; he just brackets these off, and says that they're not really the concern of the linguist or semiotician, but of the sociologist or anthropologist or historian. Saussurean semiotics shows signs taking their meaning from *other signs in the same system*.

We have seen in our first chapter that contextual functions are, however, unavoidable. *Deictic* features of language ('pointing' words such as *here, now, this, I, you*) rely to some extent on a knowledge of the context in which the utterance is used (who is meant by *I*? when is *now*?). Signs never occur in a void, but always in specific situations, where they aim to do things, to have effects, to do work, to elicit responses. And this broader context may include a lot of things which aren't signs, or at least which can't easily be included within Saussure's idea of the sign system.

We will have to examine this a bit further, because it implies a very important qualification. It points out the extent to which Saussurean semiotics has simplified what actually happens in sign use. Now let's complicate matters. Recall this example from Chapter 2:

There, we treated this sign as an utterance produced by the application of rules. We divided it up into paradigm sets, and showed how it has a clearly discernible syntagmatic structure. In doing this, we focused on certain features of the sign, the individual units (words) and their order, while ignoring others. We had nothing to say, for example, about the fact that this might be a sentence written in chalk on a blackboard, or that it might be a facsimile, in a textbook, of words in chalk on a blackboard. What we did, in fact, was examine this sign in isolation from any particular context. We didn't ask

Figure 9.1

> *The cat sat on the mat.*

any questions at all about who would be likely to use such a sentence, why, under what circumstances, in what situations, to whom, or with what possible effects. All we wanted was to get an idea of the internal structure of the utterance, the way it drew on and used a certain system of regular rules.

But is context ever really so negligible? Every utterance occurs in a situation. This one did, although we didn't say much about it then. It's a context so obvious it's easy to overlook: the book you're holding, this textbook on social semiotics and cultural studies. Within that context, the utterance is being used as an example of the type of sign-process we want to think about. What's more, it's a *cited* utterance, one which has been drawn from other contexts and transplanted here: the simple words, the repetitions, the visual style suggesting a series of chalk marks on a blackboard. Neither of these contexts is negligible, and each leads to a somewhat different meaning: as a schoolroom sentence, the utterance is naïve, but as a sentence in a semiotics textbook it is part of a more sophisticated argument. The utterance would be different again if it were given other contexts, such as, say, a clue in a cryptic crossword, or the answer to a question from the cat's owner. We could even go so far as to say that two radically different utterances can be verbally identical but differ only in context.

Every utterance has some sort of context, even though none is completely tied to a single context. Utterances may be cited in contexts and situations conceivably very distant from any given original, but they are never *without* context. Every utterance is a reaction to a situation, a response to another utterance, even if this utterance is a silence. Every utterance invites another utterance in response – even if that response is silence. Silence may be just as much a response as words. For a start, it has a very strong phatic function: it says things like, *I'm closing down all communications with you; this conversation isn't worth continuing; you're wasting my time; go away*; or, on a more positive note, silence can also help to build the relationship: *I'm thinking over what you've said.*

Consider the use which can be made of silence in a television interview. If the interviewer asks a question to which the interviewee merely responds with a 'Yes' or 'No', the interviewer may rephrase the question and try again, hoping for a more satisfactory response. More subtly, though, the interviewer may just keep silent. Eventually, in order to fill in the silence, the intervie-

wee offers more information. With any luck, this may even include information the interviewee hadn't originally been intending to say, so strong is the
import of the silence.

Even silence and withdrawal from the exchange, then, are responses. If
for Saussure the basic *object* of semiotic study is the system of *langue* and
the basic *unit* of meaning is the *syntagm*, we must now augment that:

> The basic *situation* in which meaning occurs is the **exchange**.

Exchange is not, of course, something new to the Saussurean system: with
the idea of value, it is already one of the key features of his theory of signs,
though it is limited exclusively to relations among signs. Here, we will want
to draw other consequences from the idea of exchange. Saussurean semiotics works very economically and elegantly to describe what it characterises
as the internal relations within a system. These do not, however, by any
means exhaust the relations that sentence can enter into in the real world,
or all the contextual forces which have formed it.

Citability provides the potential for signs to be and do new things. Figures
9.2 and 9.3 are two such occasions. How can we think through such poten-
tials? It may help to take as an example a process which very clearly takes on
its meaning in the sort of exchange we've just been suggesting, and have a
close look at just what is happening in it.

The gift

Whatever else it might be, a gift is very clearly a sign. It means something.
It says something about the giver's relationship to the receiver, or at least
about what the giver imagines this relationship to be – that is, it has very
important phatic, conative and emotive functions.

Sometimes the bare act of giving is a sign, regardless of what the gift itself
might actually be. Consider the peculiar practice of giving cards. Cards are
an ambiguous sort of gift, something you give when you're not actually giving
a present. Giving a card, you are giving something with very little actual use
value at all: at best a joke or witticism or attractive picture that sits on a shelf
for a week or so and then goes out with the vegetable peelings. In the obvious absence of any other use, the important thing with a card is simply the
act of giving it. With a card, you say, *I gave you something, even though it's
something which has no other use whatever than to say 'I gave you something'.*

This is not an indicator of the vapidity of greeting cards, but of the significance of the act of giving. It might be more accurate to say that it isn't the

Figure 9.2

You can never forget the feeling of a pure cotton sheet.

In Australia in the 1980s, Sheridan ran a famous series of billboards showing a male model asleep in their sheets. In their choice of a good-looking and well-muscled young man, the advertisers were clearly aimed at women, who are by far the biggest buyers of manchester goods. What the advertisers didn't seem initially to have reckoned with was that the billboards would become gay icons. More than one gay pub in Sydney displayed its own copy of the poster behind the bar.

card which is the sign, but the ritualised act of giving. The card itself is just a sort of receipt, the minimal something that has to change hands so there can be a giving. Giving a card reduces the act of giving to almost nothing *but* a sign, one which is almost pure formal function.

There is, however, a certain skill involved in gift-giving. You have to judge all sorts of things, including the interests, likes and dislikes of the person you're giving it to. You don't usually give an expensive wine to a non-drinker, or to the person who runs the shop you bought it from. You have to judge your relationship with the recipient. How close is it? Too expensive or too cheap a present may be embarrassing, for both parties. A present which a receiver feels is too expensive may be seen as a way of insisting on a closeness the receiver doesn't want; one which is too cheap may speak of a distance, and may well produce it even if there wasn't one there before.

Very importantly, you have also to consider that a gift places a debt on the receiver. If you get a gift, you *have to* reply: if you don't give a gift back, your silence will be a reply anyway. There is the same sort of skill in responding

Figure 9.3 The Mod revival

1977 saw the rise of Punk and the revival of 1960s Mod among work-ing-class British youth. It is easy to suggest contributing social causes for this: obvious ones would have to be the high and rising rate of unemployment (particularly in urban areas and particularly among youth), made more irksome by the ostentation of that year's celebra-tions of the royal Silver Jubilee. The Mode revival embraced the cloth-ing, music and lifestyle of the original 1960s movement: a sharp and immediately recognisable sartorial sense; a taste for the music of the original bands associated with 1960s Mod (such as The Who); and, of course, the lovingly restored Vespa motor scooters. Much of the Mod revival focused on music. Mod had not only its own bands, but also its own venues and independent record labels.

British cultural studies, of course, found all this intensely interesting. Its classic text on the topic is Dick Hebdige's *Subculture: The Meaning of Style*. This book reads Punk and Mod as forms of 'revolt into style', symbolic gestures of social resistance. For Hebdige, Mod fashions work by quotation: that is, they repeat in new contexts and for new purposes signs which have their origin elsewhere. He argues that the Mod revival is not just a copying of the fashions and tastes of a decade and a half ago, but a knowing, witty and (socially) critical citation of them in a contemporary framework and for contemporary purposes. The music of bands such as The Jam, for instance, took a polemical and broadly left stance against many of the features of late 1970s British society. What's more, one could say exactly the same thing about the original Mod. In their fastidious neatness, relative costliness and immediately distinctive lines, for example, the original Mod fashions in clothing are themselves reworkings, re-citations of mainstream styles, which are simultaneously playing with and against various ideas of class and respectability.

As popular music is a highly saleable and increasingly international commodity, by the end of the 1970s much of the music associated with the urban British Mod revival had made its way to other parts of the world, and taken on a life quite removed from the conditions under which it had arisen. The Mod revival itself became the object of quotation and re-citation at yet another remove. For a few years in the early 1980s in Sydney, Australia, for example, there was a thriving Mod culture, complete with bands and venues marked out as its own, and, yes, lovingly salvaged and detailed Vespas. Sydney Mods, like the originals, tended to be working-class youth, in their mid-teens to early twenties; but unlike the originals, they were taking up and reworking signs from a culture half a world and nearly a generation away. And one of the frequently circulated books of Sydney Mod was Dick Hebdige's *Subculture*: circulated and read not as sociology or a study of social semiotics, but, in a final demonstration of Hebdige's point of the very unforeseeable citability of the sign, as style guide.

to a present. Give too large a present in response, and you may escalate things. And so on.

Some of us are doubtless better at handling these situations and exchanges than others. Such skills aren't simply the result of applying rules. There's no simple ready reckoner which will tell you reassuringly that if someone of a certain degree X of closeness to you, with interests A, B and C and positive dislikes P, Q and R, has given you gift Y, worth \$$Z$, on occasion W, then the absolutely correct thing to give them for Christmas is a vinyl wallet worth \$12.95. In gift-giving there is no single correct response. What you do depends on a whole host of factors too numerous and unstable to systematise in something like *langue* (such as what you actually want to do with the relationship), and on factors which are perhaps quite unforeseeable (such as what the other party might want to do with the relationship). There's a skill in it, one you can get better at: but the skill comes into it precisely because things aren't entirely governed by a system.

While the phatic, conative and emotive functions are tremendously important in the gift-as-sign, the metalingual function (the one which suggests which system of rules to decode this by) is relatively unimportant. Although systems might to some extent exist (there are such things as books of etiquette, which may or may not be of use here), they don't cover much of the intricacy of what's happening here. What is important, though, and governs a lot of the subtlety of the exchange, is the contextual function. In gift-giving, you monitor the situation and decide accordingly. You play things by ear.

System may be a very important set of considerations if we consider the sign shorn of any context. But once we start trying to take context into account, it is no longer possible to treat sign usage as simply a matter of rules. Rather than see signs as the result of the simple application of a **system of**

rules, we must now try to think of them in terms of **strategies of behaviour**.

This doesn't mean we are now having doubts about the existence of the various regularities which we have been bringing to light, but just that we should not think of these internal relations as the sole determinant of meaning. On the one hand, there is a system of rules. On the other, there are questions of what you do with those rules, what strategies you employ. In other words, it is beginning to look as if the relationship that system has to signs doesn't so much resemble the relationship between a set of instructions and their results, as that between the rules of a game and an actual match.

Games of strategy

Let us follow the analogy, by considering a game like chess or tennis. Both are highly codified. Each has quite definite sets of rules (*langue*) which govern play (*parole*). In chess, each piece can move in certain ways and not in others; in tennis, a legal shot is one which lands in certain parts of the court and not in others; and so on. In each case, there is a relatively small number of rules, but a virtually infinite number of actual moves which can be made from them. The rules are quite independent of the players. In this case, they are even objectively codified: if there's any dispute, they can be consulted and a definitive ruling can be made.

To this extent, a game works much like a semiotic system. But there's a lot more to games than this limited comparison might imply. Knowing the rules does not account for the vast variety of ways in which the rules can be used, and the effects of those uses. Though both may be equally familiar with the rules, there's a big difference between Venus or Serena Williams and a Sunday player. Far from being what governs sign usage, the system of rules may be just one feature the user can implement – and not even necessarily the determining one. As with gift-giving, there may well be certain non-systematised (and even non-systematisible) *strategic* aspects involved.

Let us suggest, then, that sign processes *do* behave with systemic regularity, but *also* that this system is not enough to described everything involved in sign processes. From the point of view of the one who uses the signs, we could say that a knowledge of the relevant systems is a *necessary* but never *sufficient* condition of competent use. The difference is between knowing the rules and playing the game. I can know the rules of tennis without ever having played it – or quite conceivably without ever even having *seen* it played. A copy of the rules will tell me the size and shape of the court, what scores points, and what constitutes a foul. But compare that codified knowledge of the game to an actual situation in play. You are standing on the court, racquet in hand, with a ball coming at you at high speed. You have a fraction of a second in which to react. In that time, you not only have to interpose your racquet, but do it in such a way as to send the ball back over the net into your opponent's court. The best shot will be the one which lands the ball in precisely that part of the court which your opponent finds it most difficult to get to in time. A fraction of a second's hesitation, or a slight miscalculation in the placement of your body, may mean the difference between you or your opponent scoring. And at every shot, though you are playing all the time within the same set of rules, the ball comes at you in a way that's never the same twice, and you hit it back in way that's never the same twice, never perfectly replicable.

So some aspects of the game, perhaps the most important ones, can't easily be formalised. Though they refer to and involve the formal regularities of system, they are extremely fluid and depend on things that are in principle unpredictable from the system. This is not in any way to suggest that they're in some way mysterious or ineffable. On the contrary, they're often highly teachable and transmissible skills. That's why there are sports coaches. These skills are just relatively uncodified. You have to learn them on the court, rather than from a book. They're a matter of training bodies, muscles, reflexes: in other words, of everything we called *embodiment* in Chapter 7.

It's useful to think of sign use in terms of a game of strategy, a *sign-game*. We have already considered actual language use as an exchange. Now think of it in particular as a tennis game, tossing the ball of response back and forth. There may be relaxed games of tennis, where no one cares much who wins, and there may be intense, fast, fierce ones. Something similar holds for conversations. There may be situations where there's little at stake except the immediate phatic pleasure of it, and the game continues just because everyone enjoys it; or there may be a lot at stake, and the exchange continues even in the face of difficulties for one or some or all of the participants (cross examination, justification, argument, persuasion, etc.). There are situations where you live on your nerves and must reply on the instant, as hesitation will be fatal; where you can't even stop to consider what you're saying. This is the skill or strategy of language use, rather than the system.

There may be loose rules for dialogue, just as there are for gift-giving. The forms of behaviour known as *etiquette* are cases in point. Etiquette demands that one doesn't interrupt a speaker, for example. In fact, of course, interruption is something we all do very frequently. Interruption is a way of asserting domination: we interrupt those we dominate more than we interrupt those who dominate us. On the whole, men interrupt women more frequently than women interrupt men. This 'rule' about non-interruption, then, is not a directive which must be followed, and neither is it a condition for the utterance to make sense. It is more like a set of available options than a set of prescriptions about how things have to be done. Even in a literal game, with strict rules, the skill in playing is often to use the rules with the utmost flexibility, right at the very limits of legality. This is the way John McEnroe used to play tennis, or the way 1970s champion Bobby Fisher famously played chess: completely within the legal rules of the game, but employing all sorts of tactics to unnerve and disturb opponents.

Improvisation and negotiation

The examples we've been looking at (dialogue, gift, game) suggest that systematicity is simply one of the aspects available to a very flexible and only partially codified *situational play* of strategies. Of necessity, these are largely improvised, according to changes in the situation and with whatever comes to hand, whether or not it was originally intended to serve that purpose. Such improvisation is often known as **bricolage**, a term first used in anthropology.

The textures of day-to-day life are full of – indeed, almost characterised by – this sort of improvisation, which takes social givens and deflects them towards other ends, investing them with other meanings. These may be spur-of-the-moment reactions to a temporary situation: an office marker temporarily disguises the run in black tights, an egg seals a leaking radiator until the next garage, a piece of a paperclip fastens the earpiece back onto a pair of glasses. Other improvisations may become part of the semi-permanent practices of some groups, first of all on the fringes of received practice, and then either becoming absorbed into, or forcing a rupture with, the official version. Trodden pathways between buildings show where their inhabitants and users habitually decline to take the designated footpaths; walls become unofficial supports for advertising, or for personal messages, or the grafitti'd assertion of a name; shopping centres at weekends become skateboard ramps. Others may be one-offs: improvisation is addressing an envelope to Elvis Presley, Gracelands, Memphis, Tennessee, mailing it with one of the US Mail's Elvis Presley issue stamps, and getting it back again marked 'Return to Sender'.

The feel for the game

Thus semiotic events are not automatic products of the rules of a system. You can be perfectly fluent in the rules of grammar, and still be tongue-tied when called on to give a speech or to begin a letter. In all systems, there is a more or less wide margin of indeterminacy. The system will give you the rules, but will not tell you everything about how these rules can be used.

On the other hand, though, it is important to emphasise that strategy is not simply a matter of individual choice, as though all possible options were available to the user, who has only to choose freely amongst them. We have argued from the outset that sign processes are primarily social. Chapter 8 in particular investigated the ways in which the various functions of address work ideologically to offer individuals roles within social processes. Not all possibilities may present themselves equally to all individuals. In general,

Figure 9.4 On the fridge

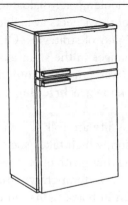

The primary purpose of the domestic refrigerator is, of course, to keep things cold. Advertisements for fridges rarely mention any other use for them. but cooling is far from their only function, as a glance at one in use readily shows. The refrigerator is a focal point of the kitchen, and the household.

The top of a refrigerator nearly always comes to serve as a shelf. For reasons of efficient management, hygiene or safety, most kitchens will have well-designed storage areas. Utensils will be put in one set of cupboard shelves, foodstuffs in others, cleaning goods in another. But because the area on top of the fridge is *not really* a storage area as such, it can serve as a miscellaneous catchment for things which don't have any other easily assignable place, in the kitchen or elsewhere. This surface is often a meter and a half or more above the ground, so it also serves as the ideal place for items which need to be kept out of the reach of children or household pets or insects.

But it's the white enamelled vertical surfaces of the refrigerator which most clearly show improvisation at work. Like a caddis-fly larva, a fridge gradually covers most of its visible surface with bits and pieces gathered from its environment: notes, magnets, advertising, information, decoration. The refrigerator becomes a clearing-centre for household information, both transient (shopping lists, notes from one household member to another) and durable (emergency telephone numbers and procedures). It is a place for filtering information which comes from outside the household: local businesses, tradespeople, power utilities and political parties all offer magnetic fridge advertising, but not all of it ends up on the fridge. It is a sort of semi-public scrapbook of personal bric-à-brac, open to and even inviting the visitor's gaze. Because of its non-designated status, visitors who would see scrutinising a host's noticeboard as intrusive will happily pore over their fridge door. Refrigerators may display personal or family mementos: cards, photographs, concert or theatre tickets, school photos, or children's drawings (that the refrigerator is such an open display may make it a symbolic reward for the child). Brightly coloured magnets even mean that the refrigerator door can be a temporary child-minder under the supervision of a parent preparing food. For the very young, it may be a walking aid. And of course, the fridge is always one of the focal points at parties.

On top:
Radio; 1/2 loaf of sliced bread; odd-shaped bottle (empty); part of fridge door handle (broken); plastic ice-cream container with small number of sweets inside; ice-cream container with a candlestick, a jar of thumbtacks, a plastic bag of magnetic letters and numbers, and the handle to a broken saucepan lid (not yet claimed on the guarantee); ice-cream container holding three containers of Play-Doh; plastic tray containing: a plastic bag of party goods (cake candles and decorations, part blowers, toothpicks); 2 packets of sparklers; Blu-Tack; jar with cake candles; 2 children's whistles, on cords; bottle-opener; 8 household candles; flower seeds; bulldog clips; lighter; 4 children's paintbrushes; more cake candles (numerals and sparkling tapers); herb slicer; picnic salt and pepper shakers; pie crust support; pastry stamp; aspirin; kitchen knife (believed lost); 5 plastic cordial bottle tops; 2 crayons; toy bottle-brush; reusable plastic iceblock sticks; mixer attachment; whistle from disused kitchen kettle; marble; 4 sweets; 2 plastic coffee measures; clothespeg; string; 2 plastic drinking straws; 2 egg rings.

Left-hand side:
Magnetic cards from local pharmacist, milk vendor, 2 plumbers, bank, ice-cream vendor, hamburger chain; takeaway menus from local pizza and seafood places; memo board with black felt pen on string; 2 school photographs; 8 non-advertising magnets (letters, numerals, animals, etc.).

Front:
Magnetic cards from gas utility, ice-cream vendor (again), hamburger chain (again) and local seafood takeaway; magnetic calendar from local Lebanese takeaway; magnetic frame with photograph of children in bath; 3 drawings by children; price list for school tuckshop; sticker from cereal packet (non-removable); 16 non-advertising magnets.

the options available in a given case are strongly linked to individuals' positions within a complex social structure, according to factors such as class, race, ethnicity, culture, gender, sexuality, age and language.

Take the case of applying for a job. Most jobs will require a formal written application, such as the one in Figure 1.1. First, before we examine the complex and sophisticated part strategy plays in such a letter, consider the main code system required by a written application. In nearly every case, it is understood that a job application is to be written in formal Standard English. The applicant's competence in using this particular form of English may assume immense importance, as it will very often be treated as an index to many other things: skills in language and communicating in general, even powers of reasoning, intellectual abilities or social skills. Obviously, in such a case an applicant who is unfamiliar with Standard English is at a disadvantage, no matter what their skills might be in other forms of English, or in abstract reasoning, management or financial affairs.

In practice, the situation is likely to be a lot more complex than a simple distinction between those who have access to a *code* and those who do not. What is going to be crucial in our job application is not just a knowledge of grammar, but something else which often gets referred to in terms such as *fluency of expression*, *stylishness* or (though it may appear to be a contradiction) *naturalness*, all of which, as we have suggested, may well be attributed metonymically to the addresser as much as to the letter. This 'something else' is considerably less easily codified than grammar and syntax, but may nevertheless provide a vital touchstone in judging both letter and addresser. It corresponds to what we earlier called a 'feel for the game', and is a matter not just of access to a code but of the way in which one *inhabits* the forms of behaviour associated with the code.

Consider the functions of address, and the subtle juggling act they require. As applicant, you may have to paint yourself as knowledgeable, but certainly not as a know-all; as respectful, but not deferential; as forceful, but not pushy; as independent and individual, but a team worker rather than a lone wolf; and so on, and so on. Optimally, you have to demonstrate that the qualities demanded by the position are not only yours, but yours by nature: that they are unlearned and unstrained natural expressions – in short, everything covered by the concept of *talent*. That is, what you have to show is that the qualities which are phatically those of the group you wish to enter are *already* yours, not by learning but by endowment. The form the letter requires is not *I can do it*, but *I have a gift for it*.

Now because these qualities tend to be represented metonymically by your 'feel for' the Standard English of the application, you will tend to be at an advantage the closer your habitual English use – the one in which you were brought up – is to Standard English. And as Standard English is an educated middle-class usage, this translates into a tendency for the procedures of the written application to favour members of the middle classes. They are the ones who tend to be the most *at home* in Standard English, for the simple reason that their English defines the standard. Written applications are nearly always required for jobs which lead to a career trajectory (promotion, salary increases, etc.), and hence to an upward social or class trajectory. What this amounts to is a sort of **gate-keeping**: the very procedures by which one can get a job associated with a certain class position tend to favour those who are already there.

It is important to remember that these links are not rigid, but matters of tendencies and probabilities. The point is not that *only* people from the middle classes get middle-class jobs; this would obviously be untrue. Individual counter-examples are easy to find. Indeed, they are often freely offered as mythic 'proof' that Western capitalist societies are genuinely free and without class. What we are talking about here is not the possibility of an individual experience so much as a distinct tendency across a group, a pattern which may show up clearly only through statistical analysis of a large number of individual cases. Neither are these links necessarily the results of conscious decisions to include or exclude. Deliberate decisions may of course be involved, but all that's necessary in the case of the job application may be a desire to find 'the best for the job', the applicant who has the best 'feel for the game'.

Habitus and disposition

The French sociologist Pierre Bourdieu uses the term **habitus** to describe the ways in which this feel for the game comes about in its various forms. The term suggests *habit*: habitus refers to the everyday, the situations, actions, procedures, demands and practices which go along with a certain walk of life and the ways in which an individual is positioned within the social world (gender, class, race, etc.). It is a form of the *embodiment* we saw in Chapter 7. The habitus in which you go about your daily affairs means that you acquire a certain set of **dispositions**. You tend to do some things rather than others – and, what's more, to do these things in certain ways rather than in others.

On the one hand, these dispositions are not so much consciously learnt as acquired through practice. They are the ways of doing things which your social environment presents to you as natural or obvious, ready at hand, commonsensical. But then on the other hand, neither are dispositions unconscious systems of rules. They're much looser, altogether less binding and more flexible than rules. Rather than proscribe what can or can't be done, they actively offer goals and means. In terms of our previous tennis analogy, habitus is like a regime of regular play, training and practice. The dispositions this inculcates are the trained speed and strategic abilities which, through immersion in the habitus, have become the second nature of the expert player.

A **habitus** is a lived network of objective social relationships and situations. Its effect is to produce agents with *dispositions* to certain practices rather than others.
Dispositions are the habituated practices or 'second nature' one gains through habitus.

Individuals make choices according to their habitus, but they do not choose the habitus. It is the product of their individual history, and depends on factors such as the place, society, class or cultural group they find themselves part of: their education, work, socio-economic status and social trajectory. Individuals belonging to the same group will largely share the same habitus, but there will always be all sorts of secondary differences among them: it is hardly possible, after all, for all members of even the most closely-knit group to have identical histories.

Habitus *disposes* individuals to make certain choices. Rather than choose practices (as free individuals) or get impelled into them (as determined), agents *fall into* practices which present themselves as the obvious and reasonable choices offered by their environment. Habitus can certainly be overridden by other considerations such as rational calculation. An individual may well realise that the way in which she is disposed to act in a certain situation may not be the best response to it. Habitus may even conceivably inculcate conflicting dispositions. In any case, what it produces is a tendency rather than a necessity: the likelihood that, *overall*, individuals sharing a habitus will react in similar ways to the same situation.

What habitus inculcates as disposition is experienced as a *sense of place*, both one's own and others'. Habitus is at work in *judgements*: 'That's not for me', 'I suppose that's the way some people choose to live', 'Give me a good honest feed any day', 'It's a real yuppie pub', 'A nice outfit, but not my style', 'You feel at home right away in this neighbourhood', 'The shop assistants seem to check you out to decide whether they're going to serve you'. Habitus is *phatic*: it makes distinctions which are constantly negotiating who is and isn't part of a given group, between who is and isn't being addressed. And as we shall see shortly, one of the most significant social arenas for this phatic contestation is *taste*.

In summary, the concept of habitus would seem to have four considerable benefits for our investigations here:

1 It lets us think not only of some of the ways in which the individual is positioned within the social, but also of the ways in which the social is already present in the individual.
2 It lets us think of these relationships between individual and social in terms of behaviours, actions, processes, and available options, rather than beliefs and ideas. One acts the way one does not primarily because one holds certain beliefs, but because certain things appear obvious, second-nature.
3 Habitus does not postulate individuals as totally free, makers of their own fates, or independent of the social world in which they exist. It is a way of thinking of the ways in which the individual is always consti-tuted by and in this social world. On the other hand, habitus does not see individuals as wholly determined by the social, powerless against forces which are forever beyond them. It gets round that rather classi-cal opposition of free will and determinism.
4 Habitus is inherently under-determining. It asks us to think of social relations as dynamic processes which are always necessarily somewhat open-ended. They are never simply resolved once and for all, but always have to be renegotiated, actively sustained, reconsidered. And it asks us to think of the individuals who act out these relations as social agents within a social world they are potentially capable of changing.

Forms of capital

In its economic sense, capital refers to what circulates in the process of economic production. When something is produced, capital is that part of the product which will be ploughed back into the cycle to ensure further production. A factory is a form of capital: it is something which is made, and which in turn is used to make other things. The raw materials it uses are another form of capital, as is the money which maintains this stock, though both of these tend to have a much shorter cycle of turnover than the factory which utilises them. Capital comes from production and goes towards feeding more production: in short, *capital reproduces production*.

Capital is a social product used in social production.

Bourdieu suggests extending this idea of capital to a number of other aspects of the social. All of them can be seen as social products which are put in circulation and are themselves used to produce further capital. As well as the familiar **economic capital** we have just been describing, there are several other types. We shall consider only three: *educational capital*, *cultural capital* and *symbolic capital*.

- **Educational capital**, of course, is what you gain through schooling. The amount depends on factors such as the length of your education, your course of study, the qualifications you receive, and the prestige of the institutions you attended. Educational capital gets exchanged for other forms of capital, particularly economic: well-paid jobs often require quite specific educational capital.

- Where economic capital is concerned mainly with products of the economy (that is, goods and money), **cultural capital** involves the circulation of cultural products and the consequent reproduction of cultural relations. It lies to varying degrees in activities such as concert- or museum- or movie-going; in a knowledge of television or movies, or even more so, film directors; in collecting (from Meissen china to the Pokemon and Dragonball Z cards which are a passion in the school-yard); in a taste for wines (or beers); in house decoration; in choice of reading matter, or style of coffee. Cultural capital may come from the possession of certain cultural artifacts, such as paintings, *objets d'art* or books. Actual physical possession, however, is not really the point. More importantly, cultural capital comes from *having access to the codes* of such artifacts: knowing how they work, what they do, what to say about them, how to appreciate, value and evaluate them: in short, how to consume them as cultural signs. To grow up in a habitus which inculcates these abilities and practical knowledges may clearly be a considerable advantage. In effect, cultural capital can be accumulated and passed on from generation to generation, just as the familiar economic capital may be.

- Cultural capital is a type of **symbolic capital**, which is a *capital of signs*. All forms of social behaviour have the potential to operate as signs of their addresser's position in social space. To wear a Rolex is a sign meaning 'large income'. To prefer beer to wine is a sign that may say 'working-class'. To prefer a small Thai restaurant to the local Pizza Hut may be read as 'yuppie'.

    Signs like the Rolex or different kinds of coffee do not necessarily provide anything like an accurate representation of social position. This is not their main function. As we know, signs are capable of producing a variety of meanings in a variety of contexts and codes, and this mobility means that symbolic capital can even be largely independent of other forms. A Rolex is a very expensive piece of equipment, and I may buy one to signify my wealth. On the other hand, though, a Rolex will still

Figure 9.5 Coffees of distinction

Coffee

BEANS
Brazil Royal
Supremo Blend
Pure Nicaraguan
Pure Guatemalan
Kenya Mocha Blend
Arabia Mocha
Golden Royal
Santos Blend
Light Turkish Blend
Dark Turkish Blend

DRINKS
Cappuccino
Flat White
Caffe Latte
Macchiato
(long/short)
Gourmet Flavoured
Coffee
Vienna Coffee
Espresso

There are two main ways in which coffee comes ready to prepare: beans (or grounds) and instant. Instant is the undistinguished one of the pair; quick, functional and without ceremony, it's what you make at home or at work when you need a fix of caffeine, or just a break. Ground bean coffee is the one around which elaborate processes of distinction arise. First there are all the various beans available (distinguished by variety and country of origin), the various types of roast to which they've been subjected, and even the additives (such as hazelnut). Then there are the methods of use, each of which requires its own regime of assembly, preparation and cleaning: pot, bag, infusor, percolator, filter, cafetière plunger, and most highly valued of all, espresso. After that, there are the ways of presenting the finished product, each with its own conventions: short black, in a small cup; long black, in a large cup; *cafe latte*, made on milk and served in a glass; and of course, *cappuccino*, coffee with steam-frothed milk, lightly sprinkled with cocoa and served in a wide shallow cup. The ability to negotiate such distinctions determines in part the effective status a coffee bar can claim. Indeed, when some coffee bars may offer the customer some 20 or so choices, status is clearly tied to an ability of *produce* distinctions.

These distinctions may be small or large, but they must in principle be clear and discernible, even if the ability to discern them does require a certain apprenticeship. On the one hand, there is the ostentation of the classical commercial espresso machine, elaborate, expensive and functioning as a very public sign of the establishment's own distinction. The espresso machine foregoes the modesty of most catering equipment, which is designed to be used unseen and unheard by the customer. It sits where it can hardly be missed, on the bar between customer and proprietor, often close to the entrance and in clear view from the street, visible (and audible) from most of the establishment, an often bulky conglomerate of fairing, tubes and duco dreaming of a 1950s Plymouth. On the other hand, there are the smaller distinctions which mark out the cognoscenti. The *macchiato* is a black coffee 'stained' (as the name implies) with the merest hint of milk. This 'staining' can serve as a figure for the distinctions which practices of taste introduce: the practice which best lends itself to distinction is the small, subtle, crucial variation.

signify 'wealth' whether I'm wealthy or not. If I'm not wealthy, I may even be able to achieve some of the effects of wealth in my dealings with others if I wear a Rolex (or better still, a cheap Rolex clone, as long as it's indistinguishable from the real thing). The sign of the thing may be just as effective as the thing itself. Far from being simply an obedient (or even misleading) representation of social position, the symbolic capital of the sign is a strategy for *negotiating* position.

That signs should lend themselves to a type of capital is hardly surprising. The system of *langue* is basically an economic model, after all: meaning is something which arises in the exchanges among signs. Bourdieu argues that economic capital is only one among many possible types. It is not even the most basic type: anthropology shows that there are societies where other forms of exchange, such as honour or the gift, are of paramount importance. But it is certainly the type that dominates today, given the dominance of western industrialised societies. In some ways, Bourdieu's conclusion is opposite to Saussure's: where Saussure suggests that semiotics is based on an economic model, Bourdieu sees symbolic capital as the grounds of possibility of all economies.

There is something quite arbitrary about symbolic capital: about *what* can be accumulated, the *type* of symbolic capital it is to function as, and its relative *value* as capital. It is far from obvious that it is intrinsically, naturally, logically or in some other way necessarily more worthy or praiseworthy to have a taste for late Beethoven quartets over country-and-western music, wine over beer, live theatre over movie-going, or Ermenegildo Zegna over Woolworths. Nevertheless, all of us have quite definite opinions and preferences on such matters; no doubt most of us have, at one time or another, even got quite heated about some of them. What is valuable cultural capital in one group is not necessarily worth much in another, once those practices are removed from the habitus which gives them value. Various forms of cultural capital compete to assert their own value, and thus the positions of those who hold them. The forms which tend to be most effective in this struggle are those which belong to the most powerful groups. These present themselves not as arbitrary capital, but as *legitimate culture*. They are the ones which then define all others in their terms (which is to say that they generally find all others lacking). To the extent that capital is arbitrary, it is defined in terms of the values of dominant groups, who thus impose both the constitution and legitimacy of capital.

Like economic capital, all of these various types of capital stand to be ploughed back into circulation to produce further capital, either of another or the same kind. The Rolex watch is not just an expenditure, but an investment in another sort of capital. When a bank sponsors a theatre season or a new wing on a gallery, economic capital is invested in symbolic capital in order to gain social or cultural capital, such as prestige. Under certain conditions this, too, may in turn be exchangeable back into economic capital, with interest. My Rolex helps me impress a client as being a corporate high-flier, with the result that I clinch a large deal for the company and get a promotion (which more than pays for the fake Rolex, and lets me think of getting a real one). In choosing to take up an opportunity to go to university, you forego several years' accumulation of economic capital in favour of a variable mixture of educational and cultural capital, according to the course of study. Gaining entry to one of the professions on graduation, you exchange educational for economic and social capital.

There are thus effective *exchange rates* among the various forms of capital. Some of these are relatively fixed. To become a medical doctor, for example, requires a certain amount of educational capital (a medical degree from an accredited institution), and there are legal and professional policings on the consistency of this exchange. Many exchange rates, though, are much more fluid: there's nothing like a standard rate of exchange between the symbolic capital of a Rolex and the economic capital of salary and promotions. Exchanges may be open to group or individual negotiations: one of the functions of unions is, after all, to negotiate between certain forms of capital.

Social space

This concept of capital lets us envisage the ways in which individuals and groups are distributed throughout what we can call *social space*. We can picture their positions in this social space as being characterised not only by the overall amount of capital they possess, but by the way that capital breaks down into various types. Individuals may possess more of one type of capital than another. An unemployed university graduate has a high educational capital she is at present unable to exchange at favourable rates for economic capital. A writer may earn as much as a tradesperson, let's say, but may have a considerably higher cultural capital, depending on the type of writing; on the other hand, writers like Stephen King and Barbara Taylor Bradford are financially highly successful and immensely popular but write mainly in genres with relatively low cultural capital (the horror story, the romantic family saga). (This is neither to judge Bradford or King as inferior authors nor to champion them for their democratic popularity; it is just to locate where they lie.)

This social space, then, compromises a series of *positions* according to volume and types of capital. It is not hard to see that each of these positions corresponds to a habitus, each producing various *dispositions*. Positions which are close together in this social space will tend to share a habitus, and the more so the closer they are. As we suggested earlier, these positions are in constant struggle and negotiation with each other, both for capital and for the relative values of the types of capital each possesses. That is, this social space is also made up of a dynamic, unstable and ever-changing series of *oppositions*.

Strategies of taste

As we have suggested, the dominant form of capital tends to be economic. High stocks of economic capital are generally worth more than high stocks of any other sort; economic capital can be more readily exchanged for other sorts than they can for it, and at more favourable rates. In short, in Western societies *power* is generally more closely bound to economic capital than any other sort.

Nevertheless, other sorts of capital can and do contest this dominance. Cultural capital in particular is the occasion for a number of highly visible and significant strategies, focusing on issues of *taste*. These work by and as **distinction**, in both of the main senses of the word:

- they *make* distinctions among things and practices, and
- they *endow* those who practice them with distinction.

Making distinctions is, of course, precisely what the sign does. A sign functions as a sign first of all because it can distinguish itself from all the other signs and things around it. In being a sign, it also produces a phatic group of addresser and addressee, and distinguishes various degrees of belonging. Because the sign is relatively independent of its referent, symbolic capital may be a way of contesting economic capital. This opens up the possibility of *symbolic struggles over representation*, where a group attempts to impose its representations and concepts of legitimacy. And again, this is a very real power of producing phatic groups, imposing social divisions, altering the objective structure of a society. Not surprisingly, Bourdieu calls this symbolic power 'the political power *par excellence*' .

Symbolic power can work in many ways, towards all sorts of ends, from a jockeying for prestige through taste, to the assertion of the rights of an oppressed group. It is *both* one of the regular mechanisms of social consumption *and* something which under the right circumstances may disrupt certain social relations. Advertising, of course, uses symbolic distinctions of taste as an indispensable strategy, producing distinctions which may be almost purely symbolic. Products sold under designer labels, for instance, may be rarely produced under the direct control of the designer whose signature they bear, and in many cases are not even designed by that person. Almost tautologically, the designer's signature may indicate only that the designer has given legal approval for the product to be marketed under that name. There may be multiple variations on a basic label, each with its own relative status: the Italian design company founded by Giorgio Armani markets a variety of Armani labels, each with its own distinctive retail outlets and clientele.

Advertising is far from the only arena of symbolic distinction, though it is of course an immensely important one. Elaborate distinctions are often made in the set of practices surrounding one single product. Wine is an obvious example: so is coffee (Figure 9.5).

Cultural capital tends to require a certain minimum of economic capital. You do need a certain freedom from economic necessity to buy books or go to the movies, even more to go to concerts, live theatre or the opera. Cultural capital is an investment of the economic capital left after you've paid the bills, and it functions as a sign of that economic freedom. Not surprisingly, accumulating it is for the most part a pursuit of those classes and class fractions which have a relatively large overall volume of capital. Nevertheless, because cultural capital is symbolic, it is partly autonomous of economic capital (remember the Rolex watch), and may thus lend itself to strategies for contesting the power and legitimacy of the more dominant economic capital.

Cultural capital tends to be used most effectively not by the most powerful groups, but by those just below them, the dominated fraction of the dominant class. **High culture** in its various forms is the cultural capital this fraction defines and seeks to impose as legitimate culture. In turn, a mastery of cultural capital distinguishes its practitioners from those with a smaller overall volume of capital, who have neither the economic freedom nor the disposition to practice culture in this way. Their cultural practices – **popular culture** – will now be seen by the practitioners of high culture in terms of a *lack* of taste.

Taste, then, attributes the effects of a set of social dispositions to personal, individual abilities. It thus provides powerful passwords, or **shibboleths**,[1] for determining who is and who is not part of a given social group. These criteria may present themselves as tests of the individual's innate ability to appreciate something universal ('quality'), but in fact the responses they evoke are products of social habitus.

---

[1] The word *shibboleth* is Hebrew. *Judges* xii, 1–6, tells how Jephthah and the Gileadites uncovered the Ephraimites in their midst by their enemies' inability to pronounce the word's *sh-* sound.

Figure 9.6 Shibboleths

In the village churchyard she lies,
Dust is in her beautiful eyes,
    No more she breathes, nor feels, nor stirs,
At her feet and at her head
Lies a slave to attend the dead,
    But their dust is as white as hers.

Was she a lady of high degree,
So much in love with the vanity
    And foolish pomp of this world of ours;
Or was it Christian charity,
And lowliness and humility,
    The richest and rarest of all dowers?

Who shall tell us? No one speaks;
No colour shoots into those cheeks,
    Either of anger or of pride,
At the rude question we have asked;
Nor will the mystery be unmasked
    By those who are sleeping at her side.

Hereafter? – And do you think to look
On the terrible pages of that Book
    To find her failings, faults and errors?
Ah, you will then have other cares,
In your own shortcomings and despairs,
    In your own secret sins and terrors!

In 1924, the Cambridge academic and literary critic I. A. Richards published under the title *Practical Criticism* the results of some experiments he had been performing with the members of his literature classes. He had presented his students with a sheet of paper bearing the text of a poem to which the student was asked to respond briefly in writing – a response Richards called a 'protocol'. The poem was left quite unidentified: no title, no poet's name, no period, and, perhaps most important of all, no indication of what Richards expected his students to feel about it. *Practical Criticism* summarises and analyses some of these protocols.

The poem reprinted above is one of those Richards used. Try it yourself, as an unseen text on which you have to comment. What is the exercise asking you to display?

At the end of the chapter, in Figure 9.8, you will find the poem identified, along with some of Richard's comments on what his students wrote.

Representation and interest

Habitus disposes individuals towards certain practices. As we have seen in the case of matters of taste, it also disposes them towards what we can call certain **representations** of these practices: perceptions, evaluations, appreciations and *knowledges* of them, particularly as they concern their own positions and those of others. These representations in turn tend to make the very features of the habitus appear as natural and commonsensical. The process is circular, and emphasises that representations are not only themselves practices, but practices which are essential to the *reproduction* of habitus.

Habitus is not coercion. As we have argued, it *offers* certain practices as self-evident and the obvious thing to do in a given situation, but it does not *force* these on the individual agents. There is always the possibility of taking up other options which are objectively present. We can say the same thing for the representations generated by habitus: representations may be contested. In fact, since representations play such a significant part in the reproduction of habitus, to contest a set of representations may be a way of altering that habitus and the objective social structures of which it is part.

Habitus disposes its agents towards certain representations, and these in turn tend to reproduce the habitus which gave rise to them, by making it appear self-evident. In other words, representation is always **interested**, to the extent that it is a product or a contestation of habitus. Again, we should take this *interest* as something which disposes agents to act in certain ways, rather than compelling them. Interest is what makes the reproduction of the original habitus somewhat more likely, the easiest path for events to fall into in the usual course of things. There may often be several conflicting interests at work in a single representation or practice. Here, one need only think of the changes the word 'black' has undergone over the last few decades as a term applied to race. Since the Civil Rights movements of the 1960s, it has gone from being a derogatory term (replaced in liberal North American usage for a long time by the more genteel 'negro') to a popular affirmation (James Brown's 'Say it loud, I'm black and I'm proud').

To say that a given representation is interested is not to say that it is untrue or a matter of false consciousness. Neither is it to say that it or its agents are consciously hypocritical or unconsciously complicit. In itself, the fact of a representation's interest says nothing about whether it is true or false. All representations are interested. Interest is not an option a discourse has, or something it slips into through a lack of vigilance; it is a necessary consequence of its positioning and the sorts of functions of address it is able to gather. Truth is not opposed to interest, but found across a variety of interests. To imagine truth as what is independent of all interests is to

Figure 9.7 The interest of knowledge

Internal and External Elements of a Language
> from Chapter V of the Introduction to *Ferdinand de Saussure, Course in General Linguistics,* trans. Roy Harris (London: Duckworth, 1983)

Our definition of a language assumes that we disregard everything which does not belong to its structure as a system; in short everything that is designated by the term 'external linguistics'. External linguistics is none the less concerned with important matters, and these demand attention when one approaches the study of languages.

First of all, there are all the respects in which linguistics links up with ethnology. There are all the relations which may exist between the history of a language and the history of a race or a civilisation. The two histories intermingle and are related one to another . . . A nation's way of life has an effect upon its language. At the same time, it is in great part the language which makes the nation.

Secondly, mention must be made of the relations between languages and political history. Major historical events such as the Roman Conquest are of incalculable linguistic importance in all kinds of ways. Colonisation, which is simply one form of conquest, transports a language into new environments, and this brings changes in the language . . . Advanced stages of civilisation favour the development of certain special languages (legal language, scientific terminology, etc.).

This brings us to a third point. A language has connexions with institutions of every sort: church, school, etc . . .

Finally, everything which relates to the geographical extension of languages and to their fragmentation into dialects concerns external linguistics . . .

It is sometimes claimed that it is absolutely impossible to separate all these questions from the study of language itself . . . In our opinion, the study of external linguistic phenomena can teach linguistics a great deal. But it is not true to say that without taking such phenomena into account we cannot come to terms with the internal structure of the language itself . . . In the case of certain languages, such as Zend and Old Slavonic, we do not even know exactly which peoples spoke them. But our ignorance in no way prevents us from studying their internal structure, or from understanding the developments they underwent. In any case, a separation of internal and external viewpoints is essential. The more rigorously it is observed, the better . . .

. . . In the case of chess, it is relatively easy to distinguish between what is external and what is internal. The fact that chess chess from Persia to Europe is an external fact, whereas everything which concerns the system and its rules is internal. If pieces made of ivory are substituted for pieces made of wood, the change makes no difference to the system. But if the number of pieces is diminished or increased, that is a change which profoundly affects the 'grammar' of the game. Care must none the less be taken when drawing distinctions of this kind. In each case, the question to be asked concerns the nature of the phenomenon. The question must be answered in accordance with the following rule. Everything is internal which alters the system in any degree whatsoever.

One of the things Saussure is doing here is launching a justification of a new discipline of study. He argues that there are aspects of language which have been ignored by all other disciplines, and which can be treated adequately only by the type of investigation he's advocating. Given that such investigations are usually done by highly trained professionals in specialised institutions – generally academics in universities – his argument is inescapably and at least in part an interested argument about careers and university budgets. What's more, it is one which does not provide any terms for talking about its own interests, as it has started by excluding social, historical and institutional factors from its object of study: though it happily admits their importance, they are the objects for *other* forms of study, not for linguistics. We cannot talk in Saussurean terms about the interests of the Saussurean system. Disinterest necessarily hides interests.

abstract from the actual situations in which we find it, which are always interested ones. The most objectively true of discourses have their own interests, without which they could scarcely exist, let alone be true. The sciences' guarantee of an objective truth is, after all, dependent upon a set of institutional, professional, financial and often political interests, which make possible its strictly controllable and relicable regimes of laboratory experimentation. *Interest*, we may say, *is the mode in which a discourse exists as practice*. It is also another version of the point we made very early in this book, and have been unfolding in its complexity ever since: *meaning is always contextual*.

EXERCISES

1 Newspapers frequently comment on grammar, spelling, punctuation and language uses, and in many ways. Columnists will often discuss it as a topic; many newspapers have a regular column devoted to language usage; educational features debate the quality of language education children receive today; and language is always a popular topic for letters to the editor.

  Gather some examples of these. What is being asserted in them, and by what means? Do some of these texts use a rhetoric of crisis? If so, how, and what does it do? Do these conflicts have bearing on class and class-fractional differences? If so, which, and how?

2 Discuss the application letter in Figure 1.1 in detail, in terms of habitus. What dispositions is it attempting to show, and in what fashion? How can the functions of address, and in particular the phatic, now be reworked in terms of habitus and disposition? Are there any advantages in this new

Figure 9.8 Richards' comments on the exercise and on his student's answers

As has been remarked before, a very wary eye is needed with any poetry that tends to implicate our stock responses. And this for two opposite reasons. If the easiest way to popularity is to exploit some stock response, some poem already existent, fully prepared, in the reader's mind, an appeal to such stock responses, should the reader happen to have discarded them, is a very certain way of courting failure. So that a poet who writes on what appears to be a familiar theme, in a way which, superficially, is only slightly unusual, runs a double risk. On the one hand, very many readers will not really read him at all. They will respond with the poem they suppose him to have written and then, if emancipated, recoil in horror to heap abuse on the poet's head. On the other hand, less emancipated readers, itching to release their own stock responses, may be pulled up by something in the poem which prevents them. The result will be more abuse for the hapless author.

Now to illustrate and justify these reflections. Here is a writer who finds only a stock experience in the poem. He is only mildly disappointed however:

13.1 This one seems to me a successful communication of an experience whose value is dubious, or which at most is valuable only on a small scale. Plainly, I think, the communication succeeds by reason of its medium; simple, straightforward, almost bald language, making no demand on any peculiar individual characteristic which might be a bar to general appreciation, as in the poetry of Blake, for instance. The reasons for my judgement of the experience-value are harder to formulate. I think one may be that *the experience does not go very much further than it would in the case of an 'ordinary man' who was not a poet*, so that its very *raison d'être* is a questionable quantity. It does, in fact, seem to me rather trite.

. . . It was very generally assumed that since the subject of the poem is solemn the treatment must be solemn too, and many readers made it as solemn as they could. Not unnaturally their results often displeased them.

13.8 *If the poem tends to check the reader from making speculations on other peoples lives then it has some value.* The poem however does not seem to do this, but *rather stimulates than quiets a man's interest in the private deeds of other people . . . *. This form of stimulation to the mind *can do it no good and may do it harm.* The poem is therefore bad.

This seems perfectly to express a possible way of reading the poem. A reading whose solemnity fully merits all the adjectives that other readers found to fling against it. Sanctimonious, didactic, pompous, portentous, priggish, seem, indeed, if the poem is looked at in this light, hardly too strong. Only one reader attempted to state the issue between this view of the poem and another view by which it would escape these charges. And he so over-states his case that he discredits it.

13.9 I am in two moods as to the intention of this poem. If the mood in which it is written is serious, *if we are meant to take the situation in profound meditation closing in self-abasing remorse,* then the whole thing is clearly vicious and preposterous. The idea of an eternity spent in turning up the files of other people's sins or crouching or cry *peccavi* for our own is *either amusing or disgusting or both.* But if the last three lines are a sudden impish whirl on the complacent moral speculation of the first three stanzas the whole is *a very delightful little whimsy . . .*

. . . If this interpretation of the poem is right, 'rude' ('the rude question we have asked', stanza 4) is simply an acknowledgement of the social convention, not in the least a rebuke . . . The word belongs to the texture of the poet's meditation and is not aimed at anyone, not even at the poet himself. It is the admission of a fact, not an attack upon anyone, or anything.

On this theory . . . the last verse would be in the same tone. Not a grim warning, or an exhortation, but a cheerful realisation of the situation, not in the least evangelical, not at all like a conventional sermon, but on the contrary extremely urbane, rather witty, and *slightly* whimsical . . . [In this reading] the poem becomes a very unusual kind of thing that it would be a pity to miss. That so few read it in this way is not surprising, for if there is any character in poetry that modern readers . . . are unprepared to encounter, it is this social, urbane, highly cultivated, self-confident, temperate and easy kind of humour.

The unseen poem is 'In the Churchyard at Cambridge', by Henry Wadsworth Longfellow (1807–82), who is best known for 'The Song of Hiawatha'. It was by far the least popular of the poems Richards presented, disliked by over 90 per cent of his students.

As these extracts show, while Richards phrases his project in terms of psychology and the abilities of more or less finely tuned individual minds, what he is discerning here can also accurately be described in terms of habitus: a dispositional, class response to poetry in particular and high culture in general. Richards's investigations helped provide a way of *testing* the student's response to literature. In showing that something as seemingly personal as this could be assessed, they helped establish 'English' as the central subject of the humanities curriculum.

conceptual apparatus? That is, does it reveal something more than the earlier model did? If so, what?

3 In what senses could we talk about *knowledge* as a form of capital? Given the boom in information technologies over the last two decades, to what extent is it possible to talk about *information* as a form of capital? Do they differ? If so, how? What relationships would both of these proposed forms of capital have with other forms of capital? What relationships would both of them have with educational capital in particular? Keeping in mind our arguments about habitus and the inculcation of dispositions, is educational capital simply a variety of the capital of knowledge? What other qualities or processes might it be useful to think of in terms of capital, and why?

4 Try I. A. Richards' 'protocol' exercise from Figure 9.6. Compare your comments with those Richards cites, a selection of which you'll find in Figure 9.8. (This is an exercise which works well in class. Do you find that on the whole the responses of your class differ from those of Richards' groups? If so, how? What does this imply, in terms of habitus? What aspects of habitus are being highlighted in Richards' comments?)

5 The very enterprise of knowledge, even of the most objective sort, has its own interests, which are minimally those of the groups who produce the knowledge. This is clearly so in the sciences and technologies, with their reliance on access to equipment, laboratories, funding, etc., but it is also no less the case in the humanities. Example 9.7 gives a sample of a text we have mentioned since the early chapters of this book, Saussure's *Course in General Linguistics*. How does it include within it a discourse on its own interests? So what about this book, *Introduction to Cultural and Media Studies*?

SOURCES AND FURTHER READING

The concepts of *capital*, *disposition* and *habitus* all come from the work of the sociologist Pierre Bourdieu. Bourdieu's work is voluminous and wide-ranging; he has written on areas such as North African and French marriage practices, taste, the French education system, literary biography, philosophy, museum-going, universities, popular culture and photography, and much of it engages in a running polemic with structuralism and academic philosophy. Bourdieu offers some initial difficulties for beginning readers; in an attempt to mirror the complexities of relationships in the material he is examining, his writing is often elaborate and demanding. One of the best and most highly approachable introductions to his work is the essays and interviews collected in *In Other Words: Essays Towards a Reflexive Sociology* (Cambridge: Polity Press, 1990). The interview 'From rules to strategies' and the essay on 'Codification' are of particular interest to the discussion in this chapter. On the strategies of taste, the massive *Distinction: A Social Critique of the Judgement of Taste* (Cambridge, MA: Harvard University Press, 1984) is almost a standard work. For an overview of Bourdieu's work, see Richard Harker, Cheleen Mahar and Chris Wilkes (eds), *An Introduction to the Work of Pierre Bourdieu: The Practice of Theory* (London: Macmillan – now Palgrave, 1990) and Richard Jenkins, *Pierre Bourdieu* (London: Routledge, 1992). You can also consult the WWW site Links to Sites Related to Pierre Bourdieu (www.utu.fi/erill/RUSE/blink.html).

Deyan Sudjic's *Cult Heroes: How to be Famous for More Than Fifteen Minutes* (New York: Norton, 1990) is mostly anecdotal rather than analytic, and it's about the designer signature and its effects rather than cult heroes, but it does have some fascinating material. Another recent study of how people work with popular cultural trends is Angela McRobbie's *In the Culture Society: Art, Fashion and Popular Music* (London: Routledge, 1999). On the ways in which people improvise and negotiate daily practices and activities within various social settings, see Michel de Certeau's *The Practice of Everyday Life* (Berkeley: University of California Press, 1984).

The term *bricolage* comes from Claude Lévi-Strauss, *The Savage Mind* (London: Weidenfeld & Nicholson, 1966). The tennis metaphor used to analyse cultural practices owes a lot to Anne Freadman's discussions of genre: see her 'Untitled: (On Genre)', *Cultural Studies*, 2(1) (1988), and Freadman and Amanda Macdonald's *What is This Thing Called 'Genre'?* (Mt Nebo, Queensland: Boombana, 1992). Finally, the extracts in Examples 9.6 and 9.8 are all from I.A.Richards' *Practical Criticism* (London: Routledge & Kegan Paul, 1964), pp. 162–4, 174–6.

Cultural studies

Other approaches, other contexts

CONTENTS

We suggested in the Introduction that the semiotic approach with which we began was far from the only approach to cultural studies. In fact, since that point we have moved a considerable distance from semiotics, as we came across issues which demanded other considerations, other types of investigation. In this final chapter, we will briefly survey some further ways of doing cultural studies.

Audience studies

As we have seen in Chapter 9, semiotic analysis may unravel the ways in which texts construct addresser and addressee positions, but it has little to say about what actual receivers do with these. One of the ways cultural studies has reacted to this has been to switch attention from analysis of texts to a study of the way actual audiences behave when they watch or read media texts. Focusing mainly on television, this research has adopted an ethnographic approach, borrowed from anthropology. **Ethnography** is a form of field research in which the researcher attempts to understand a culture by becoming part of it. Ethnographers classically try to live the lives of the subjects they study, taking extensive notes (written or tape recorded) at the same time.

Audience studies are somewhat more limited in their procedures than this. In the 1980s, David Morley and a team of researchers in Britain spent some weeks living in a number of households, watching television with family members. His book *Family Television* contains the results of this research.

Morley's work demonstrates that there is a vast difference between the ideal reader proposed in structuralist models, and the ways actual audience members behave in everyday life. He was able to show that audiences are not simply passive subjects, duped by television discourse into responding in a predictable manner. Rather, audiences use television texts for a range of purposes within domestic and other everyday contexts. For instance, the patriarchal organisation of family life means that husbands and fathers tend to override female members of the family audience when it comes to programme choice. Morley's work indicates that males and females give markedly different accounts of their viewing experience, suggesting that audiences are not homogeneous groups, but are made up of different kinds of subjectivities based on gender and other culturally defined values.

Ethnographic work in audience studies is not without its problems. The idea that researchers can become one with the audiences under study raises methodological and theoretical issues concerning speaking positions. Precisely who speaks for whom in ethnography? Does audience research really speak on behalf of the subjects it analyses, or does it reproduce its own values which it sees reflected in the context of research?

This problem is overcome to a degree with a shift from ethnography to **ethnomethodology.** In audience studies based on ethnomethodology, the focus is on explanations constructed by the participants themselves. Ethnomethodological fieldwork on audiences tends to be more modest in its requirements: group discussions rather than extensive 'live in' researcher–subject interactions are generally sufficient to display the participants' own theories and methods of audienceship (ethnomethods).

The research task is to show how this self-analysis by group participants can be read as a text involving strategies of, and against, power and domination, much like cultural studies' own analyses of the discourses and institutions of the media and other cultural forms. This work can be combined with data concerning educational, occupational and other social factors which determine many of the values which come into play when members account for their audienceship to each other.

This qualitative research, in both its ethnographic and ethnomethodological modes, leads to a different notion of audience from the one which has prevailed in more traditional social science and communication disciplines. Nonetheless it's worth discussing this traditional strand of **empiricist** audience study in some detail, because of its enormous influence over media and academic research in the past.

In these studies, mainly based on empirical data collection (surveys, interviews), audiences have been understood in terms of a massed group of individuals (hence the terms *mass media, mass communication,* etc.). The aim of this work has been to locate consistent values and trends which can then determine the character of a *typical* audience member. Such research has been used extensively in the media industry itself in an attempt to define, and hence gain control over, its audiences. In *Desperately Seeking the Audience*, Ien Ang has shown that the institutional practices of television audience measurement are not neutral and objective, but motivated by industry interests. The methodology of data collection for ratings measurement is based on an ideal notion of audience which anticipates and predetermines audience response.

Quantitative research takes place under strictly controlled circumstances guided by scientific objectives; subjects arc selected for study with a view to making general claims about social and cultural values. As a result, selection cannot be on a purely voluntary basis, because there is no guarantee that a group of volunteers will be representative of the society as a whole. Much care is needed to ensure that this kind of research is *repeatable*, as this is the prime confirmation of its objectivity. Another way of ensuring objectivity is through *triangulation*: different methods of data collection (e.g. surveys, interviews, discussions) are used in order to confirm results.

In cultural studies, quantitative audience research of this sort is not widely used. Though the two may seem a long way apart, this research has at least one crucial point in common with structuralism: both of them posit an abstract ideal reader, and thus tend to overlook the sheer diversity of actual audience behaviours.

Cultural studies' work on audiences attempts to focus on the actuality of audience behaviour. Poststructuralist notions of intertextuality, discourse, strategy and power are used to show how the 'reading' of television and other media texts is always contextual, framed by many other cultural values and institutional structures. The audience member is seen as an active participant in the reading process, able to adapt and exploit media discourse for socially defined purposes. The move here is away from the notion of audience as 'mass', with its implications of a homogeneous identity and uniform response, towards audience as part of a group or network, not necessarily defined by the social space in which the reading of media texts takes place.

Policy studies

What audiences do with television is one aspect of the wider questions of the politics of everyday life, on which we touched in Chapter 9. Through the strategic use of signs, people define, maintain and transform their cultural identities within social contexts. Research and analysis based on a critique of the politics of everyday life can expose the various signifying practices which maintain and resist structures of domination and subordination, making them available for scrutiny and possible change.

Nevertheless, this kind of critique has been questioned by many from within the ranks of cultural studies. The problem lies in whether critique on its own has the power to change the social structures which contribute to the formation of cultural identity. Critique, it has been argued, is purely an academic pursuit, isolated from the rest of society. It overlooks the importance of governmental and corporate policy in providing the social conditions necessary for cultural identity to exist in the first place. Accordingly, a school of research, policy studies, has emerged which looks for a direct connection between academic work and the policy-making procedures of government and corporate bodies. Drawing on the theoretical work of Max Weber, Michel Foucault, Norbert Elias and others, policy studies shows how the possibility of individual behaviour is always conditioned by the discourses in, and through which, individuals live their everyday life. Desire and pleasure, the hallmarks of individual self-expression, are always framed by a set of administrative procedures (either in a public sense or as a form of self monitoring), governed by institutional and social contexts.

As a consequence, policy studies works towards the development of an *ethics of citizenship*, in which the subjective, interior life of individuals is subordinate to, and conditioned by, the public arena in which individuals relate to one another as community members. This subject-as-citizen approach puts a new complexion on the study of cultural practices, because it indicates that they are subject to change in the administrative policies of the state and its corporate institutions. Academic research and argument can help bring about changes in cultural identity through direct input into policy formation at the governmental and corporate level. In this way, policy research becomes instrumentally related to the culture it seeks to define and transform.

In particular, policy studies have been active in the area of the media, becoming politically engaged with the policy-forming bodies which determine the institutional practices of media discourse. Issues such as television violence, local versus international content in television programming, and the introduction and accessibility of pay television (cable, satellite), for instance, have become topics of focused research, analysis and argument. From the perspective of policy studies, these issues need to be understood in terms of the complex interrelations between media institutions, governmental bodies and the public. Other areas to receive attention include the film industry, education, museums, community theatre and arts, and local government planning.

This form of direct intervention by the academy in outside bodies is motivated by a pragmatic desire to have a hand in the way social structures operate, leading to empowerment to change them. It argues that orthodox methods of critique, such as semiotic text analysis, are of limited use in altering the dominant ways in which cultural identity is formed.

There are, of course, risks involved in this approach. It has been argued that by surrendering critique, policy studies could very well become a compliant armature of government and corporate policy, supporting and entrenching the very practices it wishes to change. Furthermore, it has been objected that the social model promoted by policy studies privileges a bureaucratic concept in which cultural identity is entirely a matter of strict, 'top-down' institutional definition. From this point of view, policy studies seems to assume that people in everyday life accept the programmes of cultural practice instigated through policy implementation, which is to deny audiences and readers an active role in the reception of media discourse. By rejecting textual analysis, policy studies runs the danger of overlooking the ideological coding inscribed in media texts, thus neglecting the media institutions' discursive orientation to the larger socio-political contexts of which they are a part.

These objections suggest that policy studies has limits, and does not supplant work in other areas of cultural studies. In fact, policy-minded academics are increasingly striking a rapport with their counterparts in textual and critical analysis. Current work in cultural studies is moving towards integrated research projects, drawing upon policy, textual analysis and audience studies, aiming to develop a thorough account of cultural meaning and identity as socio-politically defined phenomena.

The postmodern

If work on audiences and policy has an air of cultural pragmatism, it is easy for the very idea of the postmodern to sound like science-fiction, with its suggestions that the day after tomorrow is somehow already here today. The term is somewhat difficult to pin down, and there is considerable argument about whether it's a useful, misleading or just empty term in cultural analysis. At the very least, however, it encompasses a number of divergent and even opposed arguments, the complexities of whose interrelations we certainly haven't the space to go into here. What we can do instead is focus on two broad clusters of ways in which the term is used, in each case as a figure of difference from a certain concept of the **modern**.

One way of taking those terms *modern* and *postmodern* is as **successive stages of capitalism**. For the Marxist geographer David Harvey (1989), the inaugural moment of capitalist modernity is Henry Ford's development of the production line for his car-assembly plant in 1913. Fordism had its boom years in the prosperity following the Second World War. But do its conditions still hold today? Harvey argues that the mode of capitalism has changed considerably since then, enough to result in a very different set of social relations.

Consider some of the events since the end of the Second World War in 1945. As the economies of Japan and Western Europe recovered, they began to lose their dependence on USA exports, and to increase the volume of goods they themselves exported. As a result, the US not only lost much of a significant market but found itself facing new competition. From the 1960s on, the Western labour market was gradually to be restructured as the impacts of movements such as feminism and, in the United States, civil rights made themselves felt. The rise of cheaper manufacturing industries in what had become known as the 'Third World' led to many multinational corporations establishing more profitable offshore operations, to take advantage of a cheaper non-unionised labour force. By the 1970s, the Arab–Israeli war and OPEC decisions on oil pricing had forced up energy costs for the Western nations. In 1973, a stockmarket slump heralded the biggest recession since the War, and the end of postwar buoyancy.

This spiral of increasing crisis, Harvey argues, required far more flexible (postmodern) means of accumulation and circulation of capital than (modern) Fordism could supply. An ever-increasing need for innovation now becomes paramount: new markets, products, financial services and technologies. New industries arise, particularly those connected with electronics, as an enormous expansion in information technologies has led to a situation where information itself can take on something of the status of a commodity. This in turn produces enormous changes in the ways in which knowledge is produced and circulated. There are tendencies towards a single world money market, a massive growth in private service sectors, and a corresponding diminution of the power of the state. Financial speculation is possible on a previously unheard-of scale; fortunes can be made independently of the cycle of production and consumption. Mergers and takeovers in all areas, coupled with pressures for deregulation (of media, labour relations, etc.), lead to situations such as the extraordinary present concentrations of media ownership. With high levels of structural unemployment, labour relations change; there are crises for the union movements, such as the moves towards individual labour contracts rather than awards.

The cultural effects of all this are, of course, immense. The need for innovation requires an induction of needs, through an acceleration of obsolescence and turnover time. This is in principle capable of affecting virtually all cultural commodities, from music to clothing, from film to cars, from novels to tastes in food. Out of this comes what Harvey calls the 'postmodernist aesthetic that celebrates difference, ephemerality, spectacle, fashion, and the commodification of cultural forms' (1989, p. 156).

Not everyone agrees with this analysis. Harvey and the economic regulationists on which he draws readily admit that if there is indeed a qualitative break from the modern to the postmodern, then that transition is as yet little understood and poses many problems. To begin with, it is not always easy to isolate which apparent shifts in attitudes and cultural practices are due to this particular aspect of change in the economic base, and to trace their detailed mechanisms. Furthermore, if it exists, such a break can hardly be universal and complete: many aspects of Fordist modernity would seem to survive happily and healthily into this postmodernity. Here, Harvey's schema can look just a bit too neatly dichotomous: he loves drawing up ledgers of the characteristic features of Fordist modernity versus those of flexible post-modernity.

In *The Postmodern Condition*, the philsopher Jean-François Lyotard (1984) sees modernity as a Western cultural phenomenon whose conceptual foundation is the Enlightenment faith in reason. Modernity is marked by a series of *metanarratives* or 'grand narratives', sweeping stories about history's progressive liberation, by reason, of human potential, labour, science and technology. What they have in common, he argues, is a function of **legitimation**: they endorse the present by promising liberation, though it is inevitably a liberation in a future which is perpetually deferred.

For Lyotard, the postmodern is the collapse of these grand narratives and their functions of legitimation, under the pressures of precisely the features of late capitalism Harvey describes: the acceleration of the new and the rise of information technologies. In them, all exchanges and social relations are atomised to a matter of information. What results is a thoroughgoing dele-gitimisation: the only goals this new techno-regime needs are the functional and managerial ones of success and efficiency, allowing it to appear as value-neutral. Against a writer such as Jürgen Habermas (1985), who sees modernism as the incomplete project of the European Enlightenment (and one whose urgent task of completion falls to Marxism), Lyotard argues that modernity bears its own incompleteness within itself, and thus collapses under its own weight.

This is not to say that Lyotard likes what the postmodern leaves us with. On the contrary, the apparent ethical neutrality of the postmodern demand for nothing but efficient performance is profoundly and insidiously despotic in its overriding of all other criteria. In its place, Lyotard suggests a respect for the multiplicity and irreducibility of what he calls, after Wittgenstein, *language games*. Here he approaches a topic which will be addressed in different ways in our next section, on the politics of identity and difference.

Harvey and Lyotard hardly agree in their diagnoses, or even in the ways in which they use the term *postmodern*. Nevertheless, for all their differences, one of the issues they both raise is the question of the historical *break*. That necessarily takes us back to the idea of the modern, against which, it seems, the postmodern must inevitably define itself.

The most banal use of the term *modern* is simply as a synonym for *contemporary*: modernity is just where one is now, whenever that might be. A somewhat more interesting way of using it is as a description of any period which sees itself as different from what went before. In this sense, modenity would be a matter of *progress* and *overcoming*. More than to a particular period, it refers to a *general historical figure of rupture*. This has some rather interesting consequences. If modernity is defined as a break, how can one break *from* modernity? The very act of trying to make a break is what constitutes modernity itself, by definition. If it is a matter of progress and overcoming, how do you overcome it or progress beyond it? You're never more a part of the modern than when you're declaring your intention to break with it.

The paradox may be, then, that *no simple break is possible from modernity*. This all too easily sounds apocalyptic, as though it's positing a final tyranny – or just plain inertia – against which all resistance is useless from the outset. Indeed, it has often been read this way, and responded to with heated polemic. Nevertheless, this version of the postmodern suggests a range of problems which may be of considerable importance for the ways in which cultural studies (among other things) goes about its business. Various forms of social contestation may see themselves as seeking to introduce radical breaks from existing practices. What if such opposition is already in some ways accommodated, even comfortably, within the mechanisms of social power? The urgent question in such a case would *not* be one of giving up all idea of contestation, but of finding new ways of doing it in the new and strange topologies of postmodernity. What we find here, translated to a general conceptual level, are some of the issues raised by policy studies. If there are no positions which are radically *external* to postmodernity, what strategies will allow one to unsettle it radically from within? Where does one operate from, how, and with what tools?

In a very different way, the postmodern is also related to, but not identical with, some of the questions of the politics of identity and difference we shall now discuss: what does it mean to be marginalised, as against simply excluded?

Cultural difference and identity

The investigation of cultural identities is one of the main areas in which cultural studies has been developing. As we have noted throughout, one of our key aims has been to explore practices of cultural meaning. To do so effectively and in detail entails not making generalisations about these meanings and how people understand and respond to them. A focus on an increasing variety and range of cultural identities and viewpoints, and their interactions, is one way in which such generalisations can be avoided. This task has been undertaken by many people working in the cultural studies area.

A central step in opening out the study of cultural meanings has been to question the *methods* that theorists and analysts use. An important point here is that every approach to cultural phenomena always begins from a certain perspective or *position*. As discussed above, an ethnographic approach can show just how complicated audience groupings and responses to texts can be. In a sense, someone who is studying an aspect of culture is also an audience member, observing the display of activities in front of him/her.

The position from which such activities are observed is never a given, nor is it necessarily fixed and objective. Writers on culture, like audiences, are always influenced by a complex range of cultural factors which affect they way they understand their subject matter. Basically, *there is no neutral perspective from which culture can be studied*. The position of the analyst is going to be crucial to the ideas and interpretations that are developed. The concept of analytical position raises a number of questions about the kind of study being performed:

- What is the analyst's relationship to the cultural text or activity?
- In what ways does the analyst's perspective differ from that of people involved in the text or activity (and its addressers and addressees)?
- Has the analyst been influenced by one group's experiences of the activity or text more than by those of other groups? If so, what are the effects of this influence?

These are all difficult questions to answer about the way some kind of cultural activity is being examined. The point of asking them is not simply to end up being able to identify a biased or ill-informed account of things. Rather, the aim is to be able to go on to supplement the attitude of an initial study or analysis with either a more comprehensive, or an alternative, viewpoint. Invariably, this kind of revisionary perspective operates by referring to, and often incorporating, the outlooks of one or more different cultural groups, groups that are also involved in the activities being analysed.

When we stop to think about it, cultural identity is a very complex idea. In Chapter 1, we met a letter writer, Sam West (Figures 1.1 and 1.2). Sam seemed like a more or less ordinary sort of person, perhaps similar in some ways to many of us: going to university, concerned about getting a job, having a lover, and so on. Sam's identity was neither singular nor fixed. She (or was it he?) played different roles depending on the situation: an earnest would-be banker, a somewhat impatient, lovesick friend. Outside these two texts, Sam would no doubt play many other roles as well.

There also seemed to be a range of other attributes implied about Sam. What do you think we glean about his or her age, from these two texts? Social class? Ethnic background? Sexuality? (If you try to answer these questions, ask yourself why you come up with the answers you do. What is your position, as a cultural analyst on the small social phenomenon of 'Sam West'?)

This simple example suggests that the identity of any figure is a social composite. It comprises attributes that will combine in different ratios according to the demands and pressures of the situation. Social selfhood involves *role playing*, fulfilling varying addresser and addressee positions. Further, a person may not be in charge of the roles he or she plays; they may be irresistibly imposed by the context. Identity is also structured by prevailing social discourses (how much choice, for example, does Sam have in writing a job application letter?). Questions of address (Chapter 1), genre (Chapter 5), discourse (Chapter 7) and strategy (Chapter 9) are all involved in the social construction of selfhood.

A number of factors come into play in determining cultural identities. Some of these may have come up as we pondered who 'Sam West' is: race, class, gender, ethnicity, age, sexuality. When studying an individual in social action it may appear possible to check these factors off and note which ones are dominant in different settings. But it is the *interaction* of the factors that it is most important to consider. The factors of cultural identity may work together in contradictory ways. For example, gender and class can work to produce identities that many people find difficult to handle. Men may be unsure how to treat women from a higher class, or who are professionally successful. Think of the controversy (both for and against) which has surrounded Hillary Rodham Clinton's arrival and continued presence in the political scene in the USA, first with her Presidential husband in the White House, and then as a Senator. Identity is never a neat total of factors that conveys a finite set of meanings.

If cultural identity and position are complicated in individual cases, the interactions and layers get much more involved when we turn to group situations. It is when studying the interactions of groups that issues of cultural identity have been raised in most detail. In turn, these issues affect many of the important ideas in cultural studies that we have considered in previous chapters.

Once variations of identity are acknowledged, any theory of the audience becomes much more complicated. Whom does an audience for any mass media or popular text consist of? It must comprise a wide array of groups and sub-groups, and their different cultural identities will see them produce more or less varied readings and interpretations of texts.

Cultural identity is a crucial question in considering the production of social meaning, and a key motive in the dialogism among social texts. Attention to questions of identity can alert us to a much broader range of social texts and textual producers. As we have discussed in the chapters in the second half of the book – those on genre, narrative, medium and ideology – the power of authoring texts and representing the real is a formidable social power. It is not a coincidental or natural state of affairs that prevailing historical accounts of the settlement and growth of countries like Australia and the United States are told from white male social perspectives.

By raising the notion of authors' cultural (and not simply their personal) identities and positions, we can start to see the ideological impacts of these accounts. In the first place, we may perceive the erasure of the viewpoints of other racial and ethnic groups, or the orientation of these histories around masculine values and actions. Second, we can also start to become aware that marginalised groups, including white women and men and women of colour, have their own histories and narratives to tell. Their texts challenge and subvert the dominant images of both the past and the present. These kinds of challenges take place across the whole range of contemporary social activities – for instance, investigating how female subcultures differ from male ones – and historical traditions – such as examining the resistance of native peoples to European colonists in the eighteenth and nineteenth centuries.

In studying all such activities and traditions, questions of cultural identity in terms of race, class and gender open up the *ideological stakes* of representation. This line of thinking in cultural studies reveals the **politics of identity and difference**. It makes us aware that one of the key ways in which power operates in societies is by setting up groups and versions of the **other** – figures who can be both excluded from the opportunities of support and well-being that society may offer and scapegoated as the cause of social problems.

At the same time, theories of cultural identity are also crucial in preventing the concept of the other being reduced to that of a victim. In studying the complexities of identity, the independent actions and strengths of marginalised groups emerge in their own right.

For practitioners of cultural studies, the most important lesson to be learned from analysing issues of identity and position is to try to avoid reproducing the effects of discriminatory power in one's thought and work. In this way, the notion of cultural identity foregrounds what may well be the overriding revelation of cultural studies: the complex interweavings of culture with the negotiations and contestations of social power.

Cyberculture

It is a commonplace to say that the Internet has an unprecedented ability to foster new forms of social relations. One of the most frequent ways of characterising this is through the novelty of its 'interactivity'. The term is doubtless overused, and often very uncritically, but it does usefully point to something we dealt with in our very first chapter: the ways in which address works. Interactivity generally refers to those aspects of the Internet where you are offered the role of addresser as well as addressee, of saying as well as listening – where the Internet is more like a telephone than like a television. If that addresser role is strictly controlled in many other media (radio talkback is always at the whim of the host, letters to the editor are selected and edited with care), the very architecture of the Internet works to diffuse any such control. From its beginnings as part of the US defence network, the Internet has been deliberately decentralised, so that the whole thing could continue to work regardless of the functioning of any particular one of its parts.

One of the conclusions often drawn from this is that the Internet is therefore essentially liberatory: if it is not under some centralised control, it can only be the provenance of free individuals and small groups, in an egalitarian world where the individual is unhindered by boundaries of nation, class, gender or property. A famous early example of this, since reprinted several hundred times, is John Perry Barlow's Declaration of the Independence of Cyberspace, which sees the Internet as a liberatory rupture of all forms of state power which would try to regulate it.

But does this follow? First there is the sheer economics of access and ownership. The hardware and software which give access to the Internet are for the most part proprietary products of some of the biggest corporate players in the world marketplace, and initial and ongoing costs are still very real economic restrictions. The technical infrastructure necessary for Internet connection is simply not available over most of the planet and for most of its population, but is concentrated massively in the wealthier nations. Far from 'wanting to be free' (as Barlow's Declaration would have it), information is already highly and increasingly commodified. And on top of this, ideas of cyber-liberation may simply be mistaken about the nature of power in late capitalist Western societies. The liberated individual who chooses his or her own destiny is not a threat to the social and political order, which that order must keep in check: it is the very dream of that order, the individual that order incessantly invokes and promises us we can be with its help. The interpellation late capitalism offers is not the one cyber-liberation imagines it is – *be good*, or *be obedient* – but the very thing cyber-liberation offers as a cure: *Be yourself. Where do you want to go today? Just do it.*

What the Internet raises is not so much the promise of rupture as a reconsideration of issues of community. People now conduct a lot of their business, working life, leisure and even social life online. Many, perhaps even most of these interactions take place among people who have not met face-to-face, and yet some of them take place within an atmosphere of intense community. A famous article which first appeared in 1993 in the *Village Voice* (a weekly newspaper published in New York city) details the quite real distress and sense of outrage which went through an online MUD when some software hacking let one of its participants force another's online persona to submit to actions which, had they occurred in the offline world, could only be construed as rape. Can we speak of community in cases where participants know each other only through often highly and obviously fantasised online personae, and where the flesh-and-blood participants may be living half a world away from each other?

But that absence of face-to-face contact may be irrelevant, as such contact is neither necessary nor sufficient for a feeling of community. We all live in what Benedict Anderson calls 'imaginary communities' of individuals we will never meet, yet with whom we share a very real bond of commonality: the obvious example is the nation. On the other hand, we don't usually feel any great sense of community with the people we're standing shoulder-to-shoulder with on the bus or in the queue for the automatic teller. Community is largely an imagined relation in this sense; it is not lessened by the lack of face-to-face contact, and may in some cases even be accentuated by it.

Because of that, it has been argued, the Internet may represent a newly emerging form of the 'public sphere': an arena separate from the existing political and governmental spheres, in which democratic and critical scrutiny of all aspects of the social world can take place. The Internet can operate as a way of disseminating news which is not usually covered by or available to major Western media, or which is actively repressed by the media or government of the country in which it originates. It may provide a visible presence or even focus for various minorities. A quick check of any of the big online indices to the Web, for example, will show an enormous variety of online support groups, providing resources, newsgroups, email lists, contacts and links for almost every conceivable interest. Identity politics proliferates on the Internet, from geeks and grrls to the often violently racist and homophobic 'hate sites' (and to those who oppose them). The medium is still relatively very new, and still in the process of formation. We may suspect that most of its effects are yet to be seen.

SOURCES AND FURTHER READING

Audience studies

For a comprehensive coverage of contemporary research in television audiences, see *Remote Control: Television, Audiences and Cultural Power* (London: Routledge, 1989), edited by Ellen Seiter *et al.* David Morley's *Family Television: Cultural Power and Domestic Leisure* (London: Comedia, 1986) presents a detailed ethnographic analysis of audience in a domestic context. His earlier *The Nationwide Audience: Structure and Decoding* (London: British Film Institute, 1980) is also useful. Other studies of audiences include Greg Philo's *Seeing is Believing: The Influence of Television* (London: Routledge, 1990); James Lull's *Inside Family Viewing: Ethnographic Research on Television's Audiences* (London: Comedia, 1990); Tony Wilson's *Watching Television: Hermeneutics, Reception and Popular Culture* (Cambridge: Polity Press, 1993); and Duncan Petrie and Janet Willis (eds), *Television and the Household: Reports from the BFI's Audience Tracking Study* (London: British Film Institute, 1995).

Ien Ang's *Desperately Seeking the Audience* (London: Routledge, 1991) provides an account of the institutional values of the media with respect to audience. The following works undertake related analysis: Justin Lewis, *The Ideological Octopus: An Exploration of Television and Its Audience* (New York: Routledge 1991); Shaun Moores, *Interpreting Audiences: The Ethnography of Media Consumption* (London: Sage, 1993); Virginia Nightingale, *Studying Audiences: The Shock of the Real* (London: Routledge, 1996); and Sonia Livingston, *Making Sense of Television* (London: Routledge, 1998).

For a study of the reading of popular literature, see Janice Radway's seminal work, *Reading the Romance: Women, Patriarchy, and Popular Literature* (Chapel Hill: University of North Carolina Press, 1984). Denis McQuail's *Mass Communication Theory: An Introduction* (London: Sage, 1987) contains a useful account of empirical research methods and theory. For a good introductory book on qualitative methodology, see Klaus Bruhn Jensen and Nicholas W. Jankowski (eds), *A Handbook of Qualitative Methodologies for Mass Communication Research* (London: Routledge, 1991).

Policy studies

For an introduction to the policy debate within cultural studies, see various essays by Morris, Frow, Bennett and Johnson in *Beyond the Disciplines: The New Humanities*, edited by K. K. Ruthven (Canberra: Highland Press, 1992). This debate is continued by Hunter, Meredyth, Frow, O'Regan, Cunningham, Morris and Levy, in a special issue of the journal *Meanjin* (51 (3), 1992). For a thorough account of the policy position and its relation to the humanities, see

Ian Hunter et al., *Accounting for the Humanities: The Language of Culture and the Logic of Government* (Brisbane: Institute for Cultural Policy Studies, 1991); see also Stuart Cunningham's *Framing Culture: Criticism and Policy in Australia* (Sydney: Allen & Unwin, 1992).

For an integration of critique and policy, see Stuart Cunningham and Graeme Turner (eds), *The Media in Australia: Industries, Texts, Audiences*, 2nd edn (Sydney: Allen & Unwin, 1997); Tony Bennett, Michael Emmison and John Frow, *Accounting for Tastes: Australian Everyday Cultures* (New York: Cambridge University Press, 1999); Chris Rojek and John Urry (eds), *Touring Cultures: Transformations of Travel and Theory* (London: Routledge, 1997). And once more, Grossberg, Nelson and Treichler's collection, *Cultural Studies* (New York: Routledge, 1992) contains essays from standpoints of both cultural critique and cultural policy.

The postmodern

John Frow's essay, 'What was Postmodernism?', in *Time and Commodity Culture: Essays in Cultural Theory and Postmodernity* (Oxford: Oxford University Press, 1997) offers a judicious survey of the literature and the polemics. David Harvey's argument is in *The Condition of Postmodernity: An Enquiry into the Origins of Cultural Change* (Oxford: Blackwell, 1989). Linda Hutcheon's *The Politics of Postmodernism* (London: Routledge, 1989) is well-known.

Jean-François Lyotard's *The Postmodern Condition: A Report on Knowledge* (Minneapolis: University of Minnesota Press, 1984) is his best-known statement on the matter, though the shorter pieces in *The Postmodern Explained to Children: Correspondence 1982–1985* (Sydney: Power Publications, 1992) are also important, and at times somewhat different. *The Differend: Phrases in Dispute* (Minneapolis: University of Minnesota Press, 1988) is Lyotard's most thorough statement of the implications of this for philosophy.

There is a wealth material on the postmodern online. Two of the best-known sites are Arthur and Marilouise Kroker's journal *CTHEORY*, at www.ctheory.com, and the more academic *Postmodern Culture*, at jefferson.village.virginia.edu/pmc/contents.all.html.

Cultural difference and identity

A wide range of issues involving the politics of cultural identity is raised in *Cultural Studies,* edited by Grossberg, Nelson and Treichler (New York: Routledge, 1992). Angela McRobbie's *Feminism and Youth Culture: From Jackie to Just Seventeen* (Basingstoke: Macmillan – now Palgrave, 1991) examines differences between male and female teenage sub-cultures. Two collections – Gail Dines and Jean M. Humez's *Gender, Race, and Class in Media* (Newbury Park: Sage, 1994) and Stuart Hall and Paul du Gay's

Questions of Cultural Identity (Newbury Park: Sage, 1996) – provide a detailed overview of issues of cultural identity and difference.

A wide critical survey of different notions of sexuality and identity is presented in *The Lesbian and Gay Studies Reader* (New York: Routledge, 1993), edited by Henry Abelove, Michele Aina Barale and David Halperin. Jonathan Dollimore's *Death, Desire and Loss in Western Culture* (New York: Routledge, 1998) looks at the complex ways in which sexuality has been represented in Western cultures. *The Post-Colonial Studies Reader* (New York: Routledge, 1995), edited by Bill Ashcroft, Gareth Griffith and Helen Tiffin, provides a thorough overview of theories and practices of postcolonial cultural representation. Lastly, *Black Looks: Race and Representation* (Boston: South End Press, 1992) by bell hooks studies the politics of identity in relation to race, as does Robert Ferguson's *Representing Race: Ideology, Identity, and the Media* (Oxford: Oxford University Press, 1998).

Cyberculture

John Perry Barlow's 'Declaration of the Independence of Cyberspace' can be found in many places on the Web (Google lists over 400), but in particular on his own site (www.eff.org/~barlow/Declaration-Final.html) within the Electronic Frontier Foundation, of which he is a cofounder (www.eff.org). Benedict Anderson's classic work on community is *Imagined Communities: Reflections on the Origin and Spread of Nationalism*, 2nd edn (London: Verso; 1991). The *Village Voice* article is Julian Dibbell's 'A Rape in Cyberspace: How an Evil Clown, a Haitian Trickster Spirit, Two Wizards, and a Cast of Dozens Turned a Database Into a Society' (23 December 1993). In a different form, it is now a chapter in his *My Tiny Life: Crime and Passion in a Virtual World* (New York: Henry Holt, 1999). Both versions are available on Dibbell's web site, at www.levity.com/julian/bungle_vv.html.

Mark Poster's arguments about the Internet as a public sphere are made in an essay on 'CyberDemocracy' in his *What's the Matter with the Internet?* (Minneapolis: University of Minnesota Press, 2001); this essay, as well as several others of interest, is also available from his website at www.humanities.uci.edu/mposter/. Allucquère Rosanne Stone's pages (www.actlab.utexas.edu/~sandy/) are a well-known investigation of identity politics through the new media, as is her book *The War of Desire and Technology at the End of the Mechanical Age* (Boston: MIT Press, 1995). The Cyberculture pages of Alan Liu's Voice of the Shuttle (vos.ucsb.edu/shuttle/cyber.html) provide a wealth of material. One of the most informative online discussion groups, where cultural studies and cyberculture interact, is at the CULTSTUD-L discussion list at www.cas.usf.edu/communication/rodman/cultstud/index.html.

Bibliography

Abelove, Henry, Michele Aina Barale and David Halperin (eds) (1993) *The Lesbian and Gay Studies Reader*. New York: Routledge.

Adam, Barbara and Stuart Allan (eds) (1995) *Theorizing Culture: An Interdisciplinary Critique After Postmodernism*. New York: New York University Press.

Allen, Graham (2000) *Intertextuality*. New York: Routledge.

Allen, Robert C. (ed.) (1992) *Channels of Discourse, Reassembled: Television and Contemporary Criticism*. Chapel Hill: University of North Carolina Press.

Althusser, Louis (1977) 'Ideology and Ideological State Apparatuses (Notes Towards an Investigation)'. Translator, Ben Brewster. In *Lenin and Philosophy and Other Essays*. London: NLB.

Altman, Rick (1999) *Film Genre*. London: British Film Institute.

Anderson, Benedict (1991) *Imagined Communities: Reflections on the Origin and Spread of Nationalism*, 2nd edn. London: Verso.

Ang, Ien (1991) *Desperately Seeking the Audience*. London: Routledge.

Ashcroft, Bill, Gareth Griffiths, and Helen Tiffin (eds) (1995) *The Post-Colonial Studies Reader*. New York: Routledge.

Bakerman, Jane S. (1995) *Gender in Popular Culture: Images of Men and Women in Literature, Visual Media, and Material Culture*. Cleveland: Ridgemont.

Bakhtin, M. M. (1986) 'Speech Genres'. In Caryn Emerson and Michael Holquist (eds), *Speech Genres and Other Late Essays*. Translator, Vern W. McGee. Austin: University of Texas Press.

Bal, Mieke and Inge E. Boer (eds) (1994) *The Point of Theory: Practices of Culture Analysis*. New York: Continuum.

Balkin, J.M. (1998) *Cultural Software: A Theory of Ideology*. New Haven: Yale University Press.

Barbero-Martin, J. (1993) *Communication, Culture and Hegemony: From the Media to Mediations*. Translators, Elizabeth Fox and Robert A. White. London: Sage.

Barlow, John Perry (1996) 'A Declaration of the Independence of Cyberspace'. 8 February 1996 <http://www.eff.org/~barlow/Declaration-Final.html>.

Barthes, Roland (1967) *Elements of Semiology*. Translators, Annette Lavers and Colin Smith. London: Cape.

—— (1977a) 'Change the Object Itself'. In Stephen Heath (ed. and trans.), *Image–Music–Text*. London: Fontana.

—— (1977b) 'Introduction to the Structural Analysis of Narratives'. In ditter *Image–Music–Text*. London: Fontana.

—— (1983) *The Fashion System*. Translators, Matthew Ward and Richard Howard. New York: Hill & Wang.

—— (1987) *Mythologies*. Translator, Annette Lavers. New York: Hill & Wang.

Beebee, Thomas O. (1994) *The Ideology of Genre: A Comparative Study of Generic Instability*. University Park: Pennsylvania State University Press.

Bell, Allan and Peter Garrett (eds) (1998) *Media Discourse*. Oxford: Blackwell.

Bennett, Tony and Janet Woollacott (1987) *Bond and Beyond: The Political Career of a Popular Hero*. London: Macmillan – now Palgrave.

Bennett, Tony and Michael Emmison and John Frow (1999) *Accounting for Tastes: Australian Everyday Cultures*. New York: Cambridge University Press.

Berger, Peter L. and Thomas Luckmann (1991) *The Social Construction of Reality: A Treatise on the Sociology of Knowledge*. London: Penguin.

Bignell, Jonathan (1997) *Media Semiotics: An Introduction*. Manchester: Manchester University Press.

Bishop, Wendy and Hans Ostrom (eds) (1997) *Genre and Writing: Issues, Arguments, Alternatives*. Portsmouth: Boynton.

Blonsky, Marshall (ed.) (1985) *On Signs: A Semiotics Reader*. Oxford: Basil Blackwell.

Bordo, Susan (1997) *Twilight Zones: The Hidden Life of Cultural Images from Plato to O.J.* Berkeley: University of California Press.

Bourdieu, Pierre (1984) *Distinction: A Social Critique of the Judgement of Taste*. Translator, Richard Nice. Cambridge, Massachusetts: Harvard University Press.

—— (1990) *In Other Words: Essays Towards a Reflexive Sociology*. Translator, Matthew Adamson. Cambridge: Polity Press.

Bouissac, Paul (ed.) (1998) *Encyclopedia of Semiotics* New York: Oxford University Press.

Brewer, Ebenezer Cobham (1970) *Brewer's Dictionary of Phrase and Fable*. London: Cassell.

Bright, Brenda Jo and Liza Bakewell (eds) (1995) *Looking High and Low: Art and Cultural Identity*. Tucson: University of Arizona.

Brown, M. E. (ed.) (1990) *Television and Women's Culture: The Politics of the Popular*. London: Sage.

Browne, Ray B. and Ronald J. Ambrosetti (eds) (1993) *Continuities in Popular Culture: The Present in the Past and the Past in the Present and Future*. Bowling Green, Ohio: Popular.

Carney, George O. (ed.) (1995) *Fast Food, Stock Cars, and Rock'n'Roll: Place and Space in American Pop Culture*. Lanham: Rowman Littlefield.

Certeau, Michel de (1984) *The Practice of Everyday Life*. Translator, Steven Rendall. Berkeley: University of California Press.

Chandler, Daniel (2001) *Semiotics: The Basics*. New York and London: Routledge.

—— *Semiotics for Beginners*, Media and Cultural Studies site, University of Wales, Aberyswyth. 8 January 2001 <http://www.aber.ac.uk/media>.

Chatman, Seymour (1978) *Story and Discourse: Narrative Structure in Fiction and Film*. Ithaca: Cornell University Press.

Cobley, Paul and Litza Jantz (1999) *Introducing Semiotics*. Cambridge: Icon.

Cohan, Steven and Ina Rae Hark (1992) *Screening the Male*. London: Routledge.

Cohan, Steven and Linda M. Shires (1988) *Telling Stories: A Theoretical Analysis of Narrative*. New York: Routledge.

Cohen, Tom (1998) *Ideology and Inscription: 'Cultural Studies' after Benjamin, de Man and Bakhtin*. Cambridge: Cambridge University Press.

Cohen, Stan and Jock Young (eds) (1973) *The Manufacture of News: Social Problems, Deviance and the Mass Media*. London: Constable.

Cook, Guy (1992) *The Discourse of Advertising*. London: Routledge.

Coward, Rosalind. (1984) *Female Desire*. London: Granada.

—— and John Ellis (1977) *Language and Materialism: Developments in Semiology and the Theory of the Subject*. London: Routledge.

Culler, Jonathan (1981) 'Story and Discourse in the Analysis of Narrative'. In *The Pursuit of Signs: Semiotics, Literature, Deconstruction*. London: Routledge.

—— (1986) *Saussure*. Ithaca: Cornell University Press.

CULTSTUD-L Discussion List. 1 October 2000 <http://www.cas.usf.edu /communication/rodman/cultstud/index.html>.

Cunningham, Stuart (1992) *Framing Culture: Criticism and Policy in Australia*. Sydney: Allen & Unwin.

—— and Graeme Turner (eds) (1997) *The Media in Australia: Industries, Texts, Audiences*. 2nd edn. Sydney: Allen & Unwin.

Cutting, Gary (ed.) (1994) *The Cambridge Companion to Foucault*. Cambridge: Cambridge University Press.

Danaher, Geoff, Tony Schirato and Jen Webb (2000) *Understanding Foucault*. Sydney: Allen & Unwin.

Danesi, Marcel (1999) *Of Cigarettes, High Heels and Other Interesting Things: An Introduction to Semiotics*. Basingstoke: Macmillan – now Palgrave.

Davis, Boyd H. and Jeutonne P. Brewer (1997) *Electronic Discourse: Linguistic Individuals in Virtual Space*. Albany: State University of New York Press.

Davis, Robert Con and Ronald Schleifer (eds) (1998) *Contemporary Literary Criticism and Cultural Studies*. New York: Longman.

Dery, Mark (ed.) (1994) *Flame Wars: The Discourse of Cyberculture*. Durham: Duke University Press.

Dibbell, Julian (1993) 'A Rape in Cyberspace: How an Evil Clown, a Haitian Trickster Spirit, Two Wizards, and a Cast of Dozens Turned a Database Into a Society'. *Village Voice*, 23 December 1993. 2 March 2001 <http://www.levity.com/julian/bungle_vv.html>.

—— (1999) *My Tiny Life: Crime and Passion in a Virtual World*. New York: Henry Holt.

Dijk, Teun A. van (ed.) (1997) *Discourse Studies: A Multidisciplinary Introduction*. London: Sage.

Dines, Gail and Jean M. Humez (eds) (1994) *Gender, Race, and Class in Media*. Newbury Park: Sage.

Dixon, Wheeler Windston (ed.) (2000) *Film Genre 2000: New Critical Essays*. Albany: State University of New York Press.

Dollimore, Jonathan (1998) *Death, Desire and Loss in Western Culture*. New York: Routledge.

Dubrow, Heather (1982) *Genre*. London: Methuen.

During, Simon (ed.) (1993) *The Cultural Studies Reader*. London: Routledge.

Dworkin, Dennis (1997) *Cultural Marxism in Postwar Britain: History, the New Left, and the Origins of Cultural Studies*. Durham: Duke University Press.

Eagleton, Terry (1985) 'Capitalism, Modernism and Postmodernism'. *New Left Review*, 152: 60–73.

—— (1991) *Ideology: An Introduction*. London: Verso.

Edgerton, Gary R., Michael T. Marsden and Jack Nachbar (eds) (1997) *In the Eye of the Beholder: Critical Perspectives in Popular Film and Television*. Bowling Green, Ohio: Popular.

Eldridge, John (ed.) (1993) *Getting the Message: News, Truth, and Power*. London: Routledge.

Ellis, John (1982) *Visible Fictions*. London: Routledge.

Fairclough, Norman (1989) *Language and Power*. London: Longman.

—— (1995) *Critical Discourse Analysis: The Critical Study of Language*. London: Longman.

—— (1995) *Media Discourse*. London: Edward Arnold.

Ferguson, Robert (1998) *Representing Race: Ideology, Identity, and the Media*. Oxford: Oxford University Press.

Fiske, John (1982) *Introduction to Communication Studies*. London: Methuen.

—— (1987) *Television Culture*. New York: Methuen.

—— (1989) *Understanding Popular Culture*. Boston: Unwin Hyman.

—— and Graeme Turner, and Bob Hodge (1987) *Myths of Oz: Readings in Australian Popular Culture*. Sydney: Allen & Unwin.

Foster, Hal (ed.) (1985) *Postmodern Culture*. London: Pluto.

Foucault, Michel (1972) *The Archaeology of Knowledge*. Translator, A. M. Sheridan Smith. London: Tavistock.

Fowler, Roger (1991) *Language in the News: Discourse and Ideology in the Press*. London: Routledge.

Fowles, Jib (1996) *Advertising and Popular Culture*. Newbury Park: Sage.

Freadman, Anne (1988) 'Untitled: (on Genre)'. *Cultural Studies*, 2(1): 67–99.

—— and Amanda Macdonald (1992) *What is this Thing Called 'Genre'? Four Essays in the Semiotics of Genre*. Mt Nebo, Queensland: Boombana.

Frow, John (1997) *Time and Commodity Culture: Essays in Cultural Theory and Postmodernity*. Oxford: Clarendon.

Frus, Phyllis (1994) *The Politics and Poetics of Journalistic Narrative: The Timely and the Timeless*. Cambridge: Cambridge University Press.

Fuery, Patrick and Nick Mansfield (1997) *Cultural Studies and the New Humanities: Concepts and Controversies*. Oxford: Oxford University Press.

Galtung, Johan and Marie Holmboe Ruge (1973) 'Structuring and Selecting News'. In Stan Cohen and Jock Young (eds), *The Manufacture of News*. London: Constable.

Garber, Marjorie, Paul B. Franklin and Rebecca L. Walkowitz (eds) (1996) *Field Work: Sites in Literary and Cultural Studies*. New York: Routledge.

Garber, Marjorie, Jann Matlock and Rebecca L. Walkowitz (eds) (1993) *Media Spectacles*. New York: Routledge.

Geertz, Clifford (1983) 'Blurred Genres: The Refiguration of Social Thought'. In

Local Knowledge: Further Essays in Interpretive Anthropology. New York: Basic Books.

Genette, Gerard (1980) *Narrative Discourse: An Essay in Method*. Translator, Jane E. Lewin. Ithaca: Cornell University Press.

Gledhill, Christine (ed.) (1987) *Home Is Where the Heart Is: Studies in Melodrama and the Women's Film*. London: British Film Institute.

Goodwin, Andrew and Garry Whanel (eds) (1990) *Understanding Television*. London: Routledge.

Gould, Stephen Jay (1981) *The Mismeasure of Man*. New York: Norton.

Gramsci, Antonio (1971) *Selections from the Prison Notebooks of Antonio Gramsci*. Editors and translators, Quintin Hoare and Geoffrey Nowell-Smith. New York: International Publishers.

—— (1988) *A Gramsci Reader: Selected Writings 1916–35*. Editor, David Forgacs. London: Lawrence & Wishart.

Green, Philip (1998) *Cracks in the Pedestal: Ideology and Gender in Hollywood*. Amherst: University of Massachusetts Press.

Gregory, Chris (2000) *Star Trek: Parallel Narratives*. New York: St Martin's Press.

Grossberg, Lawrence, Gary Nelson and Paula Treichler (eds) (1992) *Cultural Studies*. New York: Routledge.

Gunter, Barrie (1995) *Television and Gender Representation*. London: John Libbey.

Habermas, Jürgen (1985) 'Modernity – An Incomplete Project'. In Hal Foster (ed.), *Postmodern Culture*. Translator Seyla Ben-Habib. London: Pluto.

—— (1987) *The Philosophical Discourse of Modernity*. Translator, Frederick Lawrence. Cambridge: Polity Press.

Hall, Stuart (1980) 'Encoding/Decoding'. In Stuart Hall *et al.* (eds), *Culture, Media, Language: Working Papers in Cultural Studies, 1972–79*. London: Unwin Hyman.

—— (1997) *Representation: Cultural Representations and Signifying Practices*. Newbury Park: Sage.

—— *et al.* (1978) *Policing the Crisis: Mugging, the State, and Law and Order*. London: Macmillan – now Palgrave.

Hall, Stuart and Paul du Gay (eds) (1996) *Questions of Cultural Identity*. Newbury Park: Sage.

Harker, Richard, Cheleen Mahar and Chris Wilkes (eds) (1990) *An Introduction to the Work of Pierre Bourdieu: The Practice of Theory*. London: Macmillan – now Palgrave.

Harris, Roy (1987) *Reading Saussure: A Critical Commentary on the Cours de Linguistique Générale*. London: Duckworth.

Hartley, John (1982) *Understanding News*. London: Methuen.

—— (1992) *Tele-ology: Studies in Television*. New York: Routledge.

Harvey, David (1989) *The Condition of Post-modernity: An Enquiry into the Origins of Cultural Change*. Oxford: Blackwell.

Hawkes, Terence (1977) *Structuralism and Semiotics*. London: Methuen.

Hebdige, Dick (1979) *Subculture: The Meaning of Style*. London: Methuen.

—— (1988) *Hiding in the Light: On Images and Things*. New York: Routledge.

Hjelmslev, Louis (1969) *Prolegomena to a Theory of Language*. Translator, Francis J. Whitfield. Madison, Wisconsin: Wisconsin University Press.

Hodge, Robert and Gunther Kress (1988) *Social Semiotics*. Cambridge: Polity Press.

Holdcroft, David (1991) *Saussure: Signs, Systems, and Arbitrariness*. Cambridge: Cambridge University Press.

hooks, bell (1992) *Black Looks: Race and Representation*. Boston: South End Press.

Hunter, Ian *et al.* (1991) *Accounting for the Humanities: The Language of Culture and the Logic of Government*. Brisbane: Institute for Cultural Policy Studies.

Hurley, Ann and Kate Greenspan (eds) (1995) *So Rich a Tapestry: The Sister Arts and Cultural Studies*. Lewisburg: Bucknell University Press.

Hutcheon, Linda (1989) *The Politics of Postmodernism*. London: Routledge.

Hymes, Dell (1974) *Foundations in Sociolinguistics: An Ethnographic Approach*. Philadelphia: University of Pennsylvania Press.

Innis, Robert E. (ed.) (1985) *Semiotics: An Introductory Anthology*. Bloomington: Indiana University Press.

Jakobson, Roman (1988) 'Linguistics and Poetics'. In David Lodge (ed.), *Modern Criticism and Theory: A Reader*. London: Longman.

Jenkins, Richard (1992) *Pierre Bourdieu*. London: Routledge.

Jensen, Klaus Bruhn and Nicholas W. Jankowski (eds) (1991) *A Handbook of Qualitative Methodologies for Mass Communication Research*. London: Routledge.

Lacey, Nick (1997) *Image and Representation: Key Concepts in Media Studies*. New York: St Martin's Press.

Lévi-Strauss, Claude (1966) *The Savage Mind*. London: Weidenfeld & Nicolson.

Lewis, Justin (1991) *The Ideological Octopus: An Exploration of Television and Its Audience*. New York: Routledge.

Liebes, Tamar and James Curran (eds) (1998) *Media, Ritual, and Identity*. London: Routledge.

Liu, Alan. *The Voice of the Shuttle*. 22 February 2001 <http://vos.ucsb.edu>.

Livingston, Sonia (1998) *Making Sense of Television*. London: Routledge.

Lull, James (1990) *Inside Family Viewing: Ethnographic Research on Television's Audiences*. London: Comedia.

Lyotard, Jean-François (1984) *The Postmodern Condition: A Report on Knowledge*. Translators, Geoff Bennington and Brian Massumi. Minneapolis: University of Minnesota Press.

—— (1988) *The Differend: Phrases in Dispute*. Translator, Georges Van Den Abbeele. Minneapolis: University of Minnesota Press.

—— (1992) *The Postmodern Explained to Children: Correspondence 1982–85*. Translators, Barry Don *et al.*, editors, Julian Pefanis and Morgan Thomas. Sydney: Power Publications.

MacCannell, Dean and Juliet Flower MacCannell (1982) *The Time of the Sign: A Semiotic Interpretation of Modern Culture*. Bloomington: Indiana University Press.

Markowitz, Robin *Cultural Studies Central* 28 May 1996 <http://www.cultural-studies.net>.

McDonald, Myra (1995) *Representing Women*. London: Arnold.

McHoul, Alec (1996) *Semiotic Investigations: Towards an Effective Semiotics*. Lincoln: University of Nebraska Press.

McHoul, Alec and Wendy Grace (1993) *A Foucault Primer: Discourse, Power and the Subject*. Carlton: Melbourne University Press.

McQuail, Denis (1987) *Mass Communication Theory: An Introduction*. London: Sage.

McRobbie, Angela (1991) *Feminism and Youth Culture: From 'Jackie' to 'Just Seventeen'*. Basingstoke: Macmillan – now Palgrave.

—— (1999) *In the Culture Society: Art, Fashion and Popular Music*. London: Routledge.

Meanjin 51 (3) (1992) *Cultural Policy and Beyond*.

Milner, Andrew (1996) *Literature, Culture, and Society*. New York: New York University Press.

Modleski, Tania (1984) *Loving with a Vengeance: Mass Produced Fantasies for Women*. New York: Methuen.

Moriarty, Michael (1991) *Roland Barthes*. Cambridge: Polity Press.

Morley, David (1980) *The 'Nationwide' Audience: Structure and Decoding*. London: British Film Institute.

—— (1986) *Family Television: Cultural Power and Domestic Leisure*. London: Comedia.

Moores, Shaun (1993) *Interpreting Audiences: The Ethnography of Media Consumption*. London: Sage.

Motz, Marilyn J. *et al.* (eds) (1994) *Eye on the Future: Popular Culture Scholarship into the Twenty-First Century*. Bowling Green, Ohio: Popular.

Myers, Greg (1999) *Ad Worlds: Brands, Media, Audiences*. London: Arnold.

Neale, Steve (1980) *Genre*. London: British Film Institute.

—— and Frank Krutnick (1990) *Popular Film and Television Comedy*. London: Routledge.

New Mexico State University Libraries 'The Good, the Bad, and the Ugly: or Why It's a Good Idea to Evaluate Web Sources'. 17 November 2000 <http://lib.nmsu.edu/instruction/eval.html>.

Nightingale, Virginia (1996) *Studying Audiences: The Shock of the Real*. London: Routledge.

Noth, Winfried (1995) *Handbook of Semiotics*. Bloomington: Indiana University Press.

Nothstine, William L., Carole Blair and Gary A. Copeland (eds) (1994) *Critical Questions: Invention, Creativity, and the Criticism of Discourse and Media*. New York: St Martin's Press.

O'Neill, Patrick (1994) *Fictions of Discourse: Reading Narrative Theory*. Toronto: University of Toronto Press.

O'Sullivan, Tim *et al.* (1994) *Key Concepts in Communication Studies*. 2nd edn. London: Methuen.

Palumbo-Liu, David and Hans Ulrich Gumbrecht (eds) (1997) *Streams of Cultural Capital: Transnational Cultural Studies*. Stanford: Stanford University Press.

Petrie, Duncan and Janet Willis (eds) (1995) *Television and the Household: Reports from the BFI's Audience Tracking Study*. London: British Film Institute.

Philo, Greg (1990) *Seeing is Believing: The Influence of Television*. London: Routledge.

Pierce, John R. (1980) *An Introduction to Information Theory: Symbols, Signs and White Noise*. New York: Dover.

Poster, Mark (1995) 'CyberDemocracy'. 2 March 2001 <http://www.hnet.uci.edu/mposter/writings/democ.html>.

—— (2001) *What's the Matter with the Internet?* Minneapolis: University of Minnesota Press.

Postmodern Culture. 27 October 2000 <http://jefferson.village.Virginia.EDU/pmc>.

Potter, Jonathan (1996) *Representing Reality: Discourse, Rhetoric and Social Construction*. London: Sage.

Punter, David (ed.) (1986) *Introduction to Contemporary Cultural Studies*. London: Longman.

Radway, Janice (1984) *Reading the Romance: Feminism and the Representation of Women in Popular Culture*. Chapel Hill: University of North Carolina Press.

Richards, I. A. (1964) *Practical Criticism: A Study of Literary Judgement*. London: Routledge.

Rimmon-Kenan, Shlomith (1983) *Narrative Fiction: Contemporary Poetics*. London: Methuen.

Robey, David (ed.) (1973) *Structuralism: An Introduction*. Oxford: Clarendon Press.

Rojek, Chris and John Urry (eds) (1997), *Touring Cultures: Transformations of Travel and Theory*. London: Routledge.

Ross, Andrew (1989) *No Respect: Intellectuals and Popular Culture*. New York: Routledge.

Ruthven, K. K. (ed.) (1992) *Beyond the Disciplines: The New Humanities*. Occasional Paper 13, Australian Academy of the Humanities. Canberra: Highland Press.

Ryder, Martin 'Semiotics'. 25 February 2001 <http://carbon.cudenver.edu/~mryder/itc_data/semiotics.html>.

Saussure, Ferdinand de (1983) *Course in General Linguistics*. Translator, Roy Harris. London: Duckworth.

Savage, Dean and Jesse Reichler *Resources on Antonio Gramsci*. 10 October 1998 <http://www.soc.qc.edu/gramsci/>.

Seiter, Ellen *et al.* (eds) (1989) *Remote Control: Television, Audiences and Cultural Power*. London: Routledge.

Simpson, Paul (1993) *Language, Ideology and Point of View*. London: Routledge.

Smithson, Isaiah and Nancy Ruff (eds) (1994) *English Studies/Culture Studies: Institutionalizing Dissent*. Urbana: University of Illinois Press.

Sosnoski, James J. (1995) *Modern Skeletons in Postmodern Closets: A Cultural Studies Alternative*. Charlottseville: University of Virginia Press.

Steele, Tom (1997) *The Emergence of Cultural Studies: Adult Education, Cultural Politics and the English Question*. London: Lawrence & Wishart.

Stone, Allucquère Rosanne (1995) *The War of Desire and Technology at the End of the Mechanical Age*. Boston: MIT Press.

—— *Sandy Stone's Home Page*. 9 January 200 <http://www.actlab.utexas.edu/~sandy/>.

Strinati, Dominic (1995) *An Introduction to Theories of Popular Culture*. London: Routledge.

Sturrock, John (ed.) (1979) *Structuralism and Since: From Lévi-Strauss to Derrida*. Oxford: Oxford University Press.

Sukenick, Ronald (2000) *Narralogues: Truth in Fiction*. Albany: State University of New York Press.

Sudjic, Deyan (1990) *Cult Heroes: How to Be Famous for More Than Fifteen Minutes*. New York: Norton.

Taborsky, Edwina (1997) *The Textual Society*. Toronto: University of Toronto Press.

Thody, Philip (1999) *Introducing Barthes*. Trumpington: Icon.

Thomson, Clive and Hans Raj Dua (eds) (1995) *Dialogism and Cultural Criticism*. London: Mestengo.

Toolan, Michael J. (1988) *Narrative: A Critical Linguistic Introduction*. London: Routledge.

Trend, David (1995) *The Crisis of Meaning in Culture and Education*. Minneapolis: University of Minnesota Press.

Tulloch, John and Graeme Turner (eds) (1989) *Australian Television: Programs, Pleasure and Politics*. Sydney: Allen and Unwin.

Turner, Graeme (1988) *Film as Social Practice*. London: Routledge.

—— (1996) *British Cultural Studies: An Introduction*. 2nd edn. London: Routledge.

Underwood. Mick. *Cultsock: Cultural, Communication and Media Studies Infobase*. 2 March 2001 <http://www.cultsock.ndirect.co.uk/MUHome/cshtml/>.

van Kranenburg, Rob *Scholê: Teaching in a Nonlinear Environment*. 27 September 2000 <http://simsim.rug.ac.be/schole>.

Walkerdine, Valerie (1997) *Daddy's Girl: Young Girls and Popular Culture*. Cambridge, Massachusetts: Harvard University Press.

Williams, Raymond (1988) *Keywords: A Vocabulary of Culture and Society*. London: Fontana.

Williamson, Judith (1978) *Decoding Advertisements: Ideology and Meaning in Advertising*. London: Marion Boyars.

—— (1986) *Consuming Passions: The Dynamics of Popular Culture*. London: Marion Boyars.

Wilson, Tony (1993) *Watching Television: Hermeneutics, Reception and Popular Culture*. Cambridge: Polity Press.

Zizek, Slavoj (ed.) (1994) *Mapping Ideology*. London: Verso.

Zupko, Sarah *PopCultures (Sarah Zupko's Cultural Studies Centre)*. 18 February 2001 <http://www.popcultures.com>.

Index

Entries in **bold** indicate a boxed definition in the text. Where a range of pages on a topic includes a boxed definition, the page on which the definition occurs is also specified, in **bold**. For example, a locator of '140–**143**–146' indicates that the topic is dealt with on pages 140–46, with a boxed definition on page **143**.